THE BUSINESS OF LEISURE

The Business of Leisure

Tourism, Sport, Events and Other Leisure Industries

Second Edition

Ken Roberts

macmillan education   palgrave

First published 2016 by
PALGRAVE

Palgrave in the UK is an imprint of Macmillan Publishers Limited, registered in England, company number 785998, of 4 Crinan Street, London, N1 9XW.

Palgrave Macmillan in the US is a division of St Martin's Press LLC, 175 Fifth Avenue, New York, NY 10010.

Palgrave is a global imprint of the above companies and is represented throughout the world.

Palgrave® and Macmillan® are registered trademarks in the United States, the United Kingdom, Europe and other countries.

ISBN 978–1–137–42817–2 hardback
ISBN 978–1–137–42818–9 paperback

This book is printed on paper suitable for recycling and made from fully managed and sustained forest sources. Logging, pulping and manufacturing processes are expected to conform to the environmental regulations of the country of origin.

A catalogue record for this book is available from the British Library.

A catalog record for this book is available from the Library of Congress.

Printed in China

Contents

List of Tables

List of Boxes

Chapter 1

Introduction

Until the 1970s, a book on this topic would have had *leisure services* in the title. 'Leisure services' was in fact in the title of comparable books in that period (for example, Godbey and Parker, 1976). The title was still being used in the 1990s (for example, Godbey, 1997) but by then it bore an antiquated look. Leisure services were provided by voluntary associations and public authorities and agencies.

Throughout the 20th century, commerce (profit-seeking businesses) became increasingly important and eventually became the main leisure providers. Hence, this book's first edition was titled *The Leisure Industries* (Roberts, 2004). It argued that voluntary associations, the public sector and commerce were each making distinctive contributions. This edition uses *leisure business* as its headline term to signal convergences in how these three providers operate. The convergence has been towards commercial practices. The following chapters explain how this has come about. Equally important, this book argues that convergence in their methods does not alter the fact that each of the three kinds of providers has unique capabilities. They are driven by entirely different 'engines' and can offer distinctive leisure experiences.

LEISURE AS A SOCIAL SERVICE

Leisure was successfully claimed as a social service during the first half of the 20th century. This view of leisure was advocated by an alliance of public authorities and voluntary associations, supported by trade unions and (some) employers. When the first wave of countries became industrial and urban in the 19th century, numerous *ad hoc* efforts were made to provide the populations with opportunities to use their new leisure time in the new industrial and urban contexts. Public authorities created urban parks, designated playing fields and built swimming baths, libraries, art galleries, museums and concert halls. The aim was to subdue the unruly pastimes that first-generation urbanites brought from the countryside (see Burnett, 2000) and to create civilised cities where residents would lead civilised lives (Meller, 1976). Numerous clubs and societies were formed promoting different sports, arts, crafts and hobbies. The aim was to encourage 'rational' uses of leisure time that would build strong characters, families, communities and countries (Bailey, 1978; Metcalfe, 2006). Progressive employers joined this recreation movement by providing employees with sports and social clubs. Some built model industrial 'villages' with decent housing, water supplies, open spaces and neighbourhood amenities for cultural and sporting activities, but no pubs! Trade unions performed welfare functions with insurance funds plus social and sports clubs, as did cooperative societies.

After the First World War, the separate efforts of these bodies coalesced into national and then international recreation movements. The leisure providers of that era coordinated their efforts, proposing that leisure be treated primarily as a social service with government funding but provided mainly by voluntary associations, thereby dispersing power democratically. The aim was to create better, stronger societies in the post-First World War era. Leisure services were to be for everyone, but were regarded as particularly important for young people, especially those who left school relatively early. Providing leisure opportunities in 'slum' neighbourhoods was another priority (see Snape and Pussard, 2013). Recreation was among the great social movements of that age, alongside first-wave feminism; it was an equivalent of the green movements of the late-20th and early-21st centuries.

During the 1920s and 1930s, these recreation movements gained an international dimension. Between 1929 and 1935, the Geneva-based International Labour Office convened three international conferences on the problem of free time in Paris, Liege and Brussels. These conferences urged recognition of employees' right to leisure time, and also to opportunities to use this time beneficially. In the United States, the National Recreation Association (NRA, renamed as the National Recreation and Parks Association in 1964) launched a separate international initiative to coincide with the 1932 Summer Olympics in Los Angeles. This convention attracted around 700 delegates from 40 different countries: very respectable figures in an era when trans-Atlantic and trans-Pacific communication, not to mention travel, posed serious difficulties. Those present in Los Angeles proposed to repeat the event alongside the next Summer Olympics. So a further conference was held in Hamburg in 1936 under the title 'Joy and Peace'. This event attracted around 7,000 participants from 61 countries, and a crowd estimated at 1.5 million watched the main parade. A standing International Central Bureau was formed in Hamburg to organise future events. However, at this point, the international recreation movement fragmented. The German hosts did their best to make the Hamburg conference and the subsequent Berlin Olympics into celebrations of Nazi ideology and achievements, and Europe's Fascist countries took control of this international recreation movement. Its next conference was held in Rome, in Mussolini's Italy, in 1938, and a further conference was planned for Osaka (Japan) in 1940 but had to be cancelled due to an intensification of the Sino-Japanese war. By then, America's NRA and representatives from other democratic countries had withdrawn from this international movement. However, recreation movements continued to flourish within the democracies, especially in the United States, where by 1940 around 1,000 colleges offered courses that trained recreation leaders (Pangburn, 1940). These courses were the foundations from which leisure studies programmes were created in American colleges from the 1950s onwards. This academic subject spread into the UK in the 1970s, subsequently into Australia and New Zealand and then more thinly throughout the rest of the world.

During the 1950s, the US NRA revived the international dimension of its work. In 1952, it created an International Service, which offered advice, training and support to recreation movements in other countries, mainly developing countries in Latin America. An international conference was convened in Philadelphia in 1956 and attracted around 2,000 delegates from 37 countries. These numbers were respectable, but less impressive than those at pre-1939 events despite the greater ease of international communication and travel since 1945. There was to be no further event of this type.

However, at the 1956 event, the International Service was renamed the International Recreation Association, which became the World Leisure and Recreation Association (WLRA) in 1973, which in 2006 changed its title again to the snappier World Leisure Organization (WLO). A new and ongoing series of international conferences was launched in 1988, which, unlike the earlier series, are attended by individuals (mainly leisure researchers and teachers) who represent themselves rather than national recreation movements. For the host cities and countries, these conferences are always part of their event portfolios, and are intended to create a short-term boost and (hopefully) leave a longer-term legacy of enhanced tourist inflows.

Today, the old 'leisure services' are just one set of leisure providers. Claiming leisure as primarily a social service nowadays sounds anachronistic.

The public and voluntary sectors became the main providers of leisure services at a time when the scope for commercial (profit-seeking) leisure businesses was limited by people's lack of money that could be spent on 'luxuries'. 'Necessities' accounted for nearly the whole of most households' budgets. Until the Second World War, most working-class families lived barely if at all above a subsistence poverty line. Even so, commerce was always a provider of some leisure goods and services. During the early decades of industrialism, it specialised in leisure markets of dubious moral status – alcohol, tobacco and other drugs, gambling and sex. Profit-seeking entrepreneurs were channelled into these areas because most 'good leisure' was being served by non-profit providers. At that time, the temptations of commerce were wrongly but widely regarded as a major cause of poverty. So commerce was the enemy, the 'devil' that the recreation movements wished to keep at bay. This was despite the fact that by the end of the 19th century commerce had developed new leisure services that could be described as frivolous but surely not harmful. It was offering theatres with performing companies that staged plays throughout the year and pantomimes at Christmas. It also offered vaudeville or what was known as the music hall in Britain – shows that included a variety of entertaining acts (see Bailey, 1986). By the end of the 19th century, commerce had also developed the modern holiday away from home. Commerce (initially railway companies, then also bus operators) provided transport; hotels and private landlords and landladies provided accommodation; and commerce offered constant entertainment. Holidays were also organised by churches and cooperative societies, and some trade unions opened their own holiday centres. The first holidays away from home for industrial workers were pioneered by voluntary associations and some employers as a service to their employees, but by the beginning of the 20th century commerce had become the main provider and had reshaped the modern holiday.

During the first half of the 20th century, commerce introduced new (but now 'old') mass media – popular mass circulation daily newspapers, movies, recorded music and radio. In Europe, radio broadcasting was made public service in most countries, but the British Broadcasting *Company*, one of the very first operators in 1922, was formed by manufacturers of radio equipment whose hunch was that radio sales could be boosted by broadcasting light entertainment. This hunch proved correct! This company was nationalised and became the British Broadcasting *Corporation* (BBC) in 1927.

Throughout Europe, there were fears that in private hands radio would be used as a powerful instrument of political propaganda (like the mass circulation newspapers). There were also fears that commercial broadcasting would cater for a 'lowest common denominator'. America was more relaxed about the private ownership of radio stations, and broadcasting developed from the start as a commercial business within which there have always been public service slots. In Europe, until the 1970s, most broadcasting (television as well as radio by then) was still public service, but the most popular content had always been the light entertainment that had been developed in commercial music and concert halls and theatres. Harmless? The pre-1939 recreation movements treated commercial media as part of the 'opposition' which was encouraging 'mechanical' passive leisure. Approved leisure services promoted 'active' recreation, which was supposed to nurture healthy and enthusiastic worker-citizens.

LEISURE INDUSTRIES

Let us fast-forward to the end of the 20th century. We find that the commercial enemy that was threatening at the gates of the leisure services 50 years previously had entered and taken command of the castle.

The original leisure services had received a boost during a broader expansion of welfare spending in Western countries in the decades that immediately followed the Second World War. However, consumer spending on commercial leisure goods and services grew even more rapidly. Real incomes rose steadily with only brief interruptions until the banking crisis of 2008, and, as incomes rose, rising proportions of spending went on leisure goods and services (mainly the commercial varieties). The fastest-growing areas of leisure spending were the media, tourism and out-of-home eating and drinking.

After the Second World War, the original old media (movies, radio, recorded music and newspapers) were joined by television, which quickly became dominant, and all other media, especially radio and movies, needed to adapt. Later on, multi-channel TV gave viewers more choice, 24/7. In Europe, formerly the bastion of public service broadcasting, around 80 per cent of all broadcasting was commercial by the end of the century. By then the tourist industry had developed new exciting products. In Europe, international travel began to replace domestic holidays from the 1950s. Subsequently wide-bodied jets conveying more prosperous holidaymakers led to an expansion in long-haul vacations and opened the door to the rest of the world for holidaymaking Americans. Tour companies began to promote a variety of specialist products: adventure holidays, safaris, wine and art tours, farm tourism and even 'dark tourism' to Second World War extermination camps. The sale of broadcasting rights to sports events, and live broadcasting throughout global TV networks, led to a huge injection of new money into top sport, which became increasingly commercial. Commercial health and fitness gyms, and commercial promoters of various 'lifestyle' and 'extreme' sports competed with public authorities' and voluntary sports associations' 'traditional' facilities and activities.

By the beginning of the 21st century, leisure providers were presenting themselves and were being regarded differently than in the age of the leisure services. *The Leisure Industries* (Roberts, 2004) opened with the following quotation from the then UK prime minister, Tony Blair:

> more people work in film and TV than in the car industry – let alone shipbuilding. The overseas earnings of British rock music exceed those generated by the steel industry. (Tony Blair, 'Britain can remake it', *Guardian*, 22 July 1997)

By the end of the 20th century, all the older industrial countries had experienced de-industrialisation. Many of their former manufacturing jobs had been relocated to lower-wage-cost countries. Others had been retained only by replacing human workers with technology. The outcome was that by the end of the 20th century, manufacturing accounted for less than a fifth of all employment in these countries, and all the countries were seeking replacement jobs. In the 1950s and 1960s, public sector employment had grown. Many new jobs were created in public administration, education and health care. Then, from the 1970s onwards, governments had been struggling to restrain further growth in state spending. Finance and other business services became strong areas of employment growth in the 1970s and 1980s, but by the 1990s these businesses were introducing labour-saving technologies such as cash machines followed by Internet banking. Where would the next new jobs come from? Leisure seemed the most promising site.

Cities, regions and countries began looking to their leisure industries to regenerate their economies. Instead of investment in steel mills, they began trying to attract casinos and sports stadiums. They began to compete for business in the night-time economy and to develop cultural quarters which were supposed to make cities attractive to a new 'creative class' who would bring with them the expanding 'creative industries' whose main asset is intellectual property rights (Florida, 2002, 2012). Employment was proving resilient or growing in most leisure industries because it was (and still is) difficult to replace humans with technology without devaluing the leisure experience, and most leisure-related jobs are difficult if not impossible to export with one big exception, which is when the spenders are international tourists. Otherwise, leisure services have to be provided wherever the customers are based. By the end of the 20th century, it was leisure customers, not leisure jobs, that had become mobile. Consumers were able and willing to travel to the cities of their choice for shopping and entertainment, and to the countries of their choice for short breaks and longer vacations. Leisure had thus become an important contributor to cities', regions' and countries' trade balances. Inward tourism was a major export industry. Outward tourists were imports. Media content (films, music, TV programmes, sports broadcasts) sold to other countries was exports. Imported entertainment took money out of a city's, region's or country's economy. By the 1990s, cities and countries were competing to host events, especially sports mega-events, which were attracting huge numbers of sport tourists (spectators, players, officials and media personnel). These events were also leveraging spending on infrastructure, especially hotels and other types of accommodation plus transport networks. The planners' problem was, and still is, to build facilities that meet the needs of a one-off event and prove of longer-term value to local businesses and residents (see Malhado and Rothfuss, 2013).

During these developments, the view of leisure as a social service was replaced by leisure as a set of major industries. The public sector, voluntary associations and commercial providers ceased to be rivals and became partners, the triple pillars of leisure economies. Modernised leisure industries had to pull together. Alongside these developments, the old leisure studies courses had tended to split into programmes specialising on sport, tourism, hospitality, then sometimes into sub-fields such as events, youth sport, sport tourism, sport development, cultural tourism, and so on. These developments matched the division of labour within the leisure industries. Each was believed to want specialists, not leisure generalists. During this breakup in the academy, the programmes had tended to relocate out of social sciences and into management or business schools or, in the case of sport, into health faculties. The aim of the old recreation movements of creating better societies had been replaced by delivering economic growth and private benefits to leisure consumers. In the case of participant sport, the main benefits were improved health and fitness – more years of livelier life. Other leisure providers claimed to be able to enhance 'well-being'. In all cases, the leisure purchaser/consumer had become sovereign.

LEISURE SINCE THE FINANCIAL CRISIS

The 21st-century context

This book focuses on how the leisure industries have changed during the 21st century. In some respects, the story is of older trends continuing. The leisure industries remain as important or more important than ever in local and national economies. However, the financial crisis that began to unfold in 2006 and escalated into a global crash in 2008–09 has created an aftermath that has placed the leisure industries and all other businesses in Western Europe and North America in a new context. Much of this context can be summarised by one word – austerity. This is despite the fact that major sections of the leisure industries have continued to grow in terms of global spending and revenues. These sections include spending on travel and then at their destinations by international tourists, the global value of rights to televise sports events and the related events industry. These successes have been in the wider context of 'the crash' leading to an extended and ongoing age of austerity in public spending and in living standards for most citizens in the world's richest countries.

Public spending has been a casualty as governments have struggled to reduce public sector deficits (the gap between what they spend and what they raise in taxes and other charges). Households' real incomes and therefore living standards have been depressed, and for the first time since 1945 upcoming cohorts of young adults look unlikely to better the living standards of their parents (in fact, they are more likely to live worse) (see Roberts, 2012). This is just part of the new post-crash context in which the leisure industries now do business. Another feature of this context is ageing populations. Seniors are the leisure market that is guaranteed to expand for many decades. We know this because the cohorts currently entering retirement and about to retire are expected to live longer than their predecessors, and these cohorts are larger than current cohorts of children and young people. Today's retirees were born in an age when birth rates were higher. Wider economic inequality is another feature of the post-crash context. The pre-crash tendency for income and wealth to be sucked upwards rather than to trickle down has continued. In many countries, demand for luxury goods and services by the rich and better-off is the segment of the leisure market that is growing most strongly. Sometimes, it is the only leisure sector that is growing.

Then there is the continuation of new impacts from digital information and communication technologies (ICTs). The basic technologies themselves are now middle-aged. Computer games and personal computers (PCs) have been around since the 1970s. The World Wide Web was invented by Tim Berners-Lee in 1989. However, in 2000, the first dot-com bubble had yet to burst. Only older readers may recall Boo.com, Infospace, Pets.com and Tiscali, whose share prices soared in the late 1990s and then crashed. All readers will recognise the names of some survivors from that bubble; they include Amazon, Google and eBay. In 2000, file sharing had not begun to affect sales of recorded music. In 2000, only 3 per cent of US households had broadband connections (it was 70 per cent by 2012). Retail shopping had not begun to move online. Facebook was created only in 2004 and Twitter in 2006. In 2014, Facebook claimed over a billion active users, and Twitter had over 0.5 billion registered users. Both might become history before this book ceases to be read. In 1991, first-generation mobile phones were superseded by 2G, the design that was marketed until the end of the 20th century. In 2001, the first 3G mobile phones were marketed, and 4G arrived in 2009. Each generation has performed more functions than its predecessor. ICTs are still the proverbial 'elephant in the room' – the leisure room and many other rooms besides – liable at any time to shatter all the furniture.

The financial crash and its aftermath

We now realise that the roots of the crash of 2008–09 can be traced back to the 1970s, when governments began to deregulate financial institutions (see Calhoun and Derluguian, 2011; Tett, 2009). This was a precondition for the rise of global financialised capitalism (Lapavitsas, 2011). International finance was supposed to have become a self-regulating system in which risk was so widely dispersed that problems would be small-scale and manageable. How wrong can you be? All it took was for some loans (sub-prime US mortgages) to go bad for confidence to drain from the global financial system (see Chorafas, 2012; Davis, 2009; Sorkin, 2009; Tett, 2009). The recession that was triggered meant reductions in tax revenues and increases in government spending on unemployment and related benefits. This left governments seeking ways to close widening gaps between their revenues and spending.

Implications for the leisure industries

What has all this to do with leisure? A lot! New technology would have continued to create new products even if there had been no financial crash.

ICTs would have been finding new applications in old leisure industries while creating entirely new kinds of leisure businesses. Populations would have continued to age. Singles and childless young couples remain an important leisure market. Young adults have been postponing marriage and parenthood into their late twenties and thirties, and high rates of divorce and separation mean more returns to singles scenes. Yet the leisure industries in all countries are now addressing populations in which the fastest-growing age group is the over-eighties followed by the over-seventies, followed by the over-sixties. Some are fit and active. Others have medical conditions which do not necessarily diminish their leisure appetites. Irrespective of health status, many have above-average disposable (on leisure) incomes. All these 21st-century developments could have been anticipated and were foreseen before the end of the 20th century. Similarly, economic inequalities were already widening. In the United States, labour productivity rose by 30 per cent between 1998 and 2008, but real wages rose by only 2 per cent. Household debt as a proportion of disposable income in the United States rose from 3 per cent in 1998 to 130 per cent in 2008. Real wages were stagnating. Living standards were still rising or were being maintained only by mounting consumer debt (Castells et al., 2012). All this was known beforehand. The financial crash has been the unforeseen event. Were any businesses planning for this? Financial institutions were taken by surprise.

The commercialisation of leisure had been under way for decades. As explained above, throughout the 20th century, commerce had been the fastest-growing leisure provider. The difference since the crash is that commercialisation has become gale force.

■ Governments have been seeking to reduce their overall spending. Education, health and pensions are difficult even to cap. Spending on leisure services has usually been a victim.

■ Governments have become even keener to treat leisure as an investment which can boost their economies, especially if exports are boosted. So spending on events, heritage, culture and attractions is prioritised with tourists as the main target, and, wherever possible, media content is designed for export as well as domestic distribution.

■ The search for value for money leads governments to outsource delivery: in other words, to hand over the management and delivery of public services to voluntary associations and commercial businesses – whoever offers the best value for money. In-house teams are required to bid competitively for contracts. All this began long before the financial crash.

Leisure services were pathfinders. The model has subsequently spread into education, health care, the administration of welfare benefits and work programmes for the unemployed. Trade agreements with emerging market economies have typically required services of all kinds – gas, water, electricity – to be open to global competition. This model has now entered First World countries. Some commercial businesses specialise in winning public service contracts. An outcome is that voluntary associations that win contracts, and services that remain in-house, are obliged to operate as if they were commercial businesses. Alexandris (2008) has noted the spread of performance management tools and service quality models in all the leisure industries. The explanation, according to Alexandris, is that 'the market is getting more competitive and professional than ever and the leisure consumer is getting more demanding than ever' (p. 13). In many cases, the purchaser/consumer is a public authority rather than a service user.

Governments can reap a double dividend by outsourcing the delivery of public services. They invariably hope for more value for money spent. Simultaneously, they outsource responsibility for failure (see Sam, 2012). In England, the series of Active People Surveys began in 2005–06 with samples that were sufficiently large to yield results that were valid for local authority areas and individual sports (many of which are played by very small proportions of the total population). Local authorities and sport governing bodies received central government funding along with targets for increasing participation. Only the targets, not whether these were met, remained the central government's responsibility. Failure to meet the targets was offloaded (see Rowe, 2009).

Commercial businesses will accept state contracts only if they can anticipate profits. Voluntary associations are different. They usually hope to be able to enhance the scope or quality of their work, but they may well find that their own character changes in unanticipated ways. Commercial methods, accountability and monitoring become essential. Scope for new innovative work may well be reduced (see Sam, 2012).

Blurred boundaries

One type of blurring in the leisure industries is in how commercial, public sector and voluntary providers go about their businesses. Partnerships are not new. What is new is the similarity in how the formerly distinct leisure sectors operate. They are converging on commercial practices.

Another kind of blurring is between making provisions for different uses of leisure – sport, entertainment, tourism, the arts, and so on. The principal source of this blurring is the increased propensity of people to travel. Sport is a generator of tourism. Players travel to ski, to surf, to play golf and to compete in amateur sports events. Spectators also travel, especially for mega-events. The management of any event involves an activity, facility or object (a sport event, an arts festival, an exhibition), travel (by tourists or trippers) and hospitality (catering and accommodation) during and sometimes before and following the event. A sport event can be simultaneously a local spectacle, media content, a source of tourists and an object for gambling. Managers of sport, the arts, the heritage and tourism can no longer operate in independent silos. The splintering of leisure studies into specialisms that looked appropriate in the age of separate leisure industries is now outdated. Consumers may still see themselves as sport players or spectators, cultural or any other kind of tourist, but their management cannot be separated so clearly.

A further blurring is between the leisure industries and other business sectors. It has always been difficult to draw a clear boundary between leisure time and activities and the rest of people's lives. 'Grey' areas have always been acknowledged, and these areas are expanding, not necessarily in how people experience their lives but on the 'supply side'. There is an element of leisure in spending on motoring, fashion, furnishings, communications (radio, television, Internet, mobile phones) and food and drink. Design has become important in all these business sectors. They are all part of the 'experience economy' (Pine and Gilmore, 1999). Leisure providers know that 'the experience' has to be at the core of their appeal (see Gration et al., 2011; Morgan, 2008; Pegg and Patterson, 2010). The leisure industries do not supply just goods and services. They also market desires, and enable us to be recognised as, and to feel like, particular kinds of people as a result of what we wear, eat and drink, what we listen to and watch and where we are seen and who we are seen with. The leisure industries do not create social class, age, gender, ethnic or national divisions, but they can sharpen, deepen or diminish these divisions, and characterise the relevant groups. They do this by deciding, in their marketing, for whom a given activity, good or service, along with the associated identity, is most appropriate. The goods and services that are used in this way are not only those conventionally described as leisure industries or businesses.

Tony Veal (2011, 2012) has noted that the 'society of leisure' that was a hot topic of debate in the 1950s, 1960s and 1970s has not only failed to materialise: since the 1980s, the phrase has all but disappeared from the leisure studies literature. Maybe we have been looking in the wrong places. Leisure may not have become dominant or more central in people's lifestyles, but many other kinds of business have become more like leisure businesses. This, of course, implies that the business of leisure still has distinctive features. This book's position is that leisure businesses retain distinctive features. One is the fickleness of demand for non-essential purchases. Another is the operation of the triple engines – commerce, voluntary associations and the public sector. The core leisure industries still share features that make them different from all other businesses. Fickleness of demand applies to entire products rather than just brands. Also, the core leisure industries have continued to generate more jobs even in an age of austerity.

One indication of the extent to which all kinds of leisure provisions have collapsed into business is how eagerly all these industries stress and typically exaggerate their contributions to national economies. Sport England (2013) claims that sport in England supports 440,000 jobs, but these jobs include those paid for by subscriptions to sports-related television channels and employment in sports-related gambling. Independent analysts might well allocate some of the jobs claimed by Sport England to other business sectors. VisitBritain claims that inward tourism supports 9 per cent of the British economy (www.visitbritain.org), but this figure is based on the totals employed in what are said to be tourism-characteristic businesses – travel, accommodation and catering (Office for National Statistics, 2013). Oliver Wyman (2012) calculated that the combined leisure industries accounted for just 9 per cent of the UK economy (no more than VisitBritain claims for tourism alone). However, Wyman does not include travel, the media and emerging leisure businesses such as computer games and social media sites. Attempts to draw clear boundaries between different leisure industries and between leisure and other business sectors have been rendered more difficult than formerly by all the blurring. It has become impossible to make precise distinctions between different leisure industries in terms of exactly how many they employ and the economic value added, or between leisure industries and other business sectors. It is possible, while acknowledging a 'grey' area, to estimate the amount of leisure time that people have at their disposal. When we ask how they spend this time, and on what they spend money during this time, the answers range throughout the economy – gardening, music, fashion, eating out (and drinking), using recreational drugs, watching television, surfing the Internet – the list is endless. Nowadays, businesses in all these sectors need to prioritise the consumer experience. Purchasing and using have to be made enjoyable, and to confer or confirm desired identities whenever this is possible. This book does not claim to cover all the kinds of business from which individuals derive leisure experiences, whose goods and services they use in their leisure time or on which they spend income that is not commanded by necessities. The book illustrates its arguments by examining three of the older leisure industries (tourism, sport and the mass media), plus events whose number and size have made this into a large specialist sector, and new leisure industries that are being created with the aid of new (ICT) technologies and media.

BOOK PLAN

One of the core arguments, a thread that links all the chapters in this book, is that despite all the blurring, the commercial, voluntary and public sectors retain different, very distinctive, capabilities. We shall see that these sectors are not just alternative ways of providing much the same range of leisure goods and services. Each sector has its own 'engine', and the provisions that result can be distinctively commercial, voluntary or public sector products. It is in terms of the 'logics' of commerce, voluntarism and state intervention that we find our most powerful explanations of what the leisure industries offer. We find that we cannot explain the kind of holidays, for example, that are made available simply by searching for facts and explanations, however deeply and assiduously, solely within the field of tourism. We need to identify the main sector and thereby the main 'engine' which drives this segment of the leisure industries, which turns out to be commerce, which is always run for profit – the very same engine which also provides most of our popular entertainment, and most of our opportunities to gamble and to spend evenings out eating or drinking. Sport, in contrast, developed from a voluntary base, and most sport is still run by volunteers, acting as members of voluntary bodies. Commerce has claimed segments of top sport and, as explained in Chapter 6, in doing so it has not merely replaced one supply mechanism with another but is changing the character of the sports themselves that are made available for people to play and to watch. Likewise, we shall see in Chapter 8 that, as television has become increasingly commercial, the product itself (what is available on our screens) has changed.

There are two organising principles within this book. One is explicit in the chapter headings in Section II (Chapters 5–9). We systematically examine tourism, sport, events, the cultural leisure industries and then the emerging new leisure industries – how each industry has developed up to now, and how it is run. The other organising principle is that throughout all the examples in successive chapters the book seeks to identify and then illustrate the special capabilities in leisure of commerce, voluntary associations and the state. It aims to render explicit the strengths and limitations of each.

We therefore proceed in Section I (Chapters 2–4) by examining systematically the character of the commercial, voluntary and state-based systems of leisure provision. Commerce (driven by profit) is treated briefly at this point. It provides many different kinds of leisure goods and services and therefore features in all this book's chapters about particular kinds of leisure, but its distinctive features are simple, straightforward and easy to explain and understand. Chapter 3 deals similarly with voluntary associations – what they are, why they exist and what is special about what they offer. Chapter 4 treats public sector leisure in the same way, identifying how it is 'driven', and its special capabilities. These special capabilities of the public sector are considered again in Section III (Chapter 10), but the intervening chapters will illustrate repeatedly that the state has capabilities which are simply beyond the reach of both commerce and the voluntary sector.

A recurrent issue in this book which has already featured, and will feature again and again, and necessarily so, is the progressive commercialisation of leisure provision. This is despite the fact that in the social sciences (economics apart), commerce still tends to receive far more criticism than praise. Commerce has been accused of debasing our sports, films, music, catering, broadcasting, holidays and the arts, and promoting undesirable uses of leisure such as smoking, drinking and gambling. Commercialisation occurred at different times in different areas of leisure. So critiques of Hollywood and popular music date from the 1920s, whereas, in Europe, complaints about business taking over sport and broadcasting have mounted only during the last 30 years. The case against commerce differs somewhat from leisure industry to leisure industry, but there are numerous overlaps and crossovers in the arguments, and these are highlighted in Chapter 2. Governments, especially in recent times (when they have been influenced by new right thinking), have been criticised for creating or defending the conditions which enable commercial businesses to expand their operations willy-nilly and to do so profitably, failing to do enough themselves, failing to protect the voluntary sector and, within the latter, favouring the more commercial high-profile performing arts companies, and subsidising the construction of stadiums suited to major events while neglecting community arts and grass-roots amateur sport. Some of the more detailed critiques of

commerce are introduced in the chapters about the particular leisure industries in relation to which the arguments were originally developed.

This book's position is as follows:

- First, commercialisation is certainly a powerful trend. It developed throughout the 20th century and it is continuing, aided by new right, neoliberal policies.
- Second, commerce is not a wholly malign force in leisure. It can spread only when there are willing consumers, who always have alternatives.
- Third, commerce is still just one of three main systems that cater for leisure, and it is simply incapable of dowsing either the voluntary or the public sector unless volunteers and politicians decide to stand aside.
- Fourth, while commerce and the voluntary sector can be relied on to perform to their strengths, the public sector is different. Here, everything depends on policy-makers recognising their special capabilities in leisure.

The selection of leisure industries, and the order in which they are introduced from Chapter 5 onwards, may appear haphazard, but there is an underlying logic. We begin with tourism, a leisure industry in which commerce now has a long history as the principal provider. We then consider modern sports, which have voluntary sector roots which, as we shall see, are still largely intact. Commerce services sport, but Chapter 6 explains why it is unable to take over the core without changing the character of the sports themselves. Chapter 7 deals with events, which are always about tourism or short-stay visitors plus something else – the event – which may be based on sport, an art form, wine or anything else that attracts visitors. Chapter 8 is about the cultural industries – heritage, the arts and the media. Some of these – the printed media, films and recorded music – have always been basically commercial, whereas in Europe broadcasting was originally developed as a public service. Then, during the later part of the 20th century, there was a commercial takeover. Recent commercial inroads in sport and broadcast-ing, together with controversies about the costs and benefits for countries that host events such as the Olympics, highlight what is distinctive about each of the three main types of leisure providers. Chapter 9 – 'New leisure industries' – is about new leisure products or products which have been grown into major businesses by ICT-based media.

The book's final chapter returns to the role of the state in leisure. It also addresses the character of the jobs that leisure is creating, and the educa-tion programmes and qualifications that are intended to lead to careers in leisure. The chapter draws on evidence presented in the intervening chapters, and expands on the earlier analysis (in Chapter 4) of the public sector's special capabilities: what governments alone can realistically hope to achieve by intervening in leisure. Up to now these capabilities have never been properly identified. This is bound up with our failure to develop coherent leisure policies and, despite all the carping about commerce, to offer a strong modern alternative to the new right's analyses. An outcome is that although governments still spend a lot and do a lot in leisure, we fail to derive maximum benefit.

WHOSE BUSINESS?

This book is everyone's business, the leisure of everyone and everywhere. This is because the main trends affecting leisure are now global: commercialisation, ageing populations, information and communication technologies, national governments' neoliberal policies that are policed by transnational financial institutions and the financial crash and its aftermath. Major leisure products are now marketed globally: films, spectator sports, all kinds of events, television content and other 'branded' leisure goods and services. Even when people remain local (which most people do most of the time and sometimes for the whole of their lives), they are part of global markets.

This is not to claim that leisure is being homogenised globally. Far from it: every place presents a unique mixture including blends and hybrids of the local and the global. The processes and outcomes are known as 'glocalisation'. It is the processes, the ways of providing for people's leisure, that are global, and in localities everywhere leisure is now primarily a business. However, there are different outcomes which will persist. Many late-developing countries are now closing the gap with living standards in the West. The gap is still huge, but every country now has leisure consumers who are catered for by commercial businesses. The first-wave industrial countries of the West are different in that they have histories in which they developed relatively strong leisure services catering for members (of voluntary association) and for citizens (with rights of access to public leisure services). Latterly these older leisure services have been exposed to commercial competition and have often gone commercial in order to survive. In many late-developing countries, modern leisure provisions began to develop initially to cater for inward tourists. Public spending on leisure in these countries has always been treated primarily as a business investment. Voluntary leisure sectors are less sturdy when they have had to develop *de novo* in late-20th- and 21st-century commercial contexts. Public leisure services for local populations in late-developing, emerging market economies typically remain poor relations of investment for the benefit of inward tourists.

Leisure and leisure provisions in first-wave industrial countries remain different in many ways, but their services and businesses have acted as models for later-developing countries, especially (now former) colonies. Britain was the world's first industrial nation, and the types of leisure provision that it pioneered in the 19th and early-20th centuries have acted as models from which other countries have built their own versions. Most modern sports were invented in Britain as was the modern holiday away from home. Forms of entertainment that were invented and which first spread across Europe and North America in the late-19th and early-20th centuries – radio, television, mass circulation newspapers, recorded music and movies – were subsequently implanted throughout the rest of the world. All the following chapters provide a historical background on how the relevant leisure services and industries have developed. UK readers will usually find themselves reading about history in their own and other early-industrialising countries, but it is also the history of leisure provisions in other parts of the world to which the inventions have spread.

Leisure businesses based in the United States and Britain and other European countries now serve global markets. Locals in the United States and Britain and other European countries need to understand that 'their' provisions, including many of their favourite television programmes, are no longer made solely or even mainly for them. This also applies to their major sports teams and events. This was not the case in the past, but the present-day business of leisure is different – it is global.

Section I

Providers

Chapter 2

Commercial Leisure

INTRODUCTION

This chapter is not a tour around everything that commerce offers. Rather, this chapter simply identifies the 'engine' that drives commerce and the implications. The engine is profit. We explore how this makes a difference to the character of these leisure providers and the leisure goods and services that they offer. Note that the engine is profit, not money, which is a crucial fuel in most types of leisure provision – by the voluntary and public sectors as well as commerce. Charging customers and paying staff (whether the staff are sport players, artists, entertainers or managers) do not of themselves make something commercial. Commerce exists only when there is a separate class of owners – profit-seeking owners or a petit bourgeoisie of owner-workers – while other people are involved as hired hands, clients and customers (but not members or citizens). Having already identified the engine, this chapter proceeds to review the distinctive features of commercial leisure provisions that result, starting with the blurred boundary between leisure and other kinds of commerce.

BLURRED BOUNDARY

The previous chapter argued that it is impossible to draw a clear line between commercial businesses that address leisure and the rest of commerce. With voluntary associations it is easier. Leisure associations are joined voluntarily and members participate in their own (leisure) time. Public sector leisure providers work from or are funded by central or local government departments with recreation, leisure, sports, the arts, tourism or something similar in their titles. Commercial businesses that run cinemas, theatres, fitness gyms and ice rinks, and manufacturers and distributors of recorded music all appear to be firmly located in leisure, though we shall see below that this is not always so. Firms that package and sell holidays definitely look like leisure businesses. But suppose a tourist books online. Is the website operator a leisure business, and what about the airline and hotel that are booked? All these providers have leisure and business customers. Businesses that create and market computer games are clearly offering leisure products, but what about Microsoft, Apple, Google, Samsung and other businesses that produce the hardware and software that we use to book theatre tickets, to download music and to stay in everyday contact with friends? The engine is profit, and firms are delighted if their products find both business and leisure uses.

All firms that operate in consumer markets, and sometimes those addressing business customers, are subject to market pressures to make all aspects of engagement with the products and services, their use and purchasing, into pleasurable experiences. This is part of the 'experience economy' in which the design of a product and the environments in which it is bought and used can be crucial to commercial success (Pine and Gilmore, 1999). Businesses must try to make the experiences 'entertaining', which is defined by Moss (2009) as anything that attracts and captivates an audience, and an audience may comprise potential and actual purchasers. Vogel (2004) uses this definition to calculate that entertainment has become the world's largest business sector. Entertainment, as defined by Moss, has become the DNA of business-based advanced economies.

In some cases, the boundary between leisure and other businesses is blurred because customers may or may not use the products for leisure. The blurring is amplified when a leisure-like experience is designed into a product and its uses. In other cases, the boundary is blurred because a business has interests in leisure and other sectors. There are examples in Box 2.1. There are further examples among England's major football clubs. Since 2005, Manchester United has been owned by the America-based Glazer family which also owns the Tampa Bay Buccaneers, who play the American version of football. The Glazers' business interests are focused on sport, like those of Fenway Sports, the owner of Liverpool FC since 2010, which also controls the US baseball team Boston Red Sox. Other foreign owners of England's football teams lack comparable sport credentials. Since 2010, Blackburn Rovers has been owned by the V H Group, known as Venky's, an Indian company whose interests include poultry, food processing and animal vaccines. Since 2010, Cardiff City FC's principal investor has been Vincent Tan, a Malaysian investor with stakes in golf, property, resorts and gambling, who may be said to

---

Box 2.1 Leisure businesses?

THE VIRGIN GROUP

In 1968, 17-year-old Richard Branson (now Sir Richard Branson) and a friend opened a record shop. They called it *Virgin* because both felt that they were virgins in the business.

Branson is reported to have conceived the Virgin Group in 1970. Today, it is a global investment business that controls over 400 companies. The group is involved in the following:

- Music
- Mobile telephones
- Broadband and cable television
- Financial services (Virgin Money, which acquired Northern Rock in 2012)
- Holidays
- Space travel with Virgin Galactic. Flights are priced at $250,000 per passenger but the first passenger flight was further delayed by the disastrous end to a test flight in 2014.

SERCO INC.

This US-based group (headquarters in Reston, Virginia) specialises in providing professional, technological and management services to governments.

The subsidiary, Serco UK, is based in Hook, north Hampshire. It manages a number of leisure centres in the UK including the Manchester Aquatic Centre, which was built for the 2002 Commonwealth Games. In addition, Serco provides services for the following:

- UK Border Agency
- Rail and ferry services
- Bicycle hire
- The National Physics Laboratory
- Prisons
- UK Ballistic Missile Early Warning System
- Hospitals

---

have extended his leisure portfolio. In 2013, he added another football club, Bosnian FK Sarajevo. Since 2009, Manchester City FC has been owned by Sheikh Mansour, deputy prime minister of the United Arab Emirates (UEA) and a member of the ruling family in Abu Dhabi. Etihad Airways is the flag carrier of the UAE, and Etihad Stadium is now the name of Manchester City's stadium, formerly known as the City of Manchester Stadium, or Eastlands, and originally built for the 2002 Commonwealth Games. In 2014, another of Sheikh Mansour's companies, the Abu Dhabi United Group, announced plans to partner Manchester City Council in building up to 6,000 homes in the neighbourhood bordering the Etihad Stadium. In 2003, Chelsea FC was bought by Roman Abramovich, a Russian multi-billionaire and one of the richest people in the world. A football club may be a fun acquisition for those who can afford it. Ownership will intensify the fan experience (for the owner). It may be an image-building asset for a business group or even a country. Alternatively or in addition, it may simply be an investment seeking profits and capital appreciation. This is one aspect of the financialisation of capitalism. Finance is not tied to a specific firm or even business sector, but flows to wherever promises the best returns. A consequence is that today's boundary between leisure and other types of commerce is porous, more so than in the past.

A BRIEF HISTORY OF COMMERCIAL LEISURE

The 19th century

Our leisure may be distinctively modern but recreation has been universal, and when 19th-century Britain was transformed from a mainly rural into a mainly urban society and became the world's first industrial nation, soon followed by other European countries and the United States, the new urban residents brought with them many of their traditional village pastimes. They took their drinking, animal sports and fighting, and fairs continued to travel the country. Gradually, these pastimes were either banned, replaced or modernised. Town and city streets became places for daily shopping, so fairs lost their role as market places and henceforth specialised in entertainment, amusement and unprecedented thrills with their new mechanically powered rides. Modern sports, suitable for play in urban areas and compatible with industrial time rhythms, were invented and then popularised as participant games and spectator events. Traditional inns and alehouses were replaced by more specialised institutions – hotels, restaurants and pubs. Hobbies and other new uses of leisure were pioneered. The 'straight' theatre and music hall were separated, and the modern holiday was popularised.

These innovations were not all led by commerce. In fact, commerce was not at the forefront of developments in leisure in the 19th century. The new modern sports were run by voluntary bodies. The holiday 'away' was initially invented by Thomas Cook in 1841 and was then strenuously promoted by churches, progressive employers and other social reformers. The holiday away was associated with thrift, sobriety and family bonding. Museums, parks and art galleries were provided by local authorities. Throughout the 19th century, most leisure innovations were by local authorities and the voluntary sector. City and town councils opened bathhouses (to which swimming pools were added later on). These same local authorities created urban parks, designated playing fields and built concert halls and other cultural facilities. The 19th century was the age of the municipality, of civic pride and local council-led efforts to establish civilised ways of urban life (Meller, 1976). Clubs were formed by the various hobby enthusiasts, and the voluntary sector created the now-traditional youth organisations. Even sports which permitted professional (paid) players (mainly football) continued to be run by voluntary bodies, and professional footballers' wages were capped (until 1961 in Britain) at a level that was supposed to no more than compensate for a working man's lost earnings. As far as we can tell, the middle classes have always been the main joiners, but in 19th-century Britain it was not only the middle classes who formed and joined clubs. Churches and chapels, trade unions and the social clubs that they supported became bases for organised working-class pastimes which included sports, educational activities and a host of additional interests such as pigeon racing and brass bands. These non-commercial developments were part of the movement for 'rational recreation' that spread into Continental Europe and across North America, and was described in the previous chapter. The aim of these social reformers was to encourage the new urban populations to use their free time and money sensibly, meaning in wholesome, edifying ways which would lead to self-improvement. Their enemy was the 'dark side of leisure' at that time – drink, gambling and prostitution (all commercial and usually illegal).

Commerce was very much a subsidiary force in the development of leisure provision throughout the 19th century – understandably so once we appreciate that, for leisure goods and services to be profitable, people must have money to spend on non-essentials. Commerce offered pubs, fairs and music halls, the theatre and eventually holidays, but even these provisions were heavily regulated. Holidays were regulated (governed) by working time which, in the 19th century, left precious little time for leisure. Fairs, the theatre and the music hall were regulated by local government by-laws. Drinking was regulated by increasingly tough licensing laws and taxation. In the United States, the sale and distribution of alcohol products were prohibited between 1920 and 1933. The rest of the dark side of leisure (gambling and prostitution) was usually illegal. Commercial leisure at that time was either little above or beneath the boundary of respectability.

The music halls (theatres with programmes consisting of a variety of acts) and vaudeville, the equivalent in the United States, were probably the highest-profile type of commercial leisure that was created in the second half of the 19th century, and remained extremely popular until cinema and broadcasting began to compete just before, during and after the First World War. Music halls made fortunes for some proprietors and became renowned for the spectacular yields that investors could earn. So they became popular with speculative investors (like English football clubs and dot-com companies since the 1990s). Another parallel is that, as a matter of fact, music halls were always extremely high-risk ventures (Crowhurst, 2001). Leisure is usually a risky place to invest. Tastes can be fickle, and one brand is easily displaced by another.

Nowadays, commerce is the most powerful engine driving leisure provision, which makes it all the more important to realise that things were not always so. When the growth of commercial provision really took off, which was in the first half of the 20th century, it did so amidst established competition which was becoming ever stronger. Local authorities were extending their own leisure services – opening new swimming baths, and taking on responsibility for youth service, for example. Participant and spectator sports were also growing strongly. The campaign to treat leisure as a social service was at its height. New non-commercial uses of leisure were constantly being pioneered. As city populations overflowed into suburbs, gardening became a popular pastime, and local authorities created allotments for the use of garden-less households. The development of public transport and the bicycle opened up the countryside and enabled rambling and hiking to become popular recreations with their own voluntary bodies. In Britain, these included the Youth Hostels Association, which was formed in 1931 with, at that time, just 73 hostels and 6,000 members (it now has around 200 hostels and over 200,000 members). Commerce, when it developed, did not eliminate anything that already existed. It simply added to people's leisure options. No one had to use what commerce offered. There were alternatives. Indeed, there were, and still are, direct public or voluntary sector competitors in many fields of leisure where commerce operates.

Between the World Wars

The growth of commercial leisure in the first half of the 20th century was dependent on rising living standards, but it was aided considerably by scientific and technological innovations or, rather, by entrepreneurial responses to such innovations which led to businesses marketing bicycles, motor cars and aeroplanes (all of which could be, and were, used for leisure as well as for other purposes). Further technological developments made it possible to sell radios, record players and, later on, television sets. The last chapter explained that in Britain the BBC was nationalised in 1927 (it had previously been a private company which had already been subjected to state regulation and given a broadcasting monopoly), but only when commerce had already demonstrated that the best way to make money out of radio was to sell receivers and to broadcast popular entertainment to households. Recorded music and cinema were further technology-led innovations that commerce pioneered as leisure industries. The dance palais was another commercial innovation but, in this instance, not new technology rooted. Since the 19th century, commerce has been the main innovator among the leisure providers.

It was during the interwar years that mass markets were developed for a new range of 'white goods', most of which became viable when dwellings were connected to mains electricity. These goods included cookers, irons, refrigerators and washing machines as well as radios, gramophones and, later on, televisions. Thus consumption-based lifestyles began to spread (see Bowden, 1994; Cross, 1993). The 1920s and 1930s are best remembered – still (just) in living memory as well as in history books – for the unemployment and attendant poverty, but in Britain the unemployment was mostly outside the south of England, and people who remained in work experienced real increases in their earnings. In the United States, Henry Ford developed a mass market for his firm's mass-produced motor cars. It was between the wars that department stores began to cater for a mass rather than just an upmarket clientele (see Lancaster, 1996), and when multimedia advertising and consumer credit were first introduced. The seeds of the experience economy were being sown. Commerce was beginning to erode the boundary between leisure and other kinds of consumption.

Post-1945

However, commercial consumer culture has been the dominant leisure culture only since the Second World War, after which Western governments adopted Keynesian methods of economic management (part of the social democratic consensus which then prevailed). An outcome was the '30 glorious years' of full employment in most regions of most Western countries, and more-or-less continuous economic growth and year-on-year rises in standards of living. In the 1950s, the TV set became standard domestic equipment. The market for recorded music was enlarged considerably through products specifically designed to be sold to young people. Scooter and motorcycle sales rose. During the 1960s, most West European households followed the Americans in acquiring motor cars. Simultaneously, the markets for fashion clothing and cosmetics were expanded, and likewise the holiday industry, with a rising proportion of holidays taken abroad. The transistor radio, the music cassette, the Walkman and its competitors, then the CD, further enlarged the music market during the remainder of the 20th century. The video recorder, then satellite and cable television and the DVD led to further growth in the audiovisual and entertainment markets. Commerce has subsequently been responsible for all the technological advances that have placed households and businesses online, and with the latest smartphones it has now done the same for individuals who are on the move. Alcohol consumption per capita in Britain doubled between the 1950s and the 1990s. There was a similar rate of growth in other Western countries. The meals-out market expanded dramatically, assisted by the popularity of ethnic restaurants and the fast-food restaurants that were pioneered in the United States (see below). Nightclubs, offering combinations of different types of recorded and live music and alcohol, opened in virtually all towns and cities, which thereby acquired booming night-time economies and became 24-hour places. As employment in manufacturing has declined in the older industrial countries, as the remaining manufacturers have moved to city peripheries and as retail has either moved online or to out-of-town retail sites and shopping malls which have space for car parking, city centres have become primarily sites for consumption, for leisure, mainly commercial leisure (see Miles, 2010). By the end of the 20th century, the strength and variety of consumption-based lifestyles were helping to inspire debate about a postmodern condition (Featherstone, 1991). Commerce has now become the main, but it was not the first, and it is still far from being our sole, leisure provider.

SHOPPING

Is this leisure? In countries where most leisure has become commercial, shopping has arguably become the quintessential consumer experience. This is the clearest sign of the dissolving boundary between leisure and other kinds of spending. When asked how they feel about shopping, members of the public often say that it depends on the type: that the weekly trip for food and other household goods is different to shopping for clothes, cosmetics, gifts, furniture, smartphones, Tablets, DVDs, CDs, etc. As countries have grown more prosperous, 'essentials' have accounted for a declining proportion of all spending, and the essential/luxury boundary has frayed as supermarkets have become hypermarkets and located to shopping precincts (malls) or retail parks where batches of purchases can be loaded into a car before returning at a leisurely pace to the stores. Supermarkets themselves have introduced more and more specialty lines. Mood music and controlled temperatures can make even the journey down the grocery aisles into a pleasant excursion. Although we could do, and are doing (see below), more shopping online, we are also spending more time at the shops – up by roughly 50 per cent in Britain since the 1960s. Shopping is what we are most likely to do on our days off work and when we go for days out. Tourists can be relied on to shop. In the 1990s, relaxation of Britain's Sunday trading laws rapidly transformed Sunday into a major shopping day. Car parks at retail precincts were soon jammed, and congestion at nearby motorway turn-offs became a normal Sunday motoring experience.

Shopping for pleasure is not new. Street markets in the 19th century were lively, exciting, sociable places filled with shops, stalls, buskers and organ grinders. At the end of the working week, people experienced the pleasures of spending. The shopping arcades that were constructed in 19th-century Paris and other European cities were smart, upmarket places (see Rojek, 1997). However, the spread of department stores in major cities during the interwar years made the excursion into town a highlight of the weeks before Christmas, and maybe at Easter and Whitsun for middle- and working-class families alike. Shoppers would amble through the stores before deciding exactly what to purchase. The profusion of goods, all so close, available to touch, was a dreamland of the era.

The present-day equivalents are the out-of-town malls and retail parks which cater for the car-borne. Their architecture makes its own statements. These are the cathedrals of our time – cathedrals of consumerism. Look what the malls contain. There are so many kinds of shops – large and small, specialist boutiques and general department stores. Everything that one could possibly desire is within walking distance. Present-day shopping precincts have everything (see Box 2.2). There will be bars, restaurants, very likely a movie multiplex, even a casino. Some of these places cater for daytime and night-time interests. One can merge into the other. There are children's play areas and places for everyone to relax. And, of course, there is the mood music, the controlled temperature (very important in places where outdoor winters are intolerably cold and/or summers unbearably

Box 2.2 Trafford Centre

This is Western Europe's largest shopping centre by leasable area.

It opened in 1998 five miles west of Manchester (UK) city centre and attracts 35 million visits annually.

It contains Europe's largest food court and the UK's busiest, 20-screen cinema.

As well as shops, cinema and 54 dining options, the centre offers the following:

- Crèche and play area
- Sea life
- High ropes adventure course
- Golf
- Legoland

hot). Some shopping complexes incorporate hotels and nightclubs. It is possible to visit for a weekend and never go outdoors. Malls have become favoured sites for teenagers who want somewhere to hang out and to meet friends. The presence of groups of teenagers is sometimes regarded as troublesome, but it appears that whenever they visit, most young people spend at least some of the time shopping (if window shopping is included) (see Lowe, 2002). When they are at home watching TV (and the adverts) and when they are 'out', today's young people are likely to be learning to link leisure with buying.

It is convenient to have everything in one place but, as noted above, the new retail venues are not leading to a decline in total shopping time. We have more money to spend than in the past, and we are devoting more time to spending our money. Some older marketing aids have survived – shopping catalogues for instance – but these have been migrating online, and more people are buying online. Some viewers must be switching to the TV shopping channels. All this appears to be in addition to, rather than instead of, actually going out to shop.

However, 'online' is currently the growth marketplace. Table 2.1 plots the recent growth in the value of online sales in the United States (and the dip in 2012 when the post-crash recession was depressing consumer spending). Table 2.1 also plots the more recent trend for more online sales to be from a mobile device. People can now shop while journeying to or from work.

Consumers like to look, touch and try before they buy. As noted above, time spent shopping has not declined, but consumers are increasingly making

Table 2.1 Value of online sales in USA in $bn

	2009	2010	2011	2012	2013	2014
All online sales	168	173	256	225	263	304
Of which via mobile device				25	42	58

Source: www.statisticbrain.com

actual purchases online, from the convenience of their homes or while on the move, and they also enjoy the convenience of delivery to their homes. In 2014, just 9 per cent of global retail purchases were online, but this percentage is certain to rise steadily and substantially. In 2014, the proportions of UK retail sales that were online ranged from 15 per cent of video games to just over a half (51 per cent) of clothing. Majorities of the populations in all parts of the world already say that they have visited an online site (not necessarily to make an online purchase), but more will make more purchases in this way as more and more homes are connected to broadband, and as smartphones continue to spread. Consumers may regret the closure of high-street shops and their local shopping malls, but unless actual purchases are made at these sites, commerce will not maintain the facilities. Commerce is following the preferences and the money of households who increasingly order groceries online for home delivery and top up at local stores. Major supermarket chains are now slimming their hyper-facilities and opening more local 'convenience' shops. Sales of books have also drifted online, and most other kinds of shopping are likely to follow.

During the 21st century, there has been a series of closures of entire shopping malls across the United States (see www.buzzfeed.com). Decline has begun with difficulties in replacing retailers who pull out. Empty stores lead to reduced shopper footfall, and soon the exit becomes a stampede. After a tipping point, the mall closes, becomes a ghost precinct and is scheduled for demolition. This has happened to

- Rolling Acres Mall in Akron, Ohio, which opened in 1975 and closed in 2013.
- North Towne Square Mall in Toledo, Ohio, which opened in 1980, closed in 2005 and was demolished in 2013.
- Woodville Park Mall in Northwood, Ohio, which opened in 1969 and was demolished in 2014.
- Randall Park Mall in Randall, Ohio, which opened in 1976 and closed in 2009.

We should note that all the above malls were located in Ohio, which is part of America's belt of declining 'rust bucket' industries, but there have been mall closures in more prosperous regions:

- Hawthorne Plaza Mall in Hawthorne, California, which opened in 1977 and closed in 1999.
- Crestwood Mall in St Louis, Missouri, which opened in 1956 and was for sale and likely demolition in 2013.
- Dixie Square Mall in Harvey, Illinois, which opened in 1966 and closed in 2011.
- Turfland Mall in Lexington, Kentucky, which opened in 1967 and closed in 2008.

In all these cases, older malls have fallen victim to newer, more spectacular or better-located developments, probably next to highway interchanges. We are not witnessing the death of the mall, but retail is an intensely competitive consumer industry. Successful malls need to offer more than competitors. The 'more' may be more stores, more eating and drinking options, more play areas for children or just more relaxing, attractive environments. A current trend is towards retailtainment. A similar fate to the death of older malls awaits older sport centres, theme parks and other attractions.

Commerce is inherently dynamic. All businesses are perpetually vulnerable to smarter competition. America's dead malls are not signs of an all-round decline of shopping for pleasure but of vibrant retail sectors. There are many goods for which the online encounter is insufficient. Consumers want to see for real, touch and try. Retail developments follow the money as it flows from declining to expanding regions, and within all regions the money flows to facilities that offer the most attractive, pleasurable, entertaining retail experience.

GEORGE RITZER'S McDONALDIZATION THESIS

Commercial leisure has always attracted critics. The original critics were in the recreation movements of the late-19th and early-20th centuries who wanted to stem what they felt was a malignant rising tide. Their successors, the academics and leisure providers who meet at present-day leisure conferences, have accepted some commercial leisure sectors (mainly tourism) as part of their community. Critics have become more selective than in the past. A formidable example during the last 20 years has been George Ritzer's McDonaldization thesis. This thesis has been developed in a series of books and articles which Ritzer has written during and since the 1990s (1993, 1998, 1999, 2001). He defines McDonaldization as 'the process by which the principles of the fast food industry are coming to dominate more and more sectors of American society as well as the rest of the world' (Ritzer, 1993, p. 1).

Rationalisation

Ritzer believes that the German sociologist Max Weber (1864–1920) was broadly correct about the modern era becoming, above all else, an age of rationality. This means being systematic, cold and calculative in selecting the best means to achieve an end (profit in the case of commercial businesses). Alternative means are compared. Relative costs and returns are calculated carefully. A good or service is then provided in the most efficient and effective way. Improvements are sought constantly but they have to be justified rationally, otherwise no deviations from what is known to work best are permitted. The key principles of McDonaldization are said to be efficiency, calculability, predictability and control. Weber thought that the outcome of progressive rationalisation would be mammoth bureaucracies. Here Ritzer disagrees and nominates McDonald's as exemplifying the actual outcome of rationalisation.

Everyone is sure to have heard of McDonald's (see Box 2.3). It is basically the same menu everywhere with very limited local variations. The burgers are always the same size and shape, and are cooked to the same specifications. The premises – the back rooms and the counter equipment, the

---

Box 2.3 McDonald's

Ray Kroc had mortgaged his home and had invested his life savings to become the exclusive distributor of a five-spindled milkshake maker called the Multimixer. In 1954, he heard about a McDonald's hamburger stand in California which was running eight Multimixers. Kroc put the idea of opening several restaurants to Dick and Mac McDonald. At first Kroc's plan was to make money by selling Multimixers to the restaurants. Fortunately for him, so as to get the idea started, Kroc offered to run the restaurants, and this offer was accepted by the McDonalds.

The first McDonald's restaurant opened at Des Plaines in 1955. The first day's revenue was $366.12. This building is now a McDonald's museum.

McDonald's is now the world's largest chain of hamburger fast-food restaurants, with more than 34,000 restaurants serving 68 million customers daily in 121 countries.

furnishings and the decor – are always recognisably McDonald's. All over the world, the staff wear the same uniforms. Prices depend on local costs but are always 'value for money'. Yet, Ritzer claims, McDonald's offers not only food and drink but also an enchanting experience. Go through the door into a McDonald's and you leave behind outside, drab, mundane everyday life. McDonald's is part of the experience economy.

McDonald's was not the first fast-food business. Fish-and-chip shops have a longer history of selling fast food to eat in or to take away. McDonald's was not even the first fast-food hamburger restaurant chain. It was years behind Wimpy. McDonald's stands out because of its extraordinary success. The name is recognised all over the world. Most towns and cities on all continents now host at least one McDonald's. There were long queues when the restaurants first opened in Moscow, Warsaw and other East European cities in the early 1990s. McDonald's had become a symbol of consumer culture and the Western way of life more generally.

The claim that society is being McDonaldized (Ritzer's first book on this subject was titled *The McDonaldization of Society*) is a response to the extent to which the model is being copied. McDonald's has acted as an exemplar for many other businesses. So there are now many other fast-food chains selling burgers, pizzas, kebabs, chicken, and so on. The model has spread beyond fast food. We have branded pubs such as Wetherspoons in Britain. There are similar developments in other branches of retailing: brands such as Tie Rack, Accessorize, Hotel Chocolat, Paperchase and Sweet Express which may operate in high streets, railway stations or airports or as shops within larger stores. There are even wider applications of the McDonald's model. In the United States, chains of hospitals and clinics offer a standard tariff of treatments. Higher education is displaying symptoms. Degree programmes are divided into modules of standard weights. Leading brands (universities) franchise modules and launch mass open online courses (MOOCs). Wherever in the world you enrol, you receive the same course materials and recommended reading, and you do the same exercises. Ritzer claims that we are fast becoming a society where we can leave one standardised service only by stepping into another.

Despite the success of the business, McDonaldization has few academic supporters. Ritzer claims that his intention in highlighting the process is to stimulate a search for ways of resisting. Max Weber feared that we would become prisoners of large bureaucracies and wrestled with the problem of how to prevent this. In a similar way, sociology conferences since the 1990s have debated how to resist McDonaldization (see Smart, 1999). The core problem inherent in McDonaldization is said to be the ultimate irrationality of rationality. Humans have the ability to act rationally, but by taking this to extreme lengths we can dehumanise everything. So work is deskilled and even consumption may eventually become routine, boring. 'Rational systems inevitably spawn a series of irrationalities that limit, eventually compromise and perhaps even undermine their rationality' (Ritzer, 1993, p. 121). This is the core criticism. Another is that consumers are led to believe that they are operating freely when, in fact, great effort has been made to control their actions without them being aware of it' (Ritzer, 2001, p. 8). In his later books, Ritzer has sidelined McDonald's and concentrated on other examples – the Disney parks, Las Vegas, cruise ships, casinos and shopping malls. What they all have in common is that, according to Ritzer, like McDonald's they not only rationalise consumption but try to keep customers visiting by maintaining their enchantment, which is difficult when goods and services are standardised.

It is true that even the McDonald's restaurants continue to be enchanting places for successive cohorts of children. The stream of customers never ends. But by age 15, customers are likely to have become disenchanted. McDonald's will have become routine. How can businesses retain customers throughout their lives? Ritzer argues that businesses can try to rationalise not only enchantment but also re-enchantment. They are said to do this by constantly offering spectaculars and extravaganzas as well as best-ever, truly unrepeatable bargains. We move across an archipelago not just from one rationalised consumer setting to another, but from one spectacular to the next (so Ritzer claims), with the spectacles having to become increasingly spectacular in order to retain our interest. Every event and festival (see Chapter 7) has somehow to be more spectacular than its predecessors (see Carlsen et al., 2010).

Can this cycle continue? Ritzer sees no reason why not. The process is not displaying signs of exhaustion. 'I conclude that while McDonald's will eventually grow less important and may even disappear completely, and the label McDonaldization will become increasingly less important as a result, the underlying process of rationalization will continue apace, or even accelerate' (Ritzer, 2001, p. 3).

Criticisms

First, McDonaldization is confined to specific, and really quite limited, segments of the economy. It is impossible to McDonaldize sports spectacles. Modern sports are more rational than their predecessors. The games are governed by clear rules. The fields of play are clearly defined. Likewise the time limits. Methods of scoring should leave no room for doubt. Even so, what happens during a sporting contest is far from entirely predictable. Cultural products (whether highbrow or lowbrow) cannot be McDonaldized.

Second, in all consumer services, there are hundreds of small independent companies. This certainly applies with restaurants (see Warde and Martens, 2000). It applies in the holiday trade also. The big multinationals never have the field to themselves. All leisure markets are distinguished by the large number of small businesses, many run by enthusiasts about tropical fish, dance music, fitness or whatever. Commercial markets are unique in providing opportunities for enthusiasts to turn their leisure into paid work. They are different partly in the sheer number of small operators who are trying to carve out niches. Many of these businesses rely on flair and enthusiasts' know-how rather than marketing science. In recent years, they have pioneered scuba diving, paragliding, white water rafting, desert trekking and Arctic exploration as holidays for the adventurous. Most of the businesses are fragile. They are vulnerable to economic downturns and shifts in fashion, but there is a constant stream of new entrants (see Berrett et al., 1993; Butler, 1978; Hesmondhalgh, 1998; Rapuno, 2009; Smith and Maughan, 1997; Zegre et al., 2012).

Third, the commercial sector does not standardise what it makes available, let alone people's lives. Rather, commerce extends choice. By making available so many possible combinations of goods and services, commerce enables consumers to develop individualised lifestyles. Consumers have far more choice today than in the pre-McDonald's era.

Retail developments that have created shopping malls and precincts are products of rational marketing. They are located and designed so as to attract the maximum possible number of shoppers, and to induce them to spend as much as possible per dollar invested. However, although very likely to contain one, the malls, precincts and retail parks themselves cannot be described as McDonaldized. Each development has its own character – a unique mixture of shops, restaurants, and so on. They can be used flexibly, at times of their own choosing, by consumers who plot their own itineraries.

Note that it is only commerce that is able to develop shopping into a leisure activity. Under communism, shopping was a chore. There were always shortages. It was necessary to queue for virtually everything. This was also 'rational'. There are always many different ways of doing things that can be equally rational: so many that very little is explained. What is rational depends on an actor's objectives and on the social, cultural, economic and political contexts. Leisure shopping, wherever it occurs, has developed within a commercial context.

ACHIEVEMENTS AND LIMITATIONS OF COMMERCE

Achievements

A major strength of commerce is that it will seek out and cater for all tastes. It does not favour what the providers consider good for people. Commerce does not have an inbuilt loyalty to the relatively well-to-do. There is usually much more money to be made in mass markets. It is true that better-off individuals and households have more to spend on commercial leisure than poorer individuals and households, but often in aggregate the poorer sections of a population can out-spend the relatively rich. That said, as income and wealth have been sucked upwards in recent decades, the relatively well-to-do have become the consumers who are most sought by commerce. The world's richer countries are no longer in the age when the numerical predomin- ance of working-class households enabled these households collectively to out-spend wealthier strata, and when consumer cultures were working-class cultures. Consumer spending by teenagers and young adults is now mainly by students and higher education graduates who tend to be from middle- class homes and/or are on middle-class career tracks. The gentrification of city centre shopping (for an example, see Massey, 2005), meaning the replacement of budget stores with stockists of designer wear, occurs because merchandisers face more prosperous populations. Globally, the situation is different. The Chinese remain much poorer on average than the popula- tions of Western countries, but because China's population is so large, its tourists collectively now spend more than tourists from any other country. The number of outward tourists from China grew from around 10 million in 2000 to around 90 million in 2013 when they spent $129 billion in total compared with approximately $86 billion each by tourists from the United States and Germany (joint second on the list of tourist spenders), and the $53 billion spent by tourists from the UK.

Market researchers usually define the 'middle class' in terms of its ability to spend on 'luxuries'. Sociologists are never comfortable with this defin- ition, but it works for market research purposes. William Wilson (2013) defines the middle classes in emerging market economies as persons who earn between $10 and $100 per day. In China and India, this means that they have money to spend in excess of necessities. On Wilson's definition, in 2013, China had 150 million middle-class consumers and India had 50 million. These are small proportions of the populations of India and China (roughly 1.3 billion each in 2012), but these figures mean that such emerging markets have become the 'sweet spot' where leisure spending is now set to grow most rapidly. The United States with a total population of around 320 million and even the European Union with its 506 million cannot rival the growth rates or potential sizes of the classes of leisure spenders in the BRICs (Brazil, Russia, India, China and other emerging markets). Commerce is now following the money into these markets. Products are designed to match the tastes of consumers in these new 'sweet spots'.

Another strength of commerce is that it does not target a lowest or any other common denominator. Quite the reverse: whether building houses, publishing newspapers or opening restaurants, commerce generates diversity. Providers target specific market segments or even smaller niches. Commerce offers thousands of holiday packages and hundreds of different alcoholic beverages. Every provider tries to offer something different and either better or cheaper. So commerce produces more and more brands, whether on supermarket shelves or in leisure goods and services. Some argue (correctly) that the differences between many products are superficial and trivial, but it is the variety that makes commercial market places attractive to consumers. It is the public sector that offers standardised fare whether delivering houses, health care, education or holidays. Even though they tried, the communist authorities were never able to offer Western-type holidays. It was simply not the same when all the state-owned souvenir shops carried exactly the same range of goods.

Also, commerce is incredibly innovative. It produced radio and television broadcasting and movies. It produced PCs and, more recently, smartphones, Tablets and apps alongside e-cigarettes and table dancing.

We should note that it is commerce, not least commercial leisure, that has kept the global economy growing during and following the financial crash of 2008. Global tourism has defied successive recessions: it just keeps on growing. The value of sports broadcasting rights has continued to grow strongly, and there is no end in sight. As explained above, the strongest growth in tourism is now from emerging market economies such as China, India, Russia and Brazil, and the sale of sports broadcasting rights now has the greatest growth potential in these same markets.

Finally, commerce offers a distinctive consumer experience (being served). It stimulates people's wants, it makes access simple and it offers goods and services that are undemanding, thereby widening its markets.

Even the staunchest opponents of the commercialisation of education, health care, energy supply and public transport may take a more benign view of commercial leisure.

Limitations

Criticism of commercial leisure began long before McDonald's was conceived. Supporters of the recreation movements of the 19th and early-20th centuries accused commerce of promoting undesirable pastimes (doing the devil's work). Later, the commercial media were accused of spreading passivity and stupefying the masses. Throughout the second half of the 20th century, the litany of criticism grew:

- Harry van Moorst (1982) has claimed that, in capitalist societies, leisure is nothing more than ransom paid for industrial peace.
- John Clarke and Chas Critcher (1985) have argued that citizens are doubly exploited – at work where surplus value is creamed off by their employers, and then in their own time when they are enlisted as consumers that capitalist businesses need if they are to be profitable. They also claim that the variety in the public's uses of leisure is less a sign of freedom of choice than crude underlying inequalities.
- Jeremy Seabrook (1988) has argued that leisure is deformed by market relationships and that people can sustain richness in their lives only within their families and other small social groups.
- Betsy and Stephen Wearing (1992) have claimed that the commercialisation of leisure constrains rather than extends individual freedom.
- Somnez and his colleagues (1993) argue that the extension of market forces has corrupted earlier, more innocent, purer uses of leisure.
- Vittoria de Grazia (1992) has argued along very similar lines in sketching how people's lives have changed in Italian villages since the 1930s, when, whether the communists or Fascists were in power, the leisure ideal was the politically mobilised citizen engaged in uplifting activities. By the 1990s, affluence and commerce had invaded the villages. So had tourists. Some traditional festivals were being preserved as tourist attractions. However, everyone's leisure, the tourists' and the locals', had been depoliticised. It had become a relatively vacuous end in itself.

The wave of criticism continues:

- Today, commercial businesses stand accused of inverting older economic cultures that applauded thrift and now encourage people to borrow, to take the waiting out of wanting, thereby creating more and more consumer debt (Botterill, 2010). Consumer debt that could not be repaid was among the causes of the financial crash of 2008.

■ According to Robinson (2006) and many others, most of us could improve our lives by working less and spending less, but are encouraged by commerce to work and spend to our maximum capacity.

■ Schor (2004) draws attention to how consumer advertising has led to the commercialisation of childhood, socialising the upcoming generation into the work-and-spend cycle.

■ Aall and colleagues (2011) show that in Norway energy-intensive leisure consumption has been rising faster than general consumption, and protest that this cannot be allowed to continue.

What these criticisms overlook is that consumers can choose to live differently, and some are doing so. Commerce will market slow food, slow travel, eco-/sustainable tourism and other forms of 'ethical consumption' if and when it becomes profitable to do so. Consumer buycotts and boycotts work by activating commercial market mechanisms.

This book's position is that commerce has special capabilities, but that there will always be scope for complementary provisions because there are limits – two important limits – to what commerce can do. First, commerce will only cater for demands which can be met profitably. Commerce always seeks maximum profit. It always endeavours to expand or deepen its markets by increasing the number of customers, or persuading existing customers to purchase more often, or to spend more on each occasion. All businesses do their best to attract customers and to keep them loyal. The effect of all the advertising and other forms of marketing is to generate consumer culture – the images and beliefs that come to be associated with particular goods, places and experiences. Commerce is rather good at stimulating desire. But all this happens only when providing can be made profitable.

The second important limitation of commerce is that it requires a clear division between the provider and the customer. There can be consumer benefits here: people seem to like being served, to some extent and for some of the time, at any rate. The limitation is that commerce often, but not always, removes much of the potentially interesting work. It makes things easy and therefore maybe tempting but undemanding. Yet peak experience appears to arise only when things are challenging – hard work in fact (see Harper, 1997). Commerce simply cannot afford to allow people to do it all whether the 'all' is preparing food for their own consumption or producing a play.

CONCLUSIONS

Over the last 100 years, commerce has become far and away our main leisure provider. All the big three leisure activities in terms of time and money spent, and the proportions of the population that are involved – holidays, out-of-home eating and drinking and the media – are basically commercial nowadays. Every chapter of this book has to deal, in some way or another, and to some extent or another, with the effects of commercialisation.

This chapter has presented the many criticisms that the commercialisation of leisure has provoked. Most of these criticisms must be rejected on two grounds. First, there is the historical story which shows that commerce has always added to people's options without of itself eliminating any of the voluntary or public sector alternatives. Second, some of the harsher and most sweeping criticisms – those that accuse commerce of seeking out the rich and neglecting the masses, homogenising provisions and reducing choice and leading to leisure markets being dominated by monopolies – are simply mistaken.

Commerce is not basically malign, but this chapter has also explained that it has limitations. The next chapter will explain what is special about the voluntary sector. Then, Chapter 4 will identify the public sector's special capabilities. The strengths of commerce need to be recognised and indeed can be applauded, but not to the point of drowning the case for the maintenance of sometimes alternative, and sometimes complementary, provisions.

Chapter 3

Voluntary Associations

INTRODUCTION

Voluntary associations predate the development of welfare states in Western countries. Chapter 1 explained that it was the voluntary sector, in partnership with public authorities, which pioneered modern 'rational' uses of leisure time in the 19th and early-20th centuries, and promoted the view of leisure as a social service, and in that era the voluntary sector did far more than this. It pioneered education for all classes, ran hospitals and provided housing and financial assistance for the poor. After the Second World War, governments took over most of these responsibilities, thereby raising standards and providing similar services for all citizens. Most schools, hospitals and newly constructed housing for rent, and income maintenance systems were nationalised or municipalised. However, welfare states did not try to replace voluntary associations in catering for leisure. Quite the reverse: improved sports facilities and community amenities were made available for use by voluntary associations, and voluntary providers received more generous grant aid.

Today, once again, the context in which the voluntary sector operates has changed. The post-2008 squeeze on government spending has led to cutbacks in grant aid and reductions in spending on amenities of all types. Simultaneously, governments have become increasingly keen to pay independent (commercial or voluntary sector) providers to take over the management of public amenities (schools, sports centres, swimming pools, libraries, civic halls and community centres). This was the agenda in the UK's post-2010 coalition government when it advocated creating a 'big society' (and a smaller state). There have been further changes and additional features of the new context, all challenging rather than necessarily hostile to the voluntary sector. Delayed transitions by young people into adult employment and upward movements in typical ages of first marriages and parenthood, and the growth in size of the post-retirement age groups, have enlarged the sections of the population that are most likely to use and to become actively involved (as volunteers) in the voluntary sector. The new media allow people to participate online instead of or as well as attending meetings, while simultaneously enabling voluntary bodies to extend their reach.

Voluntary sectors have not declined since the decades when welfare states were built after the Second World War. In Britain, there was a decline in memberships among cohorts born after the Second World War (McCulloch, 2014), but this was not a result of state welfare replacing voluntary effort. The mid-20th century was the time when there was a profound change in people's lifestyles associated with the development of the mass media (especially the cinema, radio, then television) and the spread of home-centred, privatised lifestyles. Also, people were becoming more prosperous. The 'affluent society' was being born, at least in public discourse. The spread of car ownership enabled families to go out privately, and to destinations outside their immediate neighbourhoods. During these developments, people became less likely to join local clubs, but since the mid-20th century the voluntary sector has been resilient, and it never shrank to a point where voluntary sector leisure provisions were threatened. Today, in most Western countries, a half or more of the adult (16 and over) populations belong to at least one voluntary association. If trade unions are excluded, the general trend in membership in recent decades has usually been upwards. In the United States, there are now around 1.5 million voluntary associations, to which 57 per cent of the adult population belongs. In France, there has been an associational boom since the late-20th century. In Germany (where pre-war Nazi associations were disbanded after 1945), associational density (the proportion of the population that belongs) has tripled since 1960, with two-thirds of adults currently involved. Membership rates are even higher in Scandinavian countries at 80 per cent or more (Anheier, n.d.), and these countries have the world's strongest welfare states. These trends are perhaps too easily disguised by cries from within the voluntary sector that it needs 'more': more money, more members and especially more activists who are willing to take on management and other leadership roles.

This chapter proceeds by asking 'What is a voluntary association?' It reviews the history of these associations' involvement in leisure, and notes the types of leisure in which they excel. We then examine the history and current state of volunteering (it is flourishing rather than shrinking). The chapter proceeds by asking 'What drives the voluntary sector?' This turns out to be members' and users' enthusiasm. This enthusiasm is the associations' lifeblood and their principal defence mechanism, and it is not on the wane. The impetus to self-organise has not been quelled by the expansion of commerce any more than it was dampened during the earlier expansion of welfare states. The chapter explains how and why the voluntary sector is able to resist challenges from commerce and state provisions. The voluntary sector can sometimes provide things more cheaply, and it can sometimes do a better job than any other type of leisure provider, but it always does things differently. It provides a kind of leisure experience which is simply beyond the capabilities of both the state and the market. This is why the voluntary sector is not a 'thing of the past', a vestige from the time when most people could not afford commercial provisions, and before the state accepted responsibility for the economic and social welfare of the people. The chapter concludes with how the voluntary sector is meeting its current challenges. We find that this extraordinarily varied and adaptable sector of the leisure industries is responding as positively and energetically today as it did during industrialisation and urbanisation over a century ago.

OVERVIEW OF THE VOLUNTARY SECTOR

What is a voluntary association?

People who work in the voluntary sector do not all donate their time. These organisations are very likely to enlist unpaid volunteers but they may also employ paid staff. The organisations remain voluntary because the people in charge, the trustees or the committee, are not there for the money. There may be state subsidies, but the organisations are not statutory, meaning that they are not brought into existence at the behest of government. Associations which are formed or kept alive mainly by government grants, or specifically so that government activities can be hived off, are best described as quasi-voluntary or quasi non-governmental organisations (quangos). We also need to recognise, and sideline here, a category of commercial clubs (such as gambling clubs and health and fitness clubs) that are created by the host businesses. Sometimes the club is a legal requirement, as for certain types of betting, the idea being to prevent impulse gambling. Sometimes the club membership fee is a form of upfront payment, or a means of excluding the 'wrong types'. These are not genuine voluntary members' associations. However, voluntary associations may have business sponsors. They may well be business-like in their operating methods. Most clubs are perpetually fund-raising. They are indeed interested in money, but they are non-commercial in that no one is siphoning off profit: everything is ploughed back in.

History

Voluntary bodies have a long history, and in leisure they are still thriving. In Britain, the number of voluntary societies multiplied during the 19th century (Tomlinson, 1979). They then created, and proceeded to run, most of our modern sports. The Football Association was created in 1863, the All England Croquet Club in 1868 (tennis was added in 1877), the Rugby Football Union in 1871 and the Amateur Athletics Association in 1880. Voluntary effort also created the original modern youth organisations – the Boys' Brigade (founded in 1883), the Boy Scouts (1908) and the Girl Guides (1910), for example. Other clubs, thousands of them, were based on hobbies such as coin and stamp collecting, gardening, photography – the list is endless. The holiday away from home was pioneered by churches, philanthropists and 'progressive' employers before being developed primarily by commercial businesses, but voluntary associations continued to offer alternatives which were usually cheaper and always purportedly more educational (see, for example, Snape, 2004). Because Britain was the first industrial nation, it was among the first to acquire an impressive array of associations such as these. Subsequently, forming a committee, which then founds an association or club, has sometimes been seen as a distinctively British way of addressing any problem, but other European countries, and especially the United States, have equally strong voluntary sectors.

Voluntary sector leisure is neither derivative nor residual nor on the wane. The sector is not a poor relation of commerce. Nor does it exist only with permission and funding from public bodies. In catering for modern leisure, the voluntary sector was a first mover. Public sector and commercial provisions typically followed, and, in the cases of the arts and sport, have always rested on a broader voluntary base. The voluntary sector nurtures artistic and sporting talent from which professionals are recruited. It creates the interest which generates the spectators and audiences for professional performances. Likewise, the voluntary sector fosters interest in hobbies which commercial enterprises can then service. Voluntary action fills local authority arts and sports centres with users. The centres exist because of the interest, and not vice versa. Voluntary provision is more than a fallback: it is more often a base or at least an equal partner with other sectors. Most crucially, we shall see that voluntary clubs and societies provide kinds of leisure experience that are simply beyond the capabilities of commerce and the public sector.

Civil society

Voluntary associations are important within and far beyond leisure. They are the stuff of civil society on which liberal democracy rests. These associations fill the socio-cultural space between the state and market on the one side, and individuals and their primary groups on the other. Civil society is created when citizens voluntarily form themselves into associations. Sometimes the label used is 'third sector', or 'non-profit', or 'non-governmental organisation' (NGO). These terms are used interchangeably here. Some voluntary associations are run democratically, by their members. In other cases, control is vested in trustees who are required to respect the constitution and purposes for which the organisation was founded, maybe by a donor. People may form voluntary associations for recreational purposes, but the same socio-cultural space is available for, and is also populated by, churches, trade unions and political parties. The 'sector' includes charities. In the United States, some of these are sufficiently strong to take on responsibilities performed by state welfare in European Union countries (see Wright, 2000).

These associations began to be formed after the religious reformation in Europe, when Protestants and Catholics ceased persecuting each other and freedom of association to worship in the church of one's choice became a civil right. The sector can flourish only when there is tolerance – by the state and citizens of all persuasions – that fellow citizens should be free to think and believe freely, and to associate to pursue their interests (DeLisle, 2004). Voluntary sectors have proved more difficult to nurture in countries where there has been no reformation, and we should note that these countries are the majority in the present-day world.

Some socialists are enthusiastic about the voluntary sector. In their ideal society, rather than everything being run by state bureaucracies, they envisage the voluntary principle being extended, certainly in leisure, to encompass the mass media, for instance. Thus, newspapers and television channels would be run as cooperatives by their workforces on a non-profit basis, or by their readers or audiences (see Tomlinson, 1990).

Social capital

Describing voluntary organisations as a sector is convenient for this book's, and other, purposes, because all the organisations do share a great deal in common. However, it must be said that activists do not necessarily regard themselves as contributing to a sector. People are more likely to become involved through an interest in sport, more likely a particular sport, and sometimes just one particular club, rather than to contribute to any wider effort. Most of the organisations are aggressively independent – impossible to organise. Voluntary associations are not a coordinated movement. Nevertheless, each association creates social capital – social bonds and trust – on which other organisations can draw. There are different kinds of social capital. Robert Putnam (1995, 1996, 2000) distinguishes 'bonding capital' (which strengthens relationships within a group – within a neighbourhood, for instance) from 'bridging capital' (relationships which straddle different groups and which may therefore facilitate social mobility) and 'linking capital' (which links different sections of a population and helps to bind them together). 'Bridging' and 'linking' capital are considered especially valuable. Social capital is an asset. Where it is high, people tend to be wealthier and healthier, children have higher educational attainments, crime rates are lower and levels of civic participation are higher than elsewhere (Harper, 2001). Hence, social policy-makers are interested in how to boost social capital. Throughout the world, sports organisations (because these bodies have the capacity to involve so many people from all kinds of backgrounds) have been regarded as important generators of the socio-cultural capital on which democratic grass-roots politics depends. Hence Putnam's (2000) claim (but see below, p. 62) that the trend in recent years for Americans to go 'bowling alone' is weakening the country's political fabric. The existence of a virile voluntary sector is widely regarded as a hallmark of any genuinely democratic society. So the development of 'third sectors' has been used by the European Union as one of its indicators in assessing candidate countries' progress towards fulfilling the conditions for full membership.

Types of associations

There are many ways in which voluntary associations can be classified, but some bodies always straddle the boundary lines. This 'sector' is notoriously untidy. There is certainly no clear division between associations that exist for leisure and those that serve other purposes. Organisations can be grouped into those which exist to meet a common interest of the members, which may or may not be a leisure interest; those seeking to promote the welfare of another target group – the disabled or senior citizens for instance – which, again, may or may not embrace recreational programmes; and those promoting a cause or interest which, those involved are likely to claim, is for everyone's benefit. Such causes may be leisure based, in the arts or sport for example, or leisure related, such as the conservation of nature, or only indirectly if at all leisure linked, as in the case of opposition to fracking and the introduction of genetically modified foods. However, most voluntary bodies are involved in leisure to some extent in some way or another. Whatever its original purpose, running the association is likely to be a major leisure interest of the office-holders. Volunteering is a major leisure activity for some of those who are involved. The voluntary sector is unrivalled in its ability to mobilise voluntary effort. Associations which are based squarely on leisure interests may develop on their own or as offshoots from any other organisation – a school, firm, trade union or church – any place which initially draws people together.

Who joins, who benefits?

No one knows exactly how many voluntary associations exist in Britain or any other democratic country. All statistics are best estimates. One of the hallmarks of these political regimes is that citizens do not need official permission in order to bond together and can do so without registering with any authority. Handbooks which list arts, sports and other types of associations are always incomplete, and likewise local directories of voluntary societies. Researchers who try to survey the sector thoroughly invariably rely heavily on 'snowball' methods – being informed about additional associations from any starting point. This method always seems to find that every district within every town and city, and every rural village, is dense with clubs and societies. Any church, any further education college or university will have dozens of clubs. This is what Bishop and Hoggett (1986) discovered when they began to research the voluntary sectors in Bristol and Leicester. They were so overwhelmed by cases that it was necessary to restrict the study to just a section of each city. In her study of Toxteth, an inner-Liverpool district, Ruby Dixon (1991) contacted 54 different arts organisations. The district appeared to be an artistic hotbed, but there is no reason to believe that Toxteth is outstanding in this respect. On the basis of her fieldwork in Milton Keynes, Ruth Finnegan (1989) estimated that between 5 and 6 per cent of the local population was involved in making music of some type or another. Most of those involved in Milton Keynes were in contact with other musicians through a dense network of bands, orchestras, choirs and clubs of various types. Perhaps less surprisingly, Sara Cohen (1991) located scores of rock bands on Merseyside, but these groups are best understood as a periphery of the commercial pop music industry. Unlike other music-makers, amateur rock musicians depend on private resourcefulness and networks, which are linked to the professional tiers of the business, rather than a base of voluntary clubs.

It is difficult to estimate the proportion of the population that is involved in the voluntary sector. Unless a long prompt list is used, individuals may not recall all the groups to which they belong, especially when one can 'belong' simply by being an occasional attender. People will not necessarily think of their participation as being in a voluntary sector. They will not necessarily be aware if a sports centre that they use, or a museum or wildlife reserve that they visit, is under voluntary management. However, as noted earlier, surveys find that a half or more of all adults in Western countries report belonging to at least one voluntary association. The middle classes always have the higher membership rates, but the voluntary sector in leisure is certainly not the pre-serve of any distinct section of the population. Virtually everyone would notice and their leisure would be seriously affected if the voluntary sector disappeared completely. The labour market would be seriously depressed if the voluntary sector disappeared: it is responsible for 7.9 per cent of all civilian employment in European Union countries (European Commission, 2003). The working class' capacity for self-organisation has produced the trade unions and political parties which, in many countries, have been the govern-ing or main opposition parties for a century and more. Needless to say (no one with any knowledge of sociology will be surprised), members of different social classes tend to join different clubs (Hill, 2002). The voluntary sector has often played an important political role in forming social bonds between members of classes with an economic base. The social capital generated by the voluntary sector can harden divisions and may therefore contribute to the formation of included and excluded groups. Contrary to Putnam's (2000) inferences, social capital is not always beneficial, or equally beneficial, for the members of all social strata. That said, it remains the case that all sections of the population have stakes of some description in the voluntary sector.

Contributions in leisure

The voluntary sector caters for all kinds of leisure interests and activities, but its contributions are much greater in some fields than in others. Churches and trade unions still operate some holiday centres, and some holidays are arranged by voluntary groups – for children and adults with special needs, for example – but the tourist industry is primarily commercial. So is the evenings-out (eating and drinking) industry despite the contributions of working people's clubs, student unions, etc. Most voluntary associations run raffles as part of their fundraising, but the major forms of gambling – national and state lotteries, football pools, casinos and betting shops – are commercial businesses (with national and state lotteries, the businesses that operate them are required to distribute a proportion of 'the take' to good causes). Most voluntary associations are into publishing, at least to the extent of producing newsletters. Some operate local radio and even local closed-circuit television networks. Nowadays many (possibly most) have Internet sites. Even so, the main players in broadcasting and publishing are state organisations and commercial enterprises. The types of leisure where the voluntary sector is pivotal are sport, artistic production and performances, and hobbies.

In Chapter 6, we shall see that our main modern sports were invented and provided and, for the most part, are still managed by voluntary bodies. All sport, except the very top level in the most popular spectator sports, still happens only because volunteers bring it off. The extent and manner in which commerce has taken over sections of top sport in recent years, and the implications for the wider sports-interested public, are considered in Chapter 6. Suffice it to record here that the voluntary sector is still far and away the main provider in both the participant and spectator branches of sport.

The voluntary sector is also the mainstay of the arts and crafts. Most painting, pottery, drama and musical production is by amateurs. No one is paid. People do it for the enjoyment. Professional productions (where people are paid) are different and are usually structurally separate. There is a difference here between sport and the arts. Whereas even professional sport (where the players are paid) may remain under voluntary management, the professional theatre, musical productions, and so forth (where the artists and other producers are paid), are nearly always either on a commercial basis or with state funding. Whose arts benefit from state support, and why, is considered in Chapter 8. Here, we can simply note that both commercial considerations and state largesse are wholly irrelevant to most artistic production. All the work is done voluntarily, and the professional tiers of the arts industries would be weakened without the voluntary sector acting as a seedbed, nurturing the talent and interest that produce professional performers and their audiences.

Hobbies are the third type of leisure in which the voluntary sector is the main provider. Interests, hundreds of them – in coins, cars, stamps, animals, fish, plants, railways, etc. – are expressed and nurtured in voluntary societies (see Box 3.1, and also Box 4.2, p. 75, for examples). Individuals who do not belong to any club may do gardening or coin or antique collecting as hobbies, but they are most likely to use voluntary associations' publications and events. Most hobbies are served by commercial profit-seeking businesses, many run by enthusiasts who are trying, with varying degrees of success, to base paid occupations on their hobbies. The relevant businesses and voluntary societies feed off each other, but it is hobbies that are served by commerce: businesses may invent games but they do not develop these into hobbies. Likewise, hobby groups may use public sector facilities, especially meeting rooms, but local authority leisure services departments do not create hobbies. These are always the work of like-minded individuals

---

Box 3.1 Hobbies

PIGEON RACING

The specially bred homing pigeons that had been used for centuries to carry messages became redundant with the invention of the telegraph. However, the simultaneous development of railways, and the broader modernisation of leisure that was then in process, made it possible to organise pigeon racing as a hobby.

The 'sport' began in Belgium, spread to Holland, France and Great Britain, then to North America. Nowadays, the two main US pigeon-racing organisations have 15,000 registered lofts (where the pigeons are kept). In Europe, the big annual event is the Blackpool show, which is attended each year by around 25,000 pigeon fanciers, and upwards of 2,500 pigeons are on display competing for the prizes that are on offer.

Races of up to 1,000 miles (but usually no more than 500 miles) are normally between birds that 'home' in the same region so as to standardise distances travelled and weather conditions, though the sport has procedures for taking account of these variables. Nowadays, birds are normally transported to a race's start point in specially constructed air-conditioned trucks. The sport has developed its own complicated technologies and organisations to verify race results. Pigeons have been traded for prices up to $250,000.

Pigeon racing is now a veteran hobby/sport, but research is still continuing into exactly how the pigeons find their way home.

Sources: www.pigeon.org
www.rpra.org
www.pigeon-racing.co.uk

TIDDLYWINKING

This game is not 'just about flicking counters into a cup. It is a complex game of tactics and strategy which involves a fascinating mixture of manual dexterity and intellectual activity.' Who says so? You guessed!

The game was invented by Joseph Assheton Fincher of London and patented in 1888. There was a tiddlywinking craze in England during the 1890s. Many variations on the basic game were invented, and over 70 patents were issued for tiddlywink games.

However, the development of tiddlywinks into an organised hobby did not occur until the 1950s. The first known tournament was held at Cambridge University in 1955. Oxford University followed before long, and in 1962 its team returned undefeated from a tour of the United States.

A North American association was formed in 1966, and Americans then dominated world play until the 1990s. The American association has held over 150 tournaments at which over 500 competitors have competed.

There are sister national associations in England and Scotland. The first world singles championship was held in 1972, since when there have been over 40 champion challenge matches. The winner of the English, Scottish or US national championships is allowed to challenge the reigning world champion. In 2013, Patrick Barrie of Cambridge became the new world singles champion by beating Larry Kahn, the US champion, 26-23.

Sources: www.tiddlywinks.org
www.etwa.org

SUBBUTEO TABLE SOCCER

This is a relatively new hobby. The game was launched in 1947 and became an instant success for its manufacturer. The first sets comprised two cardboard teams, one celluloid ball and metal-framed goals with paper nets. Players were instructed to mark a pitch (chalk provided) on an ex-army blanket.

The game was at the peak of its popularity in the late 1970s and early 1980s. At that time, the manufacturer produced teams in over 300 club and national strips. Since then, Subbuteo has been failing to recruit younger players. It has lost out to competition from computerised games. However, there are sufficient enthusiasts to keep the game alive worldwide.

There are national associations, and an international federation. These amateur associations have drawn up their own rules of play. There are affiliated associations in over 30 countries. World championships are held annually. There are more frequent grand prix tournaments, and video recordings are available of some major events.

Sources: www.americansubbuteo.com
www.subbuteoforum.org.uk
www.peter-upton.co.uk

who get together, maybe informally to begin with, but before long it is most likely that a club with officers will have been brought into existence.

Tourism, broadcasting, publishing, gambling and evenings-out eating and drinking could all manage without any voluntary sector input. Hobbies, the arts and sport are different. They could not exist, or, at any rate, they would take quite different forms, if the voluntary sector's contributions were stripped away. This sector has unique capabilities, one of which is to attract volunteers.

VOLUNTEERING

Definition

Volunteering is difficult to define because the examples are so varied. However, the following should capture all instances of genuine volunteering:

- The action must be voluntary though this alone is insufficient because all leisure behaviour is voluntary and even wage labour is free in that a worker can quit.
- The intention and outcome of volunteering must be regarded as worthy.
- A volunteer may be paid, but the value of what is volunteered (the gift) must be regarded as exceeding any benefit to the giver. In this sense, volunteering is altruistic. It is necessary to insert 'be regarded' into this clause because a volunteer will normally experience non-material psychic benefits (feeling good for having done good, and maybe more).

Volunteering occurs within but is not confined to sport, tourism and events.

- Amateur sport clubs are run mainly by volunteers. The members who coach novice players and officiate matches are usually volunteers.
- Volunteers may act as guides and help to maintain heritage sites and other tourist and visitor attractions.
- Major events such as the Olympics need and attract thousands of volunteers (see below).
- Volunteers also work in charity shops, old people's homes, schools and hospitals.
- They work for political parties and other campaigning groups. They may do this work year in and year out or just for the duration of a campaign when they distribute leaflets, canvass by telephone, compile email lists, and so on.

Table 3.1 Volunteers in USA in 2014 by type of organisation

Civic, political, professional	5%
Educational	25%
Environment/animal care	3%
Hospital and other health	7%
Public safety	1%
Religious	33%
Social or community	14%
Sport, hobby, arts, cultural	4%
Other	4%
Unknown	3%

Source: US Bureau of Labor Statistics

Volunteers are very important in sport, the arts and hobbies. None could survive in their present forms without volunteers. However, in the United States, for example, only 4 per cent of volunteers do this for a sports, arts, cultural or hobby organisation or group. There are far more volunteers with a religious, educational or youth organisation (see Table 3.1).

Volunteering may be on a continuing, open-ended basis, or for a finite duration. It can be informal (assistance to relatives and neighbours, for example) or formal, under the auspices of an organisation. This is most likely to be a voluntary association, but volunteers are also found in public services such as hospitals and schools, and sometimes they are sponsored as part of a commercial business's ethical, socially responsible operations (or for public relations). Volunteering is normally a leisure-time activity, but not necessarily. Employers may grant time off work for employees to engage in 'skilled volunteering' which self-styled ethical, socially responsible firms are often willing, possibly keen, to support.

Most volunteering is organised by voluntary associations, but not all members and participants are volunteers. Some may be paid staff. Other members may donate money but otherwise remain inactive. Other members may really be clients or beneficiaries. The remainder, the active members, are the volunteers, but, as explained above, the voluntary sector is not the sole base of citizens who volunteer.

History

The term 'volunteer' was first used in the military in Europe around 1600 to distinguish volunteers (who joined freely) from conscripts. These methods of recruitment to armed forces were created when serfs were replaced by free labourers who were released from the traditional duty to serve. Ever since then, volunteers have usually enjoyed the higher status, better pay and better prospects of promotion within the military. Some connotations of this original military use of the term 'volunteer' survive to the present day (see Nichols, 2004). The term was first applied to civilians who volunteered to work in conflict zones during military operations, including the 'angels of the battlefield' who were organised by Clara Barton during the American Civil War (1861–1865). The term 'volunteer' was also applied to the women who sewed and collected supplies for soldiers. Clara Barton went on to form the American Red Cross in 1881, and then mobilised volunteers to assist in disasters including the Jordanstown (Pennsylvania) Flood in 1889.

During the 19th and early-20th centuries, there was a wave of efforts to mobilise volunteers to work with the disadvantaged in the expanding industrial cities. The Salvation Army was formed in London in 1865, American Rotary was established in Chicago in 1905 and the first Lions Club was formed in Illinois in 1917. All these volunteers were intended to look like 'armies' of civilians.

International volunteering from richer to poorer countries dates from the formation of the US Peace Corps in 1960, a model which has now been copied in many other countries. This is among the more controversial branches of the present-day volunteer movement. It is sometimes accused of being subservient to the foreign policies of governments in the volunteers' home countries, and of sponsoring 'voluntourism', in which the volunteers themselves are the main beneficiaries.

In a commercial age, it is probably inevitable that the value of volunteering is routinely assessed in money terms. This enables voluntary associations to headline the economic value of their work, and governments and businesses that 'invest' in the voluntary sector can justify this in terms of the returns per £, $ or € that they invest. In the United States, the value of a standard volunteer's work is usually set at $18–$20 per hour, whereas a skilled volunteer, typically someone with professional qualifications and experience, will be valued at anything between $50 and $500 per hour.

The profile of volunteers has changed over time, reflecting wider social trends. The original civilian 'do-gooders' were typically middle-class housewives. They are no longer available: most now have paid jobs. However, the youth life stage has been extended, making available large numbers of students and young adults who are between full-time education and starting their main adult careers. Also, later life has been extended, swelling the numbers who are retired and fit with time to spare, and who need to be needed (see Taylor et al., 2012). However, in the United States, the peak ages for volunteering are 35–54, the child-rearing ages. Women are more likely to volunteer than men (29 and 23 per cent), and whites are more likely to volunteer than any other ethnic group, but the main differences are by educational level: 39 per cent of adults (age 16 and over) with a bachelor degree or higher were volunteering in 2014 compared with just 16 per cent with just high school diplomas and 9 per cent of those who did not complete high school (see Table 3.2). We can also note from Table 3.2 that there was little change throughout the years that are covered. This is typical in leisure behaviour. When changes occur, this tends to be gradual over many years. The exception was when television was added to other mass media and within a decade had made a radical difference to everyday life: people were spending more time at home and were less likely to go to cinemas and theatres, and to be active members of voluntary associations. New media have not made a comparable impact (yet).

Olympic volunteers

London 1948 was the first Olympics to assemble a volunteer force. Needless to say, there had been officials and members of sports federations attending previous Olympics who were there in a voluntary capacity. London 1948 set a new model in creating a special team of Olympic volunteers, and this model has been repeated at every subsequent Games. The 1948 event became known as the Austerity Games. The event was held when clothing,

Table 3.2 US volunteers by educational attainment in percentages

	2010	2011	2012	2013	2014
Less than high school diploma	9	10	9	9	9
High school graduates, no college	18	18	17	17	16
Some college or associate degree	29	30	29	28	27
Bachelor degree or higher	42	42	42	40	39
Total	26	27	27	26	25

Source: US Bureau of Labor Statistics

foodstuffs and petrol were still rationed, and when failures of electricity supply were frequent. London had been chosen to host the 1944 Games (which were cancelled); it then volunteered to restart the series of modern Olympics in 1948. Volunteers were needed partly because of the austerity context. No new venues or accommodation were built. Competitors were housed in student accommodation and barracks that had been used by troops between 1939 and 1945. Athletes were conveyed to their events seated on benches in ex-army lorries. The Games needed volunteers who knew their way around London, and they were recruited from local schools, scout groups, sport clubs and police motorbike squadrons. There was no volunteer uniform. Clothing was rationed! Athletes were allocated extra but not officials or volunteers. However, a reward that was much appreciated by volunteers in 1948 was that you could eat as much as you wished, and there were 'luxury' foods such as steaks and imported fruits.

Sydney 2000 set a new norm for Olympic volunteering in the sheer size of the force that was assembled, the uniform that made volunteers distinctive and using volunteers in ways that enhanced everyone's experience of the Games. The Sydney volunteer force began to form as early as 1992 when the city's bid to host the Games was being prepared. The idea was to demonstrate local support for the bid and the enthusiasm of 'Sydneysiders' to welcome the world to their city. By 1999, the core volunteer force had expanded to around 500. Subsequently, they became known as the pioneer volunteers. In 2000, a final official total of 46,967 volunteers was high profile at all venues and throughout the city. In 2010, some of these volunteers attended a tenth-anniversary reunion where they recalled 'the best time of my life', helping to create 'the most fantastic atmosphere the city has ever seen', and 'meeting people from all over the world – athletes, politicians and princesses' (http://sydney2000reunion.com/ourstories.html). This is what volunteer applicants at subsequent sport mega-events have been hoping to experience.

In 2004, Athens followed the Sydney model except that there were around 150,000 applications to volunteer (a third of these were from outside Greece), from whom 45,000 were selected for the main Summer Olympics and 15,000 for the following Paralympics.

Beijing 2008 did everything on a grander scale. Approximately 100,000 volunteers were recruited from over a million applicants, most of whom were Beijing-based students including students at the Beijing Sport University, which is where the selected volunteers were trained (Zhuang and Girginov, 2012). Volunteering in China is different than in most other countries. If a class is invited to do so, all are expected to compete to volunteer, and they will be told that only the best will be chosen. This is not to suggest that the Beijing volunteers lacked enthusiasm. Student volunteers throughout the world have mixtures of motives. There are usually some 'conscripts' who feel that volunteering is expected of them, 'instrumentalists' who want the addition to their CVs as well as the pure enthusiasts (see Treuren, 2014).

The 2002 Commonwealth Games, which were held in Manchester, assembled the largest-ever volunteer force in peacetime Britain. There were over 20,000 applicants, of whom 10,500 were recruited. The number of applicants was considered astounding at the time (Ralston et al., 2003). These figures were vastly exceeded at the London 2012 Olympics (see Box 3.2). The 2012 volunteers were not unsung heroes. Their work was praised throughout the Games and has been ever since the Games ended. The 2012 volunteers were part of the closing ceremony and the post-Games parade through London.

Volunteers at mega-sports events are not typical of all volunteers. There are no common denominators except that the volunteers act voluntarily, their efforts are considered worthy and whatever benefits they receive are regarded as outweighed by what they give. There are plenty of unsung heroes who meet these criteria. They volunteer weekly or more frequently and continue to do so for many years in hospitals, hospices, schools, old people's homes, centres for the disabled, charity shops and in sports, drama and choral societies, and many more. Robert Stebbins (1992) names

---

Box 3.2 The London 2012 Olympic volunteers

Planning this volunteer force began in 2004 when London was preparing its bid for the Olympics. The volunteer force was part of the promise to involve the entire city and the wider country (and to leave a legacy).

Volunteer recruitment began in 2010. The entire volunteer programme was professionally designed and led. There were 240,000 applicants, from whom 70,000 were selected. Applicants had to be willing to work for at least 10 days with no expenses and no free accommodation. Days of rehearsal preceded the Games.

At the venues, the volunteers were high profile in their chinos and red and purple shirts. They were part of the Games, welcoming visitors to the venues and generating atmosphere. Games Masters worked at the venues while London Ambassadors were all over the city – at airports, rail terminals and main tourist sites.

From all accounts, the volunteers enjoyed a successful Olympics: making new friends and, most of all, seeing it all come right.

Afterwards, there were reports of withdrawal symptoms: bouts of crying, feeling lost and bereft.

volunteering as an example of serious leisure in which those concerned can build careers, become increasingly knowledgeable and skilled and may earn the appreciation of beneficiaries and status among fellow volunteers but neither receive nor seek any wider recognition. Olympic volunteers fall into Stebbins' 'project-based' leisure category – a task undertaken for a finite period (Stebbins, 2005). Individuals may or may not carry on with voluntary work after major events (see Bang, 2009; Doherty, 2009). If they do continue, Olympic experience is likely to raise false expectations.

THE ENGINE: ENTHUSIASM

> We believe that involvement in such groups [voluntary associations] offers people something probably unique in our society: the chance to come together with others to create or participate for collective benefit or enjoyment rather than for sale to an anonymous audience or purchaser. (Bishop and Hoggett, 1986, p. 3)

Spectator crowds and audiences generate special types of atmosphere and elation. The voluntary experience is not better or worse, more or less intense, but simply different. Shared enthusiasms bring people together and are then sustained and strengthened by their interaction. There is no intermediary. There is no division between the provider and the consumer. These roles are fused. Within such contexts, there are special satisfactions to be gained from developing skills and expertise. The intrinsic enjoyment, plus the recognition and esteem of fellow members, becomes sufficient reward. Members' enthusiasm can migrate to the associations themselves. So people are prepared to offer the same commitment, and sometimes as many hours per week, as in their paid occupations. Some club officials devote more time to their voluntary work than others (and sometimes they themselves) devote to their paid jobs. The voluntary sector is proof that money is not the only effective motivator. People will push themselves to peaks of sporting and artistic achievement for personal satisfaction, and for the respect and esteem earned among others who share their passions. Enthusiasm drives voluntary associations. It is their lifeblood. They thrive on it. For as long as enthusiasm is sustained, the associations cannot be threatened, or even seriously challenged, by either commercial or public provisions. If ever enthusiasm dries up, the associations are extinguished.

It is within voluntary associations that people are most likely to experience what Robert Stebbins (1992) calls 'serious leisure'. People can have careers in serious (as opposed to casual) leisure, gradually accumulating experience and skills. Enthusiasts inspire each other. So amateur musicians, actors, astronomers, archaeologists, comedians and sports players sometimes become as skilled and knowledgeable as professionals. Why do they do it? Why do they work so hard at their leisure interests? This does not happen to audiences at the cinema or crowds at spectator sports unless some of them form themselves into clubs. The dog enthusiasts studied by Dair Gillespie and his colleagues (2002) were devoting huge amounts of time, and large amounts of money, to their hobby. In some cases, the dogs appeared to be taking precedence over everything else. Some of the enthusiasts were sleeping with their dogs instead of their human partners! The rewards obtained from serious leisure careers are similar to those that some people obtain from paid employment: enrichment, improved self-image, feelings of accomplishment and belonging. The rewards can become deeper the longer a leisure career extends: as one-time players or performers become officials in their sports or arts, and then become organisers of local, regional, national and even international events. Stebbins claims, though up to now this remains unproven, that serious leisure, when people are engaged in it, can perform the social and psychological functions usually associated with paid jobs and can thereby avert the socio-psychological loss and damage that are otherwise likely during spells of unemployment or following retirement.

THE TWENTY-FIRST-CENTURY CONTEXT

Fewer joiners?

There is always talk of crisis in the voluntary sector. Up to now, all obituaries have proved not premature but plain wrong. There is always churning: births and fatalities, growing and contracting segments. In a mixed leisure economy, there are constant boundary adjustments between voluntary, public sector and commercial providers. There are always some voluntary societies that are experiencing limitations and pressing the limits of their capabilities. Most of the problems are symptoms of virility rather than terminal sickness.

That said, the associations face some common and seemingly perpetual problems. To begin with, most of the organisations are always short of money. Fundraising is usually perpetual. Every meeting may feature a fundraising raffle. The associations are constantly trying to hold on to, or are seeking new, places to meet or play – maybe looking to larger voluntary bodies such as churches, or for the use of local government premises. Second, the organisations invariably want more members, and especially more volunteers. This latter problem may well have become more acute than ever in recent years for some clubs. Most women, as well as men, have paid jobs nowadays. Men are doing more in their homes. Full-time employees of both sexes are as likely to be working longer as shorter hours than in the past (see Nichols, 2005; Roberts, 1999). However, there are more young people (between childhood and full adulthood) and there are also more retired people, and many of the latter still have decades of active life ahead of them after they have retired from their main occupations and relinquished their main family responsibilities. The 'young old' could become a major source of volunteers. In Britain (which is different from the United States in this respect), the over-45s, especially the women and those who are not in employment, are more likely than other age groups to be volunteers and to help others in less formal ways (Rushton, 2003). Even so, voluntary organisations complain about how difficult it is to recruit new blood. Recruiting members, and especially volunteers, may or may not have become even more difficult than it was in the past, but it has always been a problem for the societies. Few associations have ever had 'enough'.

The crucial point is that the sector is definitely not fizzling out. We have seen that over a half of all adults in Western countries including the United States and Britain belong to at least one voluntary society. There are roughly 1.5 million people in Britain who do voluntary work for sports teams and clubs on a more or less continuous basis – acting as referee, club secretary or whatever. As many as 7.5 million do a sport-related voluntary activity at some time during any year (Nichols, 2012). The number of volunteers vastly exceeds the number of sport-related paid jobs – just under a quarter of a million to just over half a million depending on whether sport-related employment in gambling, broadcasting, print media, computer games and sports clothing and footwear is included in the total (see Chapter 10). Whatever is included and excluded, the total has been rising – evidence of the growing economic importance of sport and leisure in general – but this has not been at the expense of volunteering, and the total of volunteers still vastly exceeds the number of paid employees in sport.

There are instances, whole areas of leisure in some countries, where clubs are in decline. For example, in recent years, some European countries' sports clubs have experienced a loss of members (see Deckers and Gratton, 1995). The reason is not that people are quitting physically active recreation. It is more a case of them engaging in recreational swimming, surfing, skiing, sailing, and so on, without necessarily joining clubs and teams and participating in competitions. This does not mean that competitive sport is threatened with extinction. It is more a case of a shift in the constantly moving boundary between club sport and self-organised recreation.

Robert Putnam (2000) has written a gloomy treatise on the decline of social capital in America. *Bowling Alone* is a catchy book title but bowling is just one of the more trivial examples that Putnam presents. He finds that more Americans are living singly; that families are dining together less frequently; that there is less activity in politics, and a decline in other forms of civic activity and church attendance; that fewer people are playing team sports and more are taking individual exercise. Putnam claims that although the United States has more voluntary associations than ever before, collectively they have fewer members than in the past. Moreover, he claims that members are increasingly passive members, paying donations instead of doing.

However, it is not clear that there really has been an overall decline in voluntary organisation membership across America (see Paxton, 1999), and there is no evidence of an all-round decline in Britain or in other European countries (Harper, 2001). Older associations may have lost members who are replaced by members of new clubs. In Britain, there has been a decline among males in membership of trade unions and working men's clubs but there has not been any decline in most types of leisure-related voluntary associations during the late-20th or early-21st centuries. In Britain, more people are taking individual exercise but as many as ever are playing team sports such as football, within which there has been a switch from the outdoor 11-a-side to the indoor 5-a-side version. Since the 1980s, there has actually been a decline in jogging (often a solitary activity), though more people are 'walking', doing keep-fit and yoga, cycling, golf, and weightlifting and training. Cue sports and darts have been in decline, but both versions of football (soccer and rugby union even more so) remain buoyant (see Chapter 6).

What about the Internet? Is it going to keep us online instead of going out and joining clubs? At present, the evidence is not clear-cut. In America, there is evidence of heavy Internet use leading to less face-to-face social interaction (Kraut et al., 1998). Some clubs have experienced a drift of members into online communities (see Lawrence, 2003). Virtual cyberspace relationships may sometimes replace the traditional variety. However, a study in Switzerland has found that Internet users in that country have larger social networks, and experience more face-to-face interaction, than non-users (Franzen, 2000). The impact of the Internet may vary from place to place, though convergence is likely as people in all countries become more familiar with this latest new technology (see Chapter 9). As they do so, they realise that, at present at any rate, the new technology cannot deliver the same satisfactions as face-to-face interaction.

It is true that some pundits in Europe, as in America, believe that the individualisation of biographies and trends towards privatism in daily life will drain voluntary organisations of their lifeblood, namely members and volunteers. Home-centred, family-based lifestyles and a general decline of community are frequently identified as threats to the voluntary sector. Note, however, that the 'decline of community' thesis is as old as industrialism. The character of home-centred lifestyles is sometimes misunderstood. Being home centred does not mean never going out. Extreme privatism is usually due to exceptional constraints – lack of money, and child-rearing couples juggling their domestic and paid-work schedules, for example – rather than choice (see Devine, 1992). In the absence of such constraints, the home usually acts as a base from which individuals and couples can venture out into wider social networks (see Allan and Crow, 1991). Traditional neighbourhood communities (as we now describe them) are in decline, and have been declining for many decades. People have become more mobile. Most neighbourhoods no longer provide traditional communal roots in which voluntary associations can grow. That said, the mobile middle classes are often the most enthusiastic joiners, keen to sink identities in the villages, towns and neighbourhoods where they want to feel that they really belong (Savage et al., 2005).

When people go out today, they are most likely to do so privately, by car. If they go out for a drink, this is not necessarily to 'the local'. Much the same has happened to occupational communities, and for much the same reasons. Labour is more mobile than in the past. People are no longer constrained to live within walking or cycling distance from their workplaces. But people still go out and associate with one another. They participate in interlocking rather than 'traditional' superimposed social networks in which kin, neighbours, work colleagues and friends are all largely the same people and all the participants have much the same circle of acquaintances. Interlocking networks have no definite bases in either neighbourhoods, churches or workplaces. The people who join a particular club will not necessarily have any other social bonds with one another. The older communal formations (which could be experienced as warm and friendly, or stifling) are in decline, but they are being replaced with other forms of sociability.

The squeeze on public spending

This is a challenge that most clubs and societies have faced. Grant aid has been reduced or even eliminated. User charges for amenities (sport centres, playing fields, civic halls, and suchlike) have been raised. Members have needed to pay more, and have usually done so. They will pay if they are sufficiently enthusiastic. Facilities have sometimes closed because a public authority has felt unable to afford to run them. In this event, club members appear to have been enterprising in finding somewhere else to meet or play even if this has meant travelling further and/or paying more. An alternative to closure sometimes on offer is for an association or a group of associations to take over the management of a facility. The public authority will usually offer financial support. A voluntary association may have to bid competitively for the contract. The contract awarder is invariably seeking to save on what it was spending to run the facility itself.

Some voluntary associations have risen to the challenge of facility management (see Box 3.3). These are invariably clubs with large memberships

---

Box 3.3 City of Chester Swimming Club

The Chester Amateur Swimming Club began in 1894 in a floating bath on the River Dee. The club transferred to the newly opened City Baths in 1901.

In the early days, the water polo team was a major attraction in the city, bringing in large crowds. The club's first major honour came in 1908, when member Wilf Edwards was selected to swim in the 1908 Olympics.

During the 1960s, the club's programme changed. Water polo declined in popularity, and by 1965 competitive swimming had become the club's major pursuit. In the late 1960s, the club started its first regular learn-to-swim classes, which continue to the present day.

There was a crisis in the 1970s when the local authority opened a new sports and leisure centre in which the fun pool was unsuitable for competitive events, and the local authority decided that the old swimming baths would have to close. The upshot was that the Chester Amateur Swimming Club joined with another local club, the Chester Dolphins (the clubs merged to become the present-day City of Chester Swimming Club in 1979), and took over the management of the baths in 1977.

Since the 1980s, the club has employed professional coaching staff. Management by a voluntary association has been a success for over 30 years. In 1984, a gymnasium was added by converting the old laundry room. In 1988, the club had one of its most successful years when the girls' swimming team became the national age group champions and 12 members were selected to represent their countries in international events. The club has established the City Baths as a recognised Amateur Swimming Association Teaching Centre and runs courses leading to teaching qualifications.

Source: www.cityofchesterswimmingclub.co.uk

and a core of stalwarts, preferably with professional skills and management experience. Most clubs lack these foundations. They will not necessarily have members with the expertise or commitment to draw up a bid for a contract. The outcome is that facility management is more likely to be outsourced to a commercial business or to a quasi-non-governmental organisation, that is a *quango* created 'from above' specifically for the purpose of hiving off a facility. This strategy is discussed in the next chapter. The outcome for member-based clubs is normally higher charges than in the past, with the new management offering some enhancement of the facility. All told, however, the voluntary sector is proving resilient.

Coping with success

This is not a problem for most voluntary associations that serve members' leisure interests. When it is a persistent problem, the persistence proves that an association is able to cope. Otherwise, the problems of success are easily avoided by individual members and associations.

Tensions may arise when associations are successful in obtaining grant aid, and especially when they win contracts to manage facilities. Fulfilling the terms of the awards is likely to become a priority. In other words, an association must become businesslike. If this is unacceptable to members, an association can always opt for complete independence, decline offers of grant aid and allow some other organisation to manage a facility and become just a user.

Similar problems can be created when an association is so successful in winning grants, contracts and/or sponsorship, or so successful in managing a facility, that it is able, and needs, to appoint paid staff like the City of Chester Swimming Club (see Box 3.3). The paid staff are likely to want the club to be run professionally and on commercial lines – their own jobs are at risk – and they may resent any expectation that they should volunteer some of their own time. Hanson (1982) gives examples from the railway clubs which were formed in Britain when steam engines were retired from the rail transport industry, and when, with the spread of the private motor car, many loss-making branch lines were closed. Before long, voluntary associations were taking over and restoring some of these lines, plus the old steam locomotives and their original carriages. By the 1970s, the more vigorous and successful railway clubs had developed money-raising activities. They were using their trains to convey paying passengers (mostly day trippers and tourists) as a way of covering the clubs' costs. This, more likely than not, required the appointment of paid staff to sell tickets and to maintain the tracks and rolling stock to the required safety standards, and to drive the trains.

Voluntary organisations include local camera clubs and pub quiz leagues, and also bodies with national, sometimes international, profiles – the International Olympics Committee, the Scouts and the Young Men's Christian Association (YMCA) are all basically voluntary and, nowadays, global in scale. There are many internationally renowned orchestras, opera and ballet companies and art collections that are under voluntary management. There are some forms of leisure where, in some voluntary associations, neither the professionals nor the volunteers can manage without the other. It would be impossible to stage the Olympic Games today without any paid staff, and these events would also be impossible without unpaid volunteers and the worldwide interest and participation that depend on voluntary action. There may always be some tensions, but the major sports and youth organisations now have long histories of achievement in which they have combined voluntary management and volunteer help on the one hand with the employment of paid administrators and professional players and leaders on the other.

CONCLUSIONS

One message from this chapter is that the voluntary sector is alive and well. Overall leisure has been commercialised but the expansion of commerce has been in addition to rather than at the expense of what the voluntary sector offers. Neither the expansion of commerce nor the strengthening of public provisions at the time when welfare states were being formed has undermined voluntarism. The different providers have complementary, non-substitutable capabilities. There are constant boundary adjustments, but there can be no wholesale takeover because of voluntary associations' distinctive capabilities and the distinctive satisfactions that they can offer. In recent years, commerce has developed new markets for the individualised pursuit of health and fitness through exercise, but this has not been at the expense of participant sports that remain under voluntary management (see Chapter 6, pp. 134–146). Likewise, holidays are still self-organised by members of churches, by schools, by employees at specific workplaces, by wine lovers and by Elvis worshippers. The Youth Hostels Association is still active. Commercial holidays have surrounded rather than taken over or extinguished the voluntary sector's contributions, and, as it usually does wherever it expands, commerce has widened holidaymakers' options (see Chapter 5). Commercial, public sector and voluntary provisions are not head-on competitors. They are more often mutually supportive. It is unnecessary to oppose one in order to support another.

Chapter 4

The Public Sector

INTRODUCTION

The financial crash of 2008–09 and the subsequent recession have not depressed all leisure businesses. Nor has the impact spread evenly across the commercial, voluntary and public sectors. Some major commercial leisure sectors have continued to flourish. The next chapter explains that global tourism has continued its apparently remorseless expansion with the steepest growth now from emerging market economies. No end is in sight, even on a distant horizon. Top sport has continued to prosper due to the steadily and steeply rising value of broadcasting rights. Once the broadcast rights markets in richer countries are saturated (which has not happened yet), there will remain immense scope for growth in the rest of the world. Again, this growth is expected to continue indefinitely. Old and new media are fusing, and the value of markets for hardware and software continues to expand. Again, there is no end in sight. Tablets and mobile phones with ever-increasing functions are not replacing but are actually helping to enlarge the audience for 'traditional' television (the set in the living room). Cyberspace is contested territory and has bred entirely new kinds of business for file sharers, hackers, bloggers and app and game creators (see Mason, 2008). Bedroom entrepreneurs in Asia create avatars for sale to richer North Americans (Yu-Hao Lee and Holin Lin, 2011). That said, it is not the case that the entire commercial leisure sector has escaped the recession. In Britain, visits to and spending in casinos, pubs and restaurants have declined (Roberts, 2013). After 2008, there was a drop in bookings for overseas holidays, though some domestic attractions reported increased visitor numbers. Commercial leisure markets are intensely competitive. So a multitude of dot-coms and many other businesses have floundered in generally buoyant sectors.

The voluntary sector can be resilient for as long as there are sufficient members with sufficient enthusiasm. They will always find somewhere affordable to meet, play or perform. Like commerce, the sector is volatile. Some associations grow while others shrink and fold. The new media have created new public space for new online communities. These may not perform the same functions for individuals as face-to-face interaction, but we have seen in Chapter 3 that online interaction is just as likely to complement, supplement or lead to more face-to-face meetings as to become a substitute.

It is public sector leisure that has absorbed the full force of the crash and the subsequent recession. Sovereign (government) debt rose through re-capitalising (bailing out) failing banks. Re-capitalisation has continued in some countries where it is called 'quantitative easing'. These operations transform private sector (bank) debt into government debt. The alternative in 2008–09 would have been financial meltdown, which, in a system of financialised capitalism, would have meant economic meltdown – wholesale collapse of firms and jobs. The scale of the bailing out was proportionate to the size of countries' financial sectors. Current account (annual income and spending) government deficits are different from the scale of any sovereign debt. Current account deficits widened when economies sank into recession, tax receipts fell and spending on out-of-work welfare benefits rose. Governments outside the Eurozone could have 'printed' money (in practice nowadays most money is created electronically). Governments could have allowed any sovereign debt to rise. They could have increased their own spending, cut taxes, increased the incomes of welfare recipients and thereby tried to spend their countries out of recession. Only the United States, custodian of the dollar, the world's main reserve currency (in which other governments hold most of their reserves, though some may still be held in bullion), has been able to get away with this 'spendthrift' behaviour. Other governments would be punished by the international system charging high interest rates. Eurozone governments agreed their own mutual 'austerity pact' or 'fiscal consolidation' in 2011, which prohibits running indefinite current account deficits. Governments could close current account deficits by raising taxes, but believe that this would be unpopular with voters, especially the majority who have remained in work since 2008, paying taxes, and most unpopular with the rich who pay the largest sums in tax. It would also have been unpopular with investors (capitalists), who favour low taxes on wealth and earnings on wealth. Governments' remaining option has been to reduce public spending. Some areas are notoriously difficult to cut. These include pensions in countries with ageing populations, and health care, given the constant invention of new drugs and medical treatments, plus the growth in the number of elderly who tend to need the most treatment. Spending on education is also difficult to cut. Spending on 'back-room' administration can be trimmed but only up to a point. Leisure spending has usually been a principal casualty, and within leisure, governments have tended to protect spending where there is a business case such as attracting tourists. So money is found to build facilities to host mega-events. Cultural facilities plus heritage sites that attract overseas visitors are usually protected. Community facilities are at the greatest risk.

The next section asks exactly how governments have been making savings in public sector leisure. There is always a historically laid base from which new developments and cutbacks must be made. It is never possible to restart with a 'clean slate'. Therefore, the subsequent section reviews the history of public leisure provisions which, in all countries where public social services now have a long history, have become a hotchpotch. Various facilities and programmes have been introduced at different times for all manner of reasons, some long forgotten, though proposals to close a facility or axe any programme invariably arouse vocal opposition. It is necessary to establish exactly what is at greatest risk under the present-day cost-cutting business culture. The chapter's third main section is a critical appraisal of the various motives and objectives that have lain behind the introduction of the various public leisure services which may currently be at risk.

The commercial sector has one pivotal driver, which is the pursuit of profit. If a leisure good or service can be supplied profitably, then, in a market economy, some or another enterprise will deliver. Anything that cannot be made profitable will be abandoned whatever its countervailing merits. Enthusiasm is the engine that drives the voluntary sector. The public sector is different. It will deliver whatever politicians decree, subject to the normal checks and balances, meaning the approval of political parties and parliaments. However, neither political parties nor governments have ever developed comprehensive and coherent leisure policies. At best, they have portfolios of arts, youth, tourism, sport, broadcasting policies, and so on. Intentions and objectives may sometimes be worthy but beyond the capabilities of public leisure provisions. Hence the case for identifying the public sector's unique capabilities: things that it can achieve which are simply beyond the capabilities and therefore cannot be replaced by commerce or voluntary effort, and which may therefore be considered prime candidates for protection not just from any current deficit reducing cutbacks but from the longer-term maelstrom of commercialisation.

BUSINESS METHODS

The movement towards more businesslike ways of running public leisure services (and other public services) began long before 2008. It can be traced to the spread of neoliberal ideas among governments throughout the world in the 1980s, endorsed by powerful international financial institutions such as the World Bank and the International Monetary Fund. In Britain, the movement hit public leisure services in 1989, when the central government's Audit Commission delivered a report on the management of local authority leisure services. The commission was appalled by what it found: no clear objectives, no data on costs per user of different facilities, no comparisons of the costs per swim in different pools, and so on. The government's response was to require the management of local authority leisure services to be opened to competitive tendering with in-house teams, voluntary associations and commercial businesses all able to bid. The incoming new Labour government in 1997 replaced compulsory competitive tendering with a similar 'best value' regime. Since then, the model has been spread across numerous public services – schools, hospitals, even prisons. It creates a division between the purchaser of a service (a government department) and a service provider. The model had precedents. Armed forces have always been under political control, but since the Middle Ages operational command has been delegated to military leaders. The model is intended to lead to greater clarity of objectives, measurable outcomes and more efficient and innovative delivery. Since 2008, this has been just one of the ways in which cost savings have not just been sought but imposed on virtually all public leisure services. Business culture has swept into public sector leisure departments. The ethos is no longer about meeting people's needs and ensuring access for all but about marketing, raising revenue, cutting costs, meeting targets and achieving best value. Perhaps surprisingly, we shall see that it has often proved possible to do as much (and sometimes more) for less money. In this sense, business methods can be declared successful. The question that remains is whether we lose something of value in the distinctive capabilities of public leisure provisions.

There are various ways in which public leisure services can cut and have been cutting their costs.

Close buildings

The buildings may be libraries, concert halls, civic halls, community meet-ing rooms, arts centres, swimming pools or sports centres. This is a way of making substantial savings from most leisure department budgets. Spending on staff, lighting and heating is axed. If the land and buildings can be sold for redevelopment, the proceeds can be invested in facilities that remain. Resources can be concentrated on the most popular, the most used facilities. Some buildings become superfluous as newer facilities draw swimmers, bas-ketball teams, squash and other sport players. Libraries have adapted to change by adding vinyl records, then video cassettes and DVDs and lat-terly computer and Internet facilities to their printed books. Today, however, more people are online at home, music and films can be downloaded and readers are purchasing printed and e-books instead of borrowing. Periodical politically driven cuts in the public sector are the equivalents of the down-turns in business that force commercial firms to trim. They thereby free resources with which they can later on respond to upturns with new services and products. Closure of underused public facilities can be compatible with maintained levels of use and user satisfaction. If there are accessible alterna-tives to the closed facilities, enthusiasts will find them. The public leisure services' defenders are unwise to oppose all closures. The sector makes itself defensible by being adaptable. Portfolios of public facilities need to change alongside the public's tastes and lifestyles.

All that said, there may be a heritage case for preserving some of the oldest, original public leisure facilities as a reminder to a town or country of how its ancestors lived and played, as educational aids, and possibly as heritage attractions in the 21st-century tourist industry.

Cut staff

Once again, the savings can be considerable, but some back-room staff must be retained, and fewer staff invariably means less sports coaching, art and drama tuition, and so on. These cuts are difficult to reconcile with main-taining the quality of a service. Leisure services tend to be labour-intensive. The size of a symphony orchestra cannot be cut without some loss of quality.

Reduce opening hours

The main savings are on staff time and costs. Buildings must continue to be maintained. It makes sense to close libraries and sports centres when no one is using them. The same applies to department stores and supermarkets.

However, in increasingly 24/7 societies, there are growing minorities for whom what are generally considered unsocial hours are the most convenient times to play.

Raise user charges

This has almost always been part of a search for cost savings. Regular users of facilities can be protected by membership schemes which cap their costs. There can be concessions for low-income groups. Visitor and user volumes are usually maintained because enthusiasts and habitual users for whom the higher charges are affordable will pay provided they cannot access cheaper alternatives. The risk is that fewer new regulars will be attracted.

It is sometimes argued that in a commercial age, full-cost payment is expected and accepted by those for whom full costs are affordable. Some may treat price as a guide to the value of a leisure experience. However, this would suggest that one of the unique capabilities of public leisure provision (identified below) is being eroded. People do not pay to use or view something that already belongs to them.

Scale down grants

Grant aid to voluntary bodies can be trimmed. This aid may be made proportionate to merit whether judged by user numbers, users' socio-demographic profiles or aesthetic standards. Reductions in state aid have been made across the board in most countries – to state broadcasters and performing arts companies, and galleries with international reputations, as well as to local youth, women's, sports and arts groups. Once again, enthusiasm usually guarantees survival, sometimes with reduced staff, programmes and activities. Commercial sponsors and higher member or user charges may (or may not) fill gaps left by the withdrawal of public funds. These cutbacks are more likely to act as challenges or dampeners than death sentences.

Sell assets

This is a way in which leisure departments can generate one-off injections of income rather than a method of achieving permanent closure of any gap between recurrent income and spending. The aim when 'selling the family silver' is usually to raise funds to invest in new or to upgrade the facilities that remain (see Box 4.1).

A problem is that most leisure departments have few assets with a substantial market value because they cannot be operated profitably. The UK

Box 4.1 Selling the family silver

Some local authorities in England have sought to restructure leisure services' budgets by the sale of assets.

In 2013, Croydon Council (in south London) decided to sell by auction 24 high-value vases, bowls and bottles from its antique Chinese ceramics collection. The 230-piece collection had been sold to the council by a local businessman in 1959. Croydon's intention in 2013 was to invest the proceeds by improving another of its leisure facilities, Fairfield Halls, a 50-year-old concert hall and arts centre.

Also in 2013, Northampton Borough Council decided to sell a 4,000-year-old Egyptian statue. This item had been acquired by the Second Marquis of Northampton in 1850 and was presented to the museum by his son 20 years later. The intention in 2013 was to invest the proceeds in other heritage services. Fair exchange? Or betraying the generosity of past generations to present and future ones?

A problem with selling leisure assets is that their market value can be modest compared with their cultural value and associations for local residents. Land is valuable. Selling playing fields and parkland, especially sites close to city centres or suitable for housing, can raise substantial funds. However, most leisure facilities are not like gas, electricity and telephone services which the UK privatised in the 1980s. In 2013, Birmingham City Council contemplated selling its National Exhibition Centre, which includes a 16,000-seat arena, but its value was assessed at just £300 million. The city-centre International Convention Centre, which is also home to the 2,262-seat Symphony Hall, would fetch an even more modest sum. Sport stadiums built for major events may have to be given away: they cannot be run profitably. The same applies to most community sport and leisure centres.

---

government could obtain a handsome price for the BBC but not for the monarch's royal palaces unless these had planning permission for conversion into hotels or office accommodation. The assets with a worthwhile market value tend to be, first, in museums and art galleries. Why not sell those exhibits that add little if anything to the overall value of a local or national collection? Second, there is land: playing fields and parks. Land is originally a gift of nature. A government can simply declare that it will remain available as public space. There are opportunity costs but no financial outlay. Once sold, the asset is lost to leisure forever. Politicians will always think carefully before taking this step on behalf of their own and future generations. They are disposing of assets that benefactors – individuals or an entire earlier generation of citizens – intended to be enjoyed in perpetuity by their descendants. That said, there may be overall public benefits, short term and long term, in using proceeds from the sale of playing fields on which the weather makes play impossible for much of the year to construct all-weather surfaces and indoor sport facilities.

Devolved management

This is the original neoliberal recipe for introducing market mechanisms into public services. It has now become virtually universal in public leisure services at both national and local levels. Its popularity with public authorities is because it works. Seeking to earn revenue from public services, certainly leisure services, is rarely the aim of a public authority because very few of the services can be operated to yield profits. The aim is more modest – to reduce costs and possibly to gain 'more for less'. The driver is the purchaser-provider split. Politicians offload responsibility for delivery but become explicitly responsible for policy. They must prescribe in detail (to be included in a legal contract) the services to be provided, any caps on charges, any concessions to be available, and whatever other conditions they care to include. The purchaser (the public authority) invariably needs to pay the leisure services provider to deliver: the conditions of the contract invariably mean that the contracted services cannot be operated at a profit. However, the provider has day-to-day freedom to manage within the terms of the contract. Wollenburg and his colleagues (2013) describe how in America a provider has an incentive to invest in additional facilities and to introduce new programmes, thereby generating more business and revenue which may become profit or may be available for investment in more facilities, staff and programmes.

There are two models of devolved management. The jury is still out on which is superior. One is management by a local community organisation, possibly 'hived off' from the purchaser, the public authority. Salford Community Leisure is an example (see Box 4.2). This model has the advantage of local knowledge and roots. The alternative is to devolve management to an enterprise that operates leisure services in several places. DC Leisure is one example (see Box 4.3). The Virgin Group and Serco (see Box 2.1) are additional examples. Here, there are advantages in the businesses' wider experience.

Devolved management creates an interesting convergence between leisure services that were originally created by public authorities and then subsequently became 'arm's length', and voluntary associations that have become largely dependent on state funding. One risk is that public leisure services lose their public identity and the sense of citizenship (see below) that this can foster. The risk can be avoided by insisting simply that all the services have City, Municipal, County, National or equivalent in their titles and displayed

Box 4.2 Salford Community Leisure

The City of Salford borders Manchester (UK). It is part of the conurbation that was a centre of the textile industry during the Industrial Revolution. Salford is now thoroughly de-industrialised, with all the attendant problems. The city scores high on most indices of disadvantage. However, the city has a university and some attractive outlying residential neighbourhoods.

Salford Community Leisure was created in 2003 to manage the city's leisure services. It is a cooperative, owned by members who are customers, employees and local residents. Its facilities include sports centres, one of which is a water sports centre, libraries, a museum, an art gallery, and community centres.

During the recession, despite cuts in government funding, the cooperative reopened a centre which had fallen into disuse and improved facilities in most others. In 2012–13, the facilities had record visitor and user numbers.

Core funding is provided by the city council.

This model of devolved management can claim to combine the day-to-day independence that businesslike methods require with firm roots in and responsiveness to its local public.

Box 4.3 DC Leisure

The title stands for 'developing community leisure'. This 'no-dividends' business was created in 1991 to take advantage of the compulsory competitive tendering that had recently been introduced for local authority leisure services in England and Wales. By 2013, DC Leisure was managing approximately 120 sport and leisure centres for 29 local authorities.

DC Leisure became part of the Places for People Group in 2012. This group had developed from a housing association which was formed in 1965. By 2013, the group owned or managed 143,000 homes. It had become a major property development as well as a property management company. Its homes are social housing, meant to be 'affordable'. Some are sold; most are rented to tenants.

Although there are no owners to whom profits are distributed, the group has attracted controversy on account of its executive salaries, judged by some to be excessive for a social enterprise.

What can such a group contribute to the management of community leisure facilities? It has proven expertise in property management, and in administering facilities for the communities whose housing it owns and manages. Local authorities are able to 'buy in' this proven expertise.

prominently above their entrances. What else is at risk in the apparently successful introduction of business methods and culture into public leisure services is best identified by a review of their history, and how and why the hotchpotch of current services was created.

THE DEVELOPMENT OF PUBLIC LEISURE SERVICES: THE CASE OF THE UK

Incremental growth

Britain is not a typical or representative country, but as the world's first industrial nation, its public leisure services have the longest history, and, in this and other ways, Britain has been a model for many later-industrialising countries. Britain's public leisure services (as they are now described and which, in the early-20th century, became part of an increasingly coordinated recreation movement) developed incrementally and haphazardly. From their 19th-century beginnings, the long-term growth of leisure time and spending played a part, but only as a hidden hand. In the 19th century, neither central nor local government had any intention, or even an aspiration, to cater comprehensively for the people's leisure. Proposals for state intervention in education, health care and housing were controversial. The case for public leisure services was way outside all political agendas. Public sector leisure provision developed in an *ad hoc* way, not in response to leisure demands so much as to address a variety of other problems that arose during the transformation of Britain into an urban industrial society. There was no landmark legislation comparable to the 1870 Education Act (which made elementary schooling universal). The legislation under which public leisure provision began includes the Baths and Washhouses Act of 1846 (see Box 4.4), the Public Health Acts of 1875 and 1890, the Local Government Act of 1894 and the Open Spaces Act of 1906.

Box 4.4 Baths and washhouses

These were the precursors of present-day public swimming pools. They were opened in all major towns and cities in Britain in the decades following the 1846 Baths and Washhouses Act. There were facilities for washing clothes. Typical charges in the 19th century were one penny per hour, or threepence for two hours, including drying. There were also 'slipper bath' facilities. These were so named because of the appearance of the baths when, in the interest of modesty, users draped large towels over the tubs while they bathed.

By the 1870s, local authorities were adding swimming pools to the basic facilities. Ashton Swimming Pool was among the first. It was built in 1870 at a cost of £16,000, most of which was donated by a local mill owner. The main pool (100 feet by 40 feet) was used exclusively by men except for a three-hour slot each Thursday, when it was for ladies. The latter normally had to use a smaller pool (27 feet by 15 feet).

The first association of swimming clubs, which evolved into the Amateur Swimming Association, was formed in 1869 in London. Its main initial responsibility was the management of games of football played in water (which became known as water polo). However, in 1869, there was also a one-mile race. Before long other distances were added. The first recorded diving championship was held in Scotland in 1889.

Sources: www.britishswiming.org
www.northflow.fsnet.co.uk
www.ashton-under-lyne.com/baths.htm

One problem to which 19th-century governments responded was the (lack of) cleanliness and the general unhealthiness of the urban masses. Urban parks were intended to be oxygenised oases, the lungs of the city, to which people could escape from harmful gases (Crompton, 2013). However, US city governments were also mindful that orderly, carefully laid out parks increased the taxable value of neighbouring properties (Crompton, 2007). We no longer believe that urban parks protect users from the pollution caused by modern lifestyles, but we know, although the processes remain opaque, that regular use of green open space is good for mental well-being and stimulates community spirit (Burls, 2010). Another concern when introducing public leisure facilities was to encourage respectable, edifying ways of life (Meller, 1976). Hence the public libraries, museums and art galleries. These provisions were part of the movement promoting rational recreation (Bailey, 1978). Sometimes, the problem was a specific section of the population. The youth service has its origins in 19th-century efforts to keep young people, especially young males, out of trouble. Sport was supported for all the above reasons: health, shaping character, and keeping young males out of mischief. Over time, provisions were introduced for other needy groups such as the retired and the disabled. Local authorities sometimes became leisure providers by force of circumstance. When they became responsible for children's schooling, they were obliged to make provisions for the pupils' leisure. Later on, when they began to construct council houses, they could not but give consideration to the recreation facilities that were needed on the often-sprawling estates. These public leisure amenities were treated, by some, as contributing to the development of 'local socialism' (see Bliers, 2003). Holiday resorts, of course, had particular reasons to enhance their public amenities.

Three features are noteworthy about the historical beginnings of Britain's public leisure services. First, local rather than the central government was the main provider. Second, most of the provision was and remains under permissive rather than mandatory legislation, meaning that local authorities were and still are allowed, but not required, to provide. Third, wherever possible, provision was via the voluntary sector or with major philanthropic contributions (see Boxes 4.4–4.6). This also applied during the development of state education and health care. In the second half of the 19th century, Britain's municipalities set about encouraging rational recreation and creating civilised ways of urban life by harnessing and coordinating voluntary effort, and filled any gaps with their own facilities only as a last resort (see Meller, 1976). The Philharmonic Hall (see Box 4.5) is just one of many grand buildings in Liverpool which were erected in the 19th century with most of the initiative and initial funding from the voluntary sector.

The outcome of all these *ad hoc* provisions was an untidy hotchpotch. Local authority leisure services varied considerably in quantity and quality from place to place. There were no nationally approved benchmarks or yardsticks. At the time the provisions were not known as leisure services. Local authorities added new committees and departments for each service that was introduced – parks, libraries, baths, allotments, youth clubs, and so on. Each service had its own aspirant profession. So by the 1930s there was extensive public sector leisure provision, but no omnibus leisure services

---

Box 4.5 Liverpool's Philharmonic Hall

This building is still owned and managed by the Royal Liverpool Philharmonic Society, which is one of the oldest concert-giving organisations in the world. The society gave its first performance in 1840. It is the only orchestral society in Britain which owns and operates its own hall.

The original hall opened in 1849 but was destroyed by fire in 1933. An art deco replacement was opened in 1939. It was reopened in 1995 following a complete refurbishment. The hall is now the home of the Royal Liverpool Philharmonic Orchestra, the Royal Liverpool Philharmonic Choir and the Merseyside Youth Orchestra.

Choral music predominated in the society's programme up to the First World War, and a full-time professional orchestra was established only after the Second World War. The orchestra's annual programme now includes the Summer Pops, which are regularly attended by over 30,000 people.

The 200-strong choir remains entirely amateur. It travels the length and breadth of Britain, and overseas as well, and has sung regularly at the BBC Proms in London's Royal Albert Hall.

Sources: www.rlps.co.uk
www.liverpoolphil.com

---

departments, no single leisure profession and, most crucially, no leisure policies. However, by the 1920s, efforts to promote 'good leisure' were being coordinated by national and international recreation movements.

Leisure and the welfare state

Public leisure services (as they are described today) were part, albeit minor parts, of the overhaul and strengthening of welfare states that followed the Second World War in all Western countries. In Britain, secondary education for all was introduced. The National Health Service was created. Council house building accelerated to replace the remaining slums and war-damaged properties. Local authority leisure services continued much as before. By the end of the 1950s, they offered some of the starkest examples of public squalor – Victorian swimming pools, waterlogged playing fields and water-free changing rooms – amid private affluence (the affluent consumer society was then coming into existence). The Albemarle Committee (1960) concluded that youth clubs in draughty church halls could not compete with glitzy dance palais and cafe bars.

However, by the 1960s, the central government was playing a larger role in leisure provision. As indicated above, this was part of the construction of Britain's post-war welfare state. There were similar developments in other Western countries. However, in Britain, as had happened in local government earlier on, sheer force of circumstance dictated the character of government interventions. Problems were arising which required a national response or, at any rate, national coordination. Central government already had more than a toehold in leisure. Much of 'the heritage' was owned by the government or by the Crown, and was being visited by increasing numbers of tourists and day trippers. Since 1927, the BBC had been the monopoly state broadcaster (see Chapter 8). Roads and railways (and canals) were always, in part, leisure resources, and were increasingly being used for leisure travel. Also, the government was already regulating gambling and alcohol sales, and had legislation prescribing the limits of decency that were permissible on stage, in print and on film (albeit, in the latter case, via the industry's own board of censors).

Britain's Arts Council was created in 1946. This was in recognition of the fact that the production of high culture was becoming unsustainable without state support. In 1949, legislation was passed enabling National Parks to be designated, and a National Parks Commission (now absorbed into Natural England) was created. This was a response to the fact that more and more people were visiting the countryside. They needed to be catered for, and potential conflicts between the various demands on the countryside had to be addressed. The United States had begun to designate national parks almost a century earlier. The first such park, Yellowstone, was designated in 1872, and the United States now has 59 such parks. Britain's Sports Council (now split into UK Sport, Sport England, and so on) was created in 1965 as an advisory body, and became an executive body with a royal charter in 1972. The case for central government intervention in sport was basically the same as for the traditional arts. Most (still genuinely voluntary and amateur) sports associations needed state support if they were to maintain the organisation and facilities required to produce internationally competitive players, and a push from the centre was needed if grass-roots facilities were to be improved so as to make sport attractive to young people and other sections of the population. It was under the auspices of, and with part funding by, the Sports Council that purpose-built local authority sport and leisure centres began to be constructed in the 1960s, and by the end of the century the UK had around 2,000 of these facilities. VisitBritain (the organisation's present title) dates from 1969 when it was created in recognition of the growing importance of international tourism in the country's trade balance, and to coordinate planning so as to accommodate the anticipated growing stream of visitors.

Exactly which and how different public leisure services were introduced varied from country to country, as did the balances between commercial, voluntary and public sector provisions. The United States is regarded internationally as the champion of private enterprise, less enthusiastic about state provision than European countries. However, while the US federal government has limited leisure responsibilities, the United States has other layers of government at state, city and local levels. There is a lot of government in America, and all layers are leisure providers. That said, it is true that private philanthropy has always played a larger role in America than in Europe. During the 20th century, the United States became the world's largest and most powerful economy, and created some of the world's richest individuals. This was accompanied by an expectation that the wealthy would donate and create foundations and legacies. So Americans became and have remained among the world's most generous givers (Wright, 2000). Yet despite this, as in Europe, after the Second World War, the need for stronger contributions by federal, state and local authorities became evident.

At that time, leisure appeared *en route* to becoming a full part of the welfare states in Western countries. The aim was access to good leisure for all. It was in this context that the first leisure studies courses were launched in

US colleges, and then spread to Britain in the 1970s. Thus, there were emergent leisure professions, but in America, in Britain and elsewhere, the public leisure services remained as fragmented as before. As well as there being all the state and local authorities, each with separate departments catering for different kinds of leisure, in Britain there were several central government ministries with substantial leisure responsibilities – those responsible for local government, the environment, transport, education, trade and industry, plus the Home Office. Outside commentators who surveyed this scene were appalled by the untidiness (Travis, 1979). However, untidiness was not the main obstacle to incorporating leisure into the welfare state. Since the Second World War, commerce had been overtaking the public and voluntary sectors as the main source of citizens' leisure opportunities. Afterwards, the rationalisation of public leisure services, when this began, was rapidly absorbed into the neoliberal agendas of cost-cutting and adopting business methods.

Rationalisation

The administrative rationalisation of Britain's public leisure services began in the 1970s as part of a broader reorganisation of local government which reduced the number of separate local authorities and thinned out the committee systems within them all. This was the start of a series of still-ongoing attempts to create more streamlined, joined-up local government. Most local authorities emerged from the 1970s overhaul with omnibus departments under leisure, recreation services or some similar title. The staffs of the former baths, parks departments, and so on, were also merged, and they created an umbrella professional organisation, the Institute of Leisure and Amenity Managers (ILAM), which set up its own training provisions, accredited other (higher and further education) institutions' courses and qualifications and established procedures for professional certification. In 2007, ILAM merged with the National Association of Sports Development to create the Institute for Sports, Parks and Leisure, which operates within the UK's Higher Education Academy. However, since 2012, there has also been a Chartered Institute for the Management of Sport and Physical Activity. It is still proving difficult to bind all the UK's leisure professionals together.

During the 1990s, there was an administrative rationalisation of the UK central government's leisure responsibilities, mirroring what had happened in local government 20 years earlier. In 1992, most of central government's leisure responsibilities were drawn together in a new Department of National Heritage, which in 1997 was retitled the Department for Culture, Media and Sport (DCMS). Since 1994, this department has had oversight of a greatly enlarged budget, provided by the National Lottery. Twenty-eight per cent of the National Lottery's stake money is channelled to 'good causes', which have included the arts, sport, the heritage, charities and, up to the turn of the millennium, a millennium fund, and then an additional fund that helped prepare for the 2012 London Olympics.

Actually the DCMS does not have a monopoly of state leisure policy-making and implementation in Britain. It never will. The exchequer will always retain a say in spending plans. The health ministry will always be involved, in some way or another, in promoting healthy lifestyles. The education ministry will always have some responsibility for the recreation of pupils and students. The government department responsible for trade and industry will always need to be involved in the development of what is now a major economic sector. The Home Office is unlikely to relinquish control over 'public order' matters related to alcohol, drugs, the conduct of spectators at sports events or whatever is causing concern and offence at a given time. Nevertheless, since 1992, the UK central government has possessed a lead ministry in leisure.

The UK's DCMS is a small central government department in terms of staff (roughly 380) and in terms of the size of its budget from the exchequer (roughly £1.5 billion in 2014–15 excluding television licence fees, which amounted to around £3.6 billion in 2012), to which should probably be added the £1.6 billion or thereabouts that was being raised for good causes through the National Lottery by 2013. This money is distributed by boards that make decisions independently, but within a framework of government policy directions. It all adds up to around £6.7 billion a year. The UK central government is not a big leisure spender. Local authorities used to spend much more on leisure services but now spend considerably less than the central government (just over £1 billion in 2013 and declining in the search for savings). So the total public sector spend on leisure is around £7.7 billion. Meanwhile, private consumers spend over £10 billion on sports goods and services alone (a minor leisure industry in cash terms). The gambling industry had a total take (stakes minus winnings) of £6.3 billion in 2012–13. Sport employs between 300,000 and just over half a million, depending on how broadly or narrowly sport is defined, and gambling around 100,000 compared with the DCMS' 380. The DCMS is a relatively modest player. However, the DCMS does not use most of its budget on its own leisure services. Rather, via the financial support that it offers (over 90 per cent of its budget is distributed to other service providers) and the regulations that it issues (which can be enforced by legislation if necessary), it exerts considerable influence throughout the commercial and voluntary sectors, and on the rest of public sector (mainly local authority) leisure provisions. So how does the DCMS try to use its influence?

Provision without policy

Leisure is not normally 'political' in the everyday sense because the main capabilities of state intervention (see below) are unlikely to be divisive unless political parties are based on national, ethnic or religious schisms. A consequence in most countries has been the delegation of leisure policy-making to 'policy communities' composed of interested politicians, civil servants, representatives of interest groups and other experts. They have sought consensus, thereby keeping a steady hand on decision-making. Now policy communities exist in all policy areas, but in leisure the policy communities have been only weakly attached to party political processes and thereby to public opinion. 'As with sport policy generally, sports development lacks the systemic embeddedness that exists in other service areas such as health and education where the organisation and professional roots are multiple and go deep into the infrastructure of political parties, the government and the state' (Houlihan and White, 2002, p. 231). Another problem with the leisure policy communities is that they have formed not around leisure in general but around sport, the arts, the countryside, and so on. This reflects the fragmentation of the leisure industries. There are many leisure policy communities. Even individually, they usually find consensus difficult to achieve and sustain. The interest groups based on particular sports and arts are often aggressively independent. Each tends to act as spokesperson and lobby for its own particular branch of leisure. So although there is now a lead leisure department in Britain's central government, its work is guided by a series of discrete sports, arts, heritage, and media policies, and so on, which are not orchestrated by an overarching leisure policy.

When politics leaves a policy vacuum, the space is likely to be filled by other forces. At local and national levels, leisure policy has always been exceptionally open to influence by the enthusiasms of individual ministers and councillors, plus the lobbying of interest groups. 'Incoming ministers for sport, of which there have been far too many in recent years, have a capacity to translate their particular enthusiasms into policy priorities in a way that is inconceivable in other government departments' (Houlihan and White, 2002, p. ix). The creation of the UK Sports Institute, now split into the English Institute of Sport and equivalent bodies in the other countries of the UK, but with most of the institute's original work now passed to Sport UK (see Chapter 6, p. 133), owed much to the then prime minister, John Major, being a sports enthusiast. Alternatively or in addition, ministers may decide to make their mark through seeking administrative efficiency, becoming businesslike, meaning, in practice, cutting costs, setting measurable targets and demanding that their departments, and other organisations which receive support, deliver. This has become the overarching requirement, especially since the financial crash of 2008–09. In recent years, government ministers have been keen on targets. They have spoken of 'deliverables' and expect targets to be achieved in exchange for state funding. But do we really want politicians to decide what arts organisations should deliver? In sport there must be losers as well as winners. Ministers who believe that they can control the flow of Olympic gold are deluded. They need proper leisure policies which square with the public sector's genuine capabilities. There has been a tendency to treat state leisure spending as 'investment' which should lead to jobs and overseas sales, and a willingness to allow the commercial sector to deliver everything that it is able to take on. The danger here is sidelining softer, more difficult to measure, social and cultural benefits that can accrue from state interventions in leisure. The big failure in public sector leisure provision is not operational but political. The political process has never yielded satisfactory leisure policies. Politicians need to say what the public leisure services are to achieve, and why.

Where should the search for leisure policies begin? Driver and his colleagues (1991) are helpful: they argue that public services always need to be benefits driven because the test of their effectiveness and value is never how much or exactly what they do but the results. Then, as John Crompton (2000) has added, the benefits need to be public benefits, shared by all or most of the population, not just the participants. Crompton (2008) has subsequently added that the public benefits need to be important to taxpayers, elected politicians and public officials. Public subsidies for purely private benefits such as enjoyment (or personal well-being) are unlikely to be politically sustainable in the long term however efficiently such benefits are delivered and however appreciative the individual recipients may be. This book adds that the benefits that are sought need to be consistent with the public sector's leisure capabilities, especially those capabilities that public provision alone possesses.

INCAPACITIES AND UNIQUE CAPABILITIES

Arguments that loosen government purse strings do not necessarily deliver the results that are promised, and in an era of pressure on public spending, it becomes all the more important for public leisure services to focus on what they are uniquely capable of delivering. We now have well over a century of experience on which to draw and we know that some aims, often highly laudable, are simply beyond the capabilities of public leisure services.

Incapacities

First, public provisions are unable to redistribute leisure opportunities in favour of the socio-economically disadvantaged. Some state measures – support for high culture and tourism, for example – are clearly not aiming to achieve this. It might be argued that free-to-use or subsidised provisions will be accessible, and therefore of particular value, to the disadvantaged. In practice, however, we find that it is nearly always the better-off who make the most use of free-to-use and subsidised facilities – national parks, libraries and sports centres, for instance. The social class skew varies in strength according to the type of leisure, but the higher-socio-economic strata usually do more irrespective of whether what they are doing is state supported. The reasons for the skew are straightforward: the better-off are the most likely to possess the transport, equipment, interest, skills and social networks that allow them to take advantage. Time and again, sport facilities have been opened with the declared intention of servicing the weak and have then been used by the strong. The main UK public leisure provisions that are used as much by the poor as by the rich are, first, BBC television, which is funded by what, in effect, is a regressive poll tax (the licence fee), and second (if it counts in this context) the National Lottery. It is true that most local authorities have programmes targeted specifically at disadvantaged groups such as the unemployed and the retired, and that subsidies are sometimes targeted (free admission on proof of being in receipt of unemployment or some other means-tested state benefit, for example). However, all the evaluative studies have shown that most members of the target populations are missed (Glyptis, 1989; Kay, 1987; King et al., 1985; Town, 1983). Some of the targets do not like being treated differently. A rather different problem is that selective subsidies are expensive to administer. Above all, in a market economy, leisure opportunities are among the rewards of success. Leisure providers – whether commercial, voluntary sector or public – have no option but to flow with this tide. Redistribution is a job for economic and other social policies, not the public leisure services.

A second incapacity is that state leisure provisions are unable to make people use their leisure in ways that the authorities would prefer. 'The latent energy in bars, waste ground and street corners, poised perhaps for violence, can be released effectively and enjoyably into sport and recreation' (Sports Council, 1985). Wrong! The authorities have been backing this theory for over a century. It has been tested to destruction. If people were susceptible to leisure education and state-promoted opportunities, the British would now be a nation of churchgoers and Shakespeare readers. Legal bans can make a difference, but mere 'nudges' are likely to be ignored. 'Social control' arguments still appear to be an excellent way of unlocking public funds (see Centre for Leisure and Sport Research, 2002). The willingness of the authorities to act on a manifestly false premise suggests that the official rationale of the relevant measures may perform latent functions. It enables governments to be seen to be 'doing something' about conditions in 'problem areas' whether the problem is 'the troubles' in Northern Ireland or the more widespread inner-city and council estate malaises. The wider public, if not the target populations, may thereby be persuaded that the latter's obesity, ill health and misdemeanours are outcomes of their own lifestyle choices rather than the surrounding economic and housing conditions and inequalities (Ingham, 1985). The crucial fact of this matter is that when people have a choice of commercial, voluntary and public sector leisure provisions, they will use the latter only if the provisions coincide with their own inclinations. The authorities can try and try again to persuade the public to use their leisure in what, to the authorities, appear to be rational ways. Public sector leisure professionals are still expected to act as 'soft cops', countervailing against harmful temptations. The 19th-century ideology of rational recreation lives on (see Heeley, 1986), but its measures are destined to fail at one or another of what are now well-known hurdles. The target population either declines to take part (in sport, arts programmes or whatever), or they drop out after initial visits or they stay and overwhelm the provisions with their own culture (see Skogen and Wichstrom, 1996).

A third incapacity is assisting the various sections of the public to fulfil their own leisure dreams, whatever these might be. This implausible rationale was surprisingly popular among some public sector leisure professionals during the second half of the 20th century. Some were inspired by France's state-funded *animateurs* who do 'missionary work' among the people, attempting to unlock their latent artistic creativity (see Kingsbury, 1976). Many public sector professionals like to appear non-judgemental, non-authoritarian, willing to listen and respond to the public's wishes. They have envisaged leisure professionals bringing together politicians and members of the public to identify leisure needs which can then be met (Coalter, 1990; Rapoport, 1977). The crucial fact here is that the agenda is hopelessly unrealistic. John Crompton's (2000) 'rule' applies; public subsidies are likely to be politically sustainable only if there is a public benefit, or at least a perceived public benefit, in what is being provided. Public sector leisure professionals are not going to be licensed to cater for the leisure interests of all the various sections of the population, be these philosophy, ocean cruises or sexual fetishes. The public sector is always going to be judgemental. There is a sense in which it is inherently paternal, deciding to facilitate some but not other leisure demands (see McNamee et al., 2000, 2001).

Unique capabilities

So what are the public sector's special capabilities? These are fourfold. First, public investment in leisure facilities can trigger an economic multiplier. Holiday resorts realised this ages ago. By laying out parks and generally taking care of the environment, the attractiveness of a holiday destination is enhanced, and (hopefully) the visitors' spending more than repays the investment. In more recent times, rural districts, declining industrial towns and major cities have become equally keen to attract tourists, day trippers and people on nights out. City councils vie with each other in their progress towards becoming 24-hour hot spots with booming night-time economies (including gay quarters in some places). Leisure spenders may be enticed by clean environments and open spaces, the conservation of any natural beauty and historic buildings, pop concert venues or museums and art galleries. Cities need tempting facilities and, equally important (but slightly different), nowadays they need attractive images (see Hughes and Boyle, 1992; Street, 1993). These measures can work. Private investment is just as able as public investment to attract visitors and spending, but only public bodies are able to invest in loss leaders. The local or national taxpayers pick up the bill and (they hope) recover their investment from visitors' spending on provisions that create jobs and salaries for the local population and enable local businesses to operate at a profit. This capability is consistent with treating leisure as a business. We shall see in Chapter 7 that governments which are cutting back on community recreation facilities are prepared to invest huge sums in order to attract major events which attract huge numbers of visitors.

The problem is not that the economic rationale is fundamentally flawed. Rather, the problem for most places is that leisure is a highly competitive market. Different coastal and inland resorts and cities compete against each other for market shares. It is a case of beggar-my-neighbour. There are winners and losers. There are cases where investment in culture has triggered urban regeneration but there are also examples of failure (see Bianchini and Parkinson, 1993). Leisure policies and provisions of different countries, regions and cities affect the distribution of leisure spending but not the global level, which is dependent on macroeconomic conditions. Moreover, a leisure-based local or national economy can be a mixed blessing (lots of seasonal and part-time jobs), and preoccupation with economic goals may sideline other special capabilities of public leisure provisions.

A second special public sector capability in leisure is extending citizenship – rights that we all enjoy simply by virtue of our citizenship. Public leisure provisions can be intended for, and accessible to, everyone. This is most easily accomplished with land. The state can simply designate coastline, rural tracts and urban parks for public enjoyment. All citizens can be given access. No one need be charged. The same principle can be applied to buildings: stately homes, art galleries, libraries and museums (see Box 4.6). Even people who do not visit can still enjoy the feeling that the facilities are theirs and that they themselves, their children, grandchildren, neighbours and indeed all their fellow citizens can use them if they so desire. A society can decide to conserve and open some facilities to all humankind, thus helping to create a global citizenship. Until recently in Britain, public service broadcasting enlarged citizenship. The main channels and programmes were available to all (see Chapter 8). Commercial provisions cannot create citizenship in the same way – the benefits are restricted to people who are able and willing to pay. Voluntary associations cater for their members or a target group. They are normally unable to reach out to the entire population unless enabled to do so by public subsidies.

The manner in which public facilities are managed sometimes fails to exploit their citizenship potential. For example, Parker and Ravenscroft (1999) and Parker (2007) argue that Britain's National Parks (where most of the land remains in private ownership) have always been administered in a paternal way: that the public has been made to feel that access is a

---

Box 4.6 Public libraries

Britain's first 'circulating' (lending) libraries were opened in the first half of the 18th century.

The 1850 Public Libraries Act enabled local authorities to open libraries. However, at that time, there were severe restrictions on how much the authorities were allowed to spend. At first they could rarely afford to purchase books. So even public libraries needed wealthy patrons. Andrew Carnegie (1835–1919) helped to finance over 380 libraries in Britain. By the time of his death, over half the library authorities in Britain had Carnegie libraries, and he had set up more than 2,800 libraries across the English-speaking world.

A further 18 library acts were passed between 1850 and 1900 which expanded provisions. During the 20th century, new services were added. The first mobile public library service was introduced in Perthshire in 1920. In 1935, Middlesex County Library became the first to loan gramophone records. In 1972, Cardiganshire became the first to loan cassettes. In 1995, Marylebone became the first public library to offer public access to the Internet.

Today, despite recent and ongoing decline, the UK still has over 3,300 libraries which are open to the general public plus over 650 mobile libraries. More than 60 per cent of the UK population hold library cards. There are around 350 million visits to public libraries every year – more than 6 times the number of attendances at professional football matches. It is in a public library that most children receive their first civic recognition through their right to a library card.

---

privilege rather than a right, and conditional upon their good (as defined by the authorities) behaviour. Public leisure provisions do not automatically enlarge and strengthen a population's sense of citizenship. They cannot achieve this if they are managed as if they were businesses. The situation is rather that public leisure services have a unique citizenship-enlarging capability.

A third unique public sector capability is enhancing national prestige and identity. These two usually go hand in hand. People experience pride if their country's (or a region's or a city's) historic buildings, art collections, sites of natural beauty, performing arts or sporting achievements win wider admiration. 'Sporting success for Britain makes people proud to be British. To some degree which is difficult to quantify, this justifies public investment' (Sports Council, 1985). Governments may seek to strengthen national identity and prestige by supporting traditional games (Irish, Scottish, Asian or whatever) but nowadays, like China, they are likely to be more concerned to succeed in major world sports, especially Olympic sports (see Tan Ying and

Roberts, 1995). Governments are better placed than either commercial businesses or voluntary associations to use leisure provisions for nation building. The success of a business is due to, and benefits most of all, its own investors, managers and workers. A voluntary association's achievements bring credit to its members – their skills and enthusiasm. Governments alone can act for their countries.

A fourth special capability is that state leisure policies and provisions can articulate a clear moral and aesthetic order. Public provisions may be unable to change the public's tastes and behaviour, but they can send out clear messages about what is approved of and what is deplored. State support places leisure activities on the 'bright side'. High culture and sport clearly benefit from these rays. Types of leisure that are outlawed, restricted or taxed heavily (alcohol, tobacco, cannabis and other recreational drugs, commercial sex and, until recently, most gambling) are thereby placed on the 'dark side'. People may still participate but if they do, they know that they are venturing into the shade. Governments must inevitably make moral choices over what to support and what to prohibit. The state is always the arbiter of last resort. It must intervene when there are conflicts over the use of water space or urban precincts (between those who want lively night-time economies and those who prefer peace and quiet, for example). 'Leisure is part of the struggle for the control of space and time in which social groups are continuously engaged' (Wilson, 1988, p. 12). Governments are inevitably drawn into these conflicts (such as that between those opposed to and those who wish to practise so-called country sports) and are thereby required to define which uses of leisure are to be admired and applauded, and which should be deplored.

CONCLUSIONS

The financial pressures that public leisure services are experiencing are not outcomes of leisure policy analysis. They stem from general squeezes on government spending in which cuts to leisure services encounter less political and public resistance than cuts to education, pensions and health care. These squeezes have been superimposed on a longer-running neoliberal agenda which claims that markets are the best decision-makers, and that commerce usually offers best value.

The consequences for public leisure services are not wholly malign. Periodic pressure to trim forces managements to establish priorities and eliminate unnecessary costs. In the short term, user numbers may withstand higher charges, reduced grant aid to voluntary bodies, closure of some facilities and reduced opening hours and/or staffing at others. The longer-term implications for the recruitment of new regular, habitual users, members, enthusiasts, players and audiences are unknown. The purchaser-provider split appears to be doing more good than harm. The business culture reinforces the case for investing in loss leaders where the gains in leisure business repay the investment. Such investment grows ever more important in societies where leisure accounts for a growing share of the economy. The relevant investments are likely to be in prestige assets which strengthen local or national pride and identity, and which attract visitors.

The unique public sector capabilities that are most at risk are leisure opportunities which individuals may or may not choose to use but which are theirs to enjoy simply as rights of citizenship, and speaking for a society on those uses of leisure which are considered of greatest intrinsic merit. However, Chapter 10 will explain how, provided politicians recognise the public sector's special capabilities in leisure, these can still be exercised effectively even in an increasingly commercial age in which public leisure services are under unremitting pressure to continue to do as much or even to do more than in the past with less government money.

Section II

Provisions

Chapter 5

Tourism

INTRODUCTION

Tourism best illustrates all the distinctive features of commercial leisure in the 21st century. The industry has grown steadily for over 100 years and is now one of the world's largest industries. It illustrates how commerce blurs the boundary between leisure and other kinds of business while creating new commercially useful classifications. The sheer size of tourism throws general trends in the present-day business of leisure into sharp relief: the switch in the balance of business from the West towards the rest of the world; ageing consumers; wider inequalities of wealth and income (which are good for tourism); the penetration of ICT into most nooks and crannies of the business; and the intense competition for shares in the trade.

The tourism statistics produced by national governments and international agencies today are nearly all about international travel: there is no distinction between travel for leisure and other purposes. It is all business to the airlines, hotels and booking agencies. Academics know that travel can be part work and part pleasure, but they also know the difference between what can be charged to expenses and what is paid from their own salaries. Vacations spent with relatives without crossing international borders, those spent in country dachas in Eastern Europe and camping and caravanning within the travellers' own countries are simply ignored in what now counts as tourism in most official statistics. The key statistics for national governments are the flows of money between countries, not how many of their citizens are enjoying holidays away from home. Statistics on international travel are of numbers of arrivals and departures, not the numbers of persons who are involved. A single person may be responsible for multiple overseas trips in any year. Each journey counts as an addition to the tourism total, which is what matters commercially rather than how many different spenders are responsible.

The international travel/tourism business is enormous in financial terms, and it has once again proved recession-proof. There was a dip in traveller numbers in 2008–09 and then an immediate recovery, which continued to a record of 1.097 billion passenger arrivals in 2013. This compares with just 25 million in 1950 and 222 million in 1975. The growth rate has been spectacular and is continuing in the 21st century (Becker, 2013). The total spent on and during this travel now amounts to $1,300 billion, equivalent to around 30 per cent of all services that count as exports. The $1,300 billion becomes meaningful only when compared with, for example, annual worldwide cinema box-office receipts at just over $35 billion, and the annual global value of television sports rights at $27 billion, which excludes irregular (not annual) events such as the global television rights to the London Olympics, which were worth $2.6 billion in 2012. International tourism dwarfs every other type of leisure business in terms of money spent and the long period over which it has grown steadily. There were setbacks prior to 2008: events such as the 9/11 terrorist attack in New York in 2001 and the Indian Ocean tsunami in 2004, but in each case international tourism soon resumed its onward and upward trajectory.

These spectacular numbers make it all the more important to bear in mind that most holidays are still spent at home or within the vacationers' own countries. In 2012, UK citizens made 55 million trips abroad, but they also took 58 million domestic holidays, and since the international figure includes all travellers, the domestic equivalent should include an additional 19 million business trips, and maybe 45 million trips that involved stays with families or friends (Deloitte/Oxford Economics, 2013).

Holidays away, including at least one trip abroad, have become normal for citizens in Western Europe, but we must bear in mind that over 90 per cent of the global population does not travel internationally in any year. Also, Americans tend to holiday within their own large country. International tourism is not huge – it is still tiny, in terms of the proportion of the global population that is involved. It is still a privilege of those who are relatively well off. Others have the 'privilege' of servicing the tourists. There are many countries in which tourism is now the main industry and the main source of local employment.

The growth of international tourism has been nuanced by trends which have been and are still affecting the whole of leisure. First, tourism has become increasingly commercial. Holiday centres run by churches, youth organisations and trade unions have been closing or now operate on a reduced scale.

Second, the main growth in international tourism is now outwards from the emerging market economies. China now dispatches more tourists than any other country. It is followed by Germany, the United States and the UK. The new rich and middle classes are still very small proportions of the populations in countries such as China, Brazil and India, but less than 10 per cent of China's population amounts to around 130 million persons, greater than the population of any European Union country, and there were 70.5 million passenger departures from China in 2011 (all statistics from the World Tourism Organization: ww2.unwto.org). In 2013, the UK welcomed 31.2 million visitors, a record number and a 6 per cent increase on 2012. Gratifyingly, there was an above-average increase of 10 per cent in visitors from the 'rest of the world' (outside Europe and North America). This is gratifying for the UK because it indicates that the country is benefiting from the swing in international tourism towards more departures from the 'rest of the world', and also because these tourists spend more per head per day than tourists from North America and Europe. This statistic, spending per head per day, and how the sum can be maximised, is as important as total tourist numbers in calculating the commercial value of tourism (see Kozak et al., 2008).

There are interesting differences in the ranking of countries by numbers of arrivals, tourism receipts and spending by the countries' own outward tourists. In 2013, France (87.7 million) was the world leader as the 'most visited' country. The United States was second (69.8 million visitors). Yet France ($56.1 billion) earned less than the United States ($138.6 billion) and Spain, the third most visited country ($60.4 billion), from its inward tourists. Visitors to the United States and Spain must stay longer or spend more per day than visitors to France. China is now easily the leading country in terms of how much its outward tourists spend ($128.6 billion in 2013). The United States is second: its outbound tourists spent $83.5 billion. Amazingly, Macau, whose main industry is gambling, and which is now part of China, was earning almost as much as the rest of the country from inward tourism in 2013 ($51.6 billion and £51.7 billion). This will last for only as long as the Beijing government sees Macau's casinos as a net asset for China, earning foreign revenue, rather than a place where China's own new rich can launder wealth acquired in dubious ways.

Third, young singles and childless couples are still travelling, but the main growth is now among the expanding 'woopies' (well-off older people).

Fourth, inequalities of income and wealth have been and are still widening globally, which benefits tourism because it is the well-off who travel. As they become even better off, they take more vacations, travel further and spend more. In the UK, the proportion of the population that goes on holiday (at home or abroad) in any year has risen from 70 per cent to 80 per cent since 1970. However, even in a relatively rich country such as Britain, a fifth of the population still does not take any holiday (domestically or internationally) (ABIA Consumer Survey, 2013, available at www.abia.com). If the poor are given more money, they spend it on basics. If the rich become richer, they spend the extra on luxuries such as travel.

Fifth, all branches of the tourist business have needed to absorb ICT. This applies to booking agencies and all destinations and businesses that wish to attract tourists – resorts, cities, hotels, entertainments, and so on.

Sixth, tourism is now an intensely competitive business. Countries, cities, resorts, hotels and travel agencies all compete for customers. It is beggar-my-neighbour. The overall size of the industry keeps growing, but specific segments are always shrinking. Older resorts become unfashionable or too expensive. Disney parks make older attractions less attractive. In 2013, one of Europe's oldest theme parks closed: Vidámpark in Budapest (Hungary). Visitor numbers had fallen from around 2.7 million a year in the 1970s to just 250,000. However, the park's roller coaster, the longest wooden roller coaster still operating anywhere in the world, is being preserved.

Overarching all these nuances is the crucial role that the public sector has always played in promoting tourism. It has always funded loss leaders. This was the case with the first modern holiday destinations – the English seaside resorts where the local authorities laid out gardens, built promenades and financed all the necessary infrastructure (water, drains, electricity supplies, and so on). Local authorities also promoted themselves as tourist destinations by advertising in the media and issuing brochures. The public sector continues to play basically the same role today, but managing 21st-century tourism has become more complicated and more expensive in today's larger and intensely competitive tourist industry. However, public tourist agencies should bear in mind that, for some travellers, the place is not the main attraction. Tom Griffin (2014) estimates that at least a quarter of all international travel is to visit friends and relatives. This suggests that long-term international migration is among the generators of tourist business.

The present chapter proceeds with how the modern holiday was invented in the 19th century (it is a social invention). The following section then explains how these foundations were built upon by adding new holiday options during the 20th century. Then we see how, in the late-20th century, a tipping point was reached when the scale of tourism and its importance to so many cities, regions and countries, all in the context of the ICT revolution, led to an intensification of competition, and an elevated role for the cultural dimension of tourism (the cultural construction of all kinds of tourist destinations and services, and of tourists themselves). This leads to an assessment of whether, and if so how, tourism can be managed in a 21st-century context.

A few cautionary notes are necessary before proceeding. Tourist authorities and businesses in all countries like to stress how their industry contributes to the economy. They tend to overlook the downside. In the UK, for example, there were around 31 million visits to Britain in 2013 but there were 55 million trips abroad by Britons. Tourism is a net loser for the UK economy (www.euromonitor.com). The outbound figure was 18 per cent down on its pre-crash peak in 2007. When it is claimed that tourism supports 9 per cent (or thereabouts) of all employment and economic activity in Britain, this total is in 'tourism-characteristic' sectors (travel, accommodation and catering), not just those jobs in these industries that rely on tourists' spending (Office for National Statistics, 2013). Also, in Britain, the benefits of international tourists' spending are distributed very unequally around the country: 53 per cent of this spending is in London (www.visitbritain.org). The larger the size of the global tourist industry, the keener countries become to maximise their shares, but globally tourist inflows and outflows are always in balance. The UK, Germany, China and Russia are among the net losers. France and the United States are among the winners. One country's gain is always another country's loss. Tourism could boost the global economy only if productivity in tourism exceeded the average throughout the economy. This may be the case with air transport, but in accommodation and catering (the other main industries where tourists spend their money), employees in the UK tend to be younger, less educated and non-white and migrants, and they are paid less per hour, than the labour force as a whole (Office for National Statistics, 2013). One might argue that the most prosperous countries' citizens will travel (because they can afford to do so) and spend their money in lower-labour-cost countries. Thus, a negative trade balance on tourism will be a sign of a country's relative economic strength. Overall, throughout the global economy, tourist spending is more realistically treated as consumption rather than an economic input. However, businesses with interests in tourism, and tourism academics also, are likely to prefer tourism to be seen as good for all concerned, especially people in their own countries.

CREATING THE MODERN HOLIDAY

Beginnings

The modern holiday is possible only amid three conditions:

■ Working time must be compartmentalised and standardised with at least one major break of sufficient length to enable workers to 'go away'.
■ There must be transport – mechanical transport – to convey the holiday-makers.
■ Workers must be able to afford a holiday.

All three conditions were met in Britain during the second half of the 19th century, and they have been met in more and more countries as their economies have modernised. Britain led in holidaymaking and in many other types of modern leisure simply because Britain was the very first industrial nation. Employers in Britain, pressured by the trade unions that were formed in the second half of the 19th century, gradually reinstated the holiday weeks that had been abolished when the population moved from the countryside into the expanding industrial towns and cities. At the same time, that is, in the later half of the 19th century, the construction of railways made the journey 'away' possible. Railways were faster than the canal boats, and the river and coastal steamers, which had carried some of the earlier holiday pioneers. The steamers were the original reason for constructing piers at Britain's seaside resorts. By the end of the 19th century, most piers had lost their original function but new piers were still being built as promenades and sites for entertainment. Later on (but still before the era of mass private motoring), the motor coach became the railways' main rival as a means of holiday travel. The third condition for mass holidaymaking was met when manual workers' real earnings and living standards rose during and after the 1870s. This brought holidays within the means of the working masses. So, by the end of the 19th century, Britain's seaside resorts were booming (during the summer months) and all the basic elements of the present-day holiday were in place.

By the closing decades of the 19th century, the holiday had become a primarily commercial type of leisure, but it was not commerce that first pioneered holidays away from Britain's industrial towns and cities. Or rather, commerce was not at the forefront in the first half of the 19th century. Thomas Cook organised the first holiday 'tour' by rail from Leicester to Loughborough in 1841, and this is sometimes taken to be the start of the modern holiday industry (see Box 5.1). Until the 1850s in Britain, churches

---

Box 5.1 Thomas Cook (1808–1892)

Thomas Cook was not the first person to organise leisure travel. The business that he founded was not the first tourist company. That status goes to Cox and Kings, established in 1758.

However, in 1841, Thomas Cook became the first entrepreneur to charter a train, which was to transport temperance campaigners from Leicester to a rally in Loughborough (just 11 miles away), and to make tickets available to the general public. This was followed by further organised outings for temperance societies and Sunday School children.

In 1850, Cook organised the first overseas tour, from Leicester to Calais. After this, he led Grand Circular Tours of Europe, and in the 1860s he began to take parties to Switzerland, Italy, Egypt and the United States. At that time, international travel was an adventure and was a privilege of the exceptionally wealthy. We are now in a different era of mass tourism, and tourists who expect to travel and stay in comfort. Nevertheless, his achievements earn Thomas Cook the position of pioneer of modern tourism.

---

and progressive employers along with idealists such as Thomas Cook arranged most holidays, which were then very much the exception for the industrial working class. The holiday was conceived as a rational form of recreation (see Box 5.2). It was considered desirable for workers to escape from the city grime and, in particular, from urban temptations, especially drink. Holidaymaking was associated with saving, sobriety and the family (see Walvin, 1978). The early idealistic holiday pioneers did not plan the Blackpools that were to come.

Box 5.2 The Co-operative Holiday Association

This association was formed in the late 19th century by a Congregationalist minister, T. A. Leonard (1864–1948) of Colne (Lancashire), who wanted to promote rational countryside holidays for working-class people. In 1891, Reverend Leonard organised a walking holiday in the Lake District for his local walking club, and this venture was subsequently expanded on a national scale as the Co-operative Holiday Association (CHA). This was to provide 'a holiday of another kind … a happy brotherhood spending its days on tramp and its evenings in social intercourse with music and chatty lecturettes'. Initially the CHA used empty cottages for accommodation and school halls for evening activities but it soon acquired its own centres in Keswick, Whitby and elsewhere. Apart from founding the CHA, the Reverend Leonard is widely regarded as the principal pioneer of rambling as a modern leisure pastime. The CHA was just one means by which this form of rational recreation was promoted.

By the early 20th century, the CHA had expanded: to 8,400 members in 1904 and 30,000 in 1914, by when it had centres in Germany, France and Switzerland. Accommodation was primitive. Meals were taken at trestle tables. Sleeping quarters were divided into cubicles with makeshift curtains. Alcohol was forbidden. Lights out was at 10.30 PM. Rambles were accompanied by lecturers who would provide wayside talks on the natural history and artistic connections of a region. The association was based on ideals of utopian socialism, Wordsworthian high thinking and plain living. Its motto was 'simple and strenuous'. To extend the social relationships formed on holidays, CHA members established local branches with winter programmes of walking and indoor cultural pastimes.

Although intended mainly for working-class people, the CHA was meant to be a classless organisation. Social distinctions were to be neutralised. Holiday parties included schoolteachers, shop assistants, warehousemen, clerks, carpenters, dressmakers and university lecturers. In practice, however, the CHA always drew the majority of its members from the middle class. It proved particularly suited to the needs of professional young adults, and especially the single young women to whom it offered a safe and respectable environment.

Source: Snape, 2004

Antecedents

The modern holiday had pre-industrial antecedents. During the 17th century, sons of the gentry (and much more rarely the daughters) had begun undertaking the 'grand tour', which took in all the main European centres of civilisation. They would set forth, often with servants and letters of introduction to distant relatives and other family acquaintances. This tour, intended to be educative, could last for well over a year. During this same period, well-to-do English families had started visiting London or the fast-developing spa towns (Buxton, Harrogate, Bath, and so on) for the (summer) season, or for at least a month. These were social occasions when the well-to-do also became well-connected, and, of course, the spa waters were supposed to be medicinal. Towards the end of the 18th century, the seaside began to rival the inland spas. Brighton's popularity was boosted by the Prince of Wales' regular visits. Sea air and water were believed to confer health benefits, but not the sun: sunbathing did not become fashionable until the end of the 19th century.

Going to the seaside

It was the seaside towns that were adopted as holiday destinations by Britain's working class during the 19th century. There is still debate as to whether the decline of Britain's spas was due to the overwhelming natural attractions of the coast, or whether failure to invest in the spas led to their decline. Inland resorts have remained popular in many European countries and in North America, but in these countries people are likely to live further from the coast than in Britain. The debate about why Britain's spas declined rumbles on (see Bacon, 1997). Whatever the reason, by the end of the 19th century, it was Britain's seaside resorts that were in full swing. Commerce was providing all the main ingredients. Private railway companies offered travel. Landladies provided board and lodging. Showmen and other entrepreneurs opened fairgrounds, piers, amusement arcades, stalls selling holiday paraphernalia, theatres and pubs. At that time, holidaymakers usually remained within their home regions. Towns would close for the holiday week. People who worked and lived together would travel together or, at any rate, meet each other while on holiday. Families sometimes visited the same resort, maybe stayed at the same boarding house, year upon year.

Blackpool was by far the most popular holiday resort in north-west England. It was the holiday place for families from the Lancashire textile towns. Blackpool Tower (inspired by the Eiffel Tower, see Box 5.4) was opened in 1894, and the town's pleasure beach also opened during the 1890s. Skegness was an east coast equivalent. Skegness was an insignificant coastal village before it was connected to the railway system at the end of the 19th century. Then things took off. Skegness became a favoured holiday destination for East Midlands families. At one time, it was not unusual for 60 trains to arrive in a single day. This was during 'the season', which lasted for just six to ten weeks. Skegness's popularity peaked in the 1930s. By then it had four cinemas, four theatres and five dance halls. Most of these have now been converted into amusement arcades, nightclubs, shops, car parks and bingo halls.

As the working class 'invaded' resorts close to the industrial cities, Britain's well-to-do families went further afield – overseas to the Mediterranean or to the 'English Riviera' in the south-west. They also adopted mountains, lakes and snow as alternative holiday destinations to the spas and seaside (Hill, 2002). Most resorts were keen to attract the masses (and their money), but some places, including Bognor Regis, preferred to remain exclusive and took care to stay off the (railway) track. Torquay was among the south-west resorts that deliberately sought to establish a superior, distinctly upmarket, appeal (Morgan and Pritchard, 1999).

Local authorities played a crucial role in attracting the expanding tourist trade. They laid out parks and promenades and kept the streets spick and span. How to attract tourists has now become a science. Researchers try to identify features that make holiday destinations attractive, and try to calculate exactly how much people will be prepared to pay and still visit and use all the facilities. It appears that cities are most attractive to tourists when they have historic buildings, plenty of shops and places to eat and drink and attractive countryside nearby (Martin and Mason, 1988). Destinations now try to image themselves so that they appeal to tourists (see McCrone et al., 1995; Morgan and Pritchard, 1998; Sheller and Urry, 2004). Nowadays, marketing a tourist place is a far more sophisticated business than just issuing a brochure containing information and photographs. The destination itself may need a radical facelift. If they are not already present, beaches or traditional mountain chalets may be constructed, and an appealing history can always be discovered, if required. The image may sometimes become the reality in the minds of tourists and even locals, though some claim that we are now into the age of the sceptical tourist who sees behind the images. In the 19th century, resorts had to rely basically on what was already there plus whatever commerce added. To begin with, the crucial assets were simply sea, sand and a railway station.

By the 1890s, countries on the opposite side of the English Channel were creating English-type seaside resorts for their own holidaymakers: Ostend in Belgium, Boulogne-sur-Mer and Deauville in France and Heiligendamm on Germany's Baltic coast. The first English-type seaside resorts in America were created in Atlantic City (New Jersey) and Long Island (New York).

Holidaymaking habits have certainly changed over the last 100 years, but when we see photographs of Blackpool at the end of the 19th century, we have no difficulty in recognising it as a holiday resort. The basic ingredients of what remains the largest segment of a now much more diverse holiday industry remain unchanged: going away for a week or two, probably to the seaside, sitting on the beach, venturing into the sea, being catered for in hotels, boarding houses and restaurants and having a wide choice of entertainment. Blackpool at the end of the 19th century bore less resemblance to either a stage on the grand tour or the pre-industrial spas than to its 21st-century self.

TWENTIETH-CENTURY DEVELOPMENTS

The holiday industry has always been innovative, and the innovators have not always been commercial businesses. By the beginning of the 20th century, voluntary associations were organising cycling and rambling holidays, and some churches and trade unions, as well as the Co-operative Holiday Association (see Box 5.2), were opening their own centres. However, the most successful and enduring innovations have been commercial. There has been a constant stream of new holiday 'products', though none have over-hauled the basic shape and features of the modern holiday.

Holiday camps

The holiday camp was an interwar innovation. The idea was to provide everything – accommodation, food, recreation and entertainment – on-site and for an all-in price. The first purpose-built holiday camp – Butlins at Skegness – opened in 1936. It was soon followed by other Butlinses and competitors (see Bandyopadhyay, 1973). The holiday camp then enjoyed what proved to be a brief period of popularity, which was ending by the 1960s. By then, more and more British holidaymakers were venturing abroad. Those who were still taking their holidays in Britain were seeking something less regimented. In any case, the facilities in the existing camps were too basic for post-war tastes. However, there are still Butlins 'resorts' at Minehead, Bognor Regis and Skegness, and there are even more Pontins holiday villages. The scaled-down UK camp industry (though the word has now been dropped) specialises in family holidays.

The true present-day counterparts of the original holiday camps are probably the hotels which have their own swimming pools, choices of restaurants, child care and organised recreation and entertainment for those so inclined, and the holiday 'villages' (operated by Center Parcs, among other companies) where the core attraction (in non-tropical countries) is most likely to be an enclosed tropical facility. Club Med has villages all around the Mediterranean (and in other parts of the world) which offer different holiday 'menus' at different sites and at different times – family holidays, adults-only, singles, couples, and activity holidays. Sandals is more specialised. It caters exclusively for 'couples in love' at ten idyllic beachfront resorts on the Caribbean's most exotic islands (adjectives from publicity materials). Gay couples are now accommodated. Absolutely everything is part of the package including a choice of gourmet dining.

The overseas package

From the 1950s onwards, the British masses began deserting domestic resorts in favour of guaranteed sun. They followed the trail that the well-to-do had pioneered when domestic resorts began to cater for the working class. The very first true overseas package holiday from the UK was to Corsica in 1950, organised by Horizon. By the 1960s, the jet engine and charter flights had made the Mediterranean as accessible, and usually as cheap, as Blackpool.

In North America, 1958 is a key date in the history of holidaymaking. This was the date of the first trans-Atlantic flight, from New York to Brussels by Pan Am, that did not make a refuelling stop (Becker, 2013). Wide-bodied jets have subsequently brought down the costs of long haul, and more and more holidaymakers from all countries have been travelling further afield. Of course, the long-term rise in incomes has helped. In 2012–13, UK residents took an average of 1.2 overseas holidays. Ever since the 1950s, America's and Britain's domestic resorts such as Atlantic City, Blackpool and Skegness have been trying, unsuccessfully, to arrest their decline. This is despite the fact that domestic holidaymaking has not declined in either America or Britain. In 2012–13, UK residents took an average of 1.9 holidays within their own country, more holidays than were taken abroad (ABTA Consumer Survey 2013, available at ww.abia.com). However, in Britain, domestic breaks now tend to be second holidays rather than main holidays, and destinations are no longer mainly the older coastal resorts, which have all lost visitors. Holidaymaking visitors to Britain, whose numbers have increased, are rarely seeking seaside sun. In the United States, they do not head for Atlantic City. Blackpool recorded its all-time peak number of visits (17 million) in the early 1970s. At that time, Blackpool was the largest resort in Europe. By 2001, the number of visits had declined to 10.9 million but had stabilised and remained above 10 million in 2013, which is still an impressive figure but smaller than in the past and the visitors were staying for shorter periods and spending less. The economic effects in Blackpool have been devastating even though the town is still the UK's number one resort (Cavill, 2002). Blackpool Pleasure Beach still claims to be among the UK's most popular attractions with around 6 million visitors a year.

When not just the British but other Europeans (mainly from northern Europe) began going abroad for their main holidays, 'the package' became the staple holiday product, and in 2012–13, 46 per cent of UK holidaymakers still bought a package for their main vacations. Thomas Cook's time finally arrived with the jet plane. The basic package has always been simple: air travel, transfers and accommodation. There are numerous variations. The travel may be by air, ship, train or motor coach. The accommodation may be hotel or self-catering. Excursions may be included. A package may be to just one place or a tour with one or two nights at a series of destinations. Customers can select from an endless mixture of places and grades of accommodation. There are specialist packages for families with young children, senior citizens, young singles, wine lovers, those after sex, mountains, white water, city culture, desert treks, *ad infinitum*. Specialist packages continue

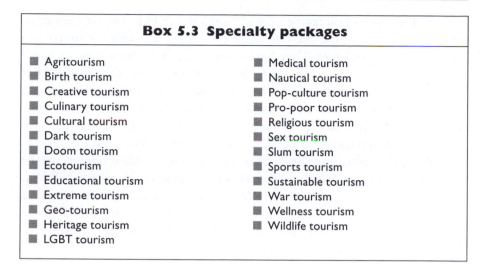

Box 5.3 Specialty packages

- Agritourism
- Birth tourism
- Creative tourism
- Culinary tourism
- Cultural tourism
- Dark tourism
- Doom tourism
- Ecotourism
- Educational tourism
- Extreme tourism
- Geo-tourism
- Heritage tourism
- LGBT tourism

- Medical tourism
- Nautical tourism
- Pop-culture tourism
- Pro-poor tourism
- Religious tourism
- Sex tourism
- Slum tourism
- Sports tourism
- Sustainable tourism
- War tourism
- Wellness tourism
- Wildlife tourism

to be created. Some of those currently available are shown in Box 5.3. For most overseas holidaymakers during the last 40 years of the 20th century, whatever their home countries, going away meant buying a package, increasingly a specialist package, put together by a tour company, advertised in its brochure and probably sold by a high-street travel agent. Although travel agents have been disappearing from high streets as more people book online, and although it is now easier than ever to put your own package together – to book the air travel, then a hotel or hotels, to book a hire car – and then holiday singly, as a couple, as a family or as a group of friends, nearly a half of main holidays by UK residents are still group packages. This is a holiday product that enjoys enduring success.

D-I-Y holidays

However, since the 1970s, there has been a countervailing trend. More and more holidaymakers have been deciding to do more for themselves. In Britain, this trend began in domestic tourism. By 1973, 80 per cent of all holidaymakers in Devon and Cornwall were car-borne, and 49 per cent of all holidays in the region were self-catering (South-West Economic Planning Council, 1976). Families were towing their own accommodation – tents and caravans. More accommodation became room-only rather than full board or half board. Rooms could be rented by the night rather than only by the week. People were opting to pick and mix, creating their holidays as they travelled. They could decide *en route* where to stop and where to eat.

Then, Europeans holidaying abroad began doing likewise. By the beginning of the 21st century, the Internet was making it simple for tourists to build their own packages. They have been able to take their own or hire a car, which enables them to travel independently, away from the congested hot spots. Visitors to Britain and to other European and American destinations have been acting in this way. Nowadays, over 70 per cent of incoming tourists have visited Britain previously (www.visitbritain.com). Their first visit may have been a package to London, Stratford-upon-Avon and Edinburgh. Next time, the visitors are likely to want something a bit different, maybe customised to their particular interests. They are becoming more confident, maybe prepared to hire a car and plan their own routes. The holiday has not been de-commercialised but it has been partly de-commodified – only partly, because we have seen that nearly a half of main holidays by UK residents are still packages.

COMPETING FOR BUSINESS

The tipping point

After the 1970s, the tourist industry crossed a tipping point. This was a consequence of the following:

■ Holidaymakers enjoying a wider choice of destinations by air and private motor car as well as by rail and motor coach.
■ The availability of a wider choice of holiday products as a result of the development of holiday camps/villages, the marketing of specialist packages, the option of towing or carrying your own accommodation (caravans and tents) and then the option of going online and constructing a customised package.
■ As standards of living rose for citizens in the advanced economies, a growing proportion of consumer spending was devoted to leisure goods and services, among which 'the holiday' or increasingly 'the holidays' were often by far the largest items.
■ The older industrial countries began to undergo economic restructuring. The earlier transition from agriculture to manufacturing was being followed by steep declines in manufacturing jobs and a need to expand employment in service sectors. This was the context in which virtually all countries, regions and cities sought to promote inward tourism as part of their economic regeneration strategies.

■ The world's poorer countries found that attracting airborne tourists from richer parts of the world was a way in which they could develop their own economies.

Thus, competition for tourists intensified. They are now sought everywhere rather than just by a limited number of specialist holiday destinations. Central and local governments' leisure policies have been reoriented with less emphasis on meeting the needs of locals and more attention to attracting and servicing visitors. This has become a source of new conflicts. Promoting tourism has also become more difficult because everywhere, nowadays, there is some opposition from locals. People complain about religious and cultural traditions being debased, environments degraded, the congestion that tourists create and also, in some cases, residents' rights being subordinated to tourists' interests. Initial waves of tourists object to further development of tourism, which threatens their idylls. First-wave second-home-owners in Ireland object to building additional tourist accommodation (see Mottiar and Quinn, 2003). So everywhere the search is now for ecologically sound, sustainable tourism (see Cole, 2006; Donohoe and Needham, 2006). This is partly a matter of not blemishing the features of a place that attract tourists, but equally of harmonising tourism with the economic, social and cultural interests of all sections of a host population. It is never easy. In 1990, 74 per cent of visitors attempted to climb Ayers Rock in Australia. Aboriginals consider this behaviour inappropriate for reasons of cultural respect. Western culture seeks to control and subjugate nature, thereby achieving progress and improved living standards. Aboriginal culture is different. It respects the sacredness of all life and connectedness with nature, and has a strong sense of place. Since 1990, visitors have become more aware of and responsive to Aboriginals' feelings, and nowadays only around 20 per cent of visitors attempt to climb the rock, but the cost has been a drop in visitor numbers (see Box 5.4).

The competition for tourists forces all places to search for or to create features that will enhance their attractiveness as tourist destinations. 'Attractions' are one such feature. Another is 'heritage' (see Chapter 8). Everywhere has a history that, locals are likely to believe, can be developed into an asset in promoting inward tourism.

Attractions

How do you attract tourists? One tactic is to create an attraction. In some places, the natural environment or the historic buildings may be sufficient.

Box 5.4 Popular attractions

THE EIFFEL TOWER

This was the winning entry from 700 proposals. It was built for the 1889 World Exposition (World Fair), which celebrated the centennial of the French Revolution. The tower is 302.6 metres high. Gustave Eiffel always referred to it as the 300-metre tower. His critics, who were opposed to its construction, called it the Eiffel Tower and this name has stuck.

Nowadays, the Eiffel Tower receives around 7 million visitors each year. There have been over 250 million visitors since the tower opened.

Source: www.toureiffel.paris/en.

AYERS ROCK

This is a red sandstone monolith, the world's largest. It is 9.4 kilometres around with steep slopes rising to 340 metres. The rock is situated in Central Australia, 335 kilometres south-east from Alice Springs. For many thousands of years, the rock has been the focus for religious, cultural, territorial and economic interrelationships among the Aboriginal peoples of Australia's Western Desert. Caves around the base of the rock were once used for shelter and are decorated with paintings.

In 1993, the area in which the rock is located was renamed the Uluru-Kata Tjuta National Park, reflecting the Aboriginal heritage of the site. However, the rock has featured prominently in recent years in Australia's efforts to promote international tourism. Visitor numbers to the rock rose to over 300,000 per year in the early 2000s but have since fallen back to around 200,000. Above all else, the rock is now a tourist attraction.

Source: uluru-australia.com/about-ayers-rock

If not, attractions can always be created. This has happened throughout the history of modern holidaymaking. Blackpool Pleasure Beach (a funfair) and Blackpool Tower are both over a century old. Blackpool's tower was inspired by the Eiffel Tower (see Box 5.4). Blackpool had noted that the Eiffel Tower was attracting a never-ending stream of visitors and hoped to replicate this.

Pleasure beaches – basically fairgrounds – were another early, much-replicated and an enduring type of attraction. However, the attractions that have attracted far and away the most attention from academics are the Disney parks, which were the original theme parks (Becker, 2013). There is now a Disney literature (see, for example, Bryman, 1995; Rojek, 1993). Disneyland opened in southern California in 1955. It was followed in 1971 by Florida's

Disney World, by Tokyo Disneyland in 1983 and Euro-Disney (20 miles east of Paris) in 1992. There are now 11 Disney theme parks and resorts, which attracted a total of 126 million visitors in 2012. These are all commercially successful. They are among the very few cases where a built attraction is a holiday destination. Other theme parks, zoos, stately homes and castles attract day visitors and tourists during their holidays. They may add to the appeal of a holiday destination, but it is really only the Disney parks that have become holiday destinations in their own right. Sociologists have noted that the Disney parks celebrate a particular moral and political order. They exalt the American way of life, present a depoliticised view of the world, applaud the triumph of the individual, especially the little man (Mickey Mouse), and provide an escape into an asexual world of fantasy. Academic interest has been heightened by the fact that the Disney organisation itself takes its social mission seriously, and the company is extremely protective towards the public image that it presents. Any outsiders who study Disney do so without cooperation from the business. Disney vets and supervises its staff carefully, and tries to ensure that no one beyond those immediately affected hears of someone being robbed, let alone sexually assaulted, while visiting one of the parks. George Ritzer uses Disney as an example of rationalisation (see Chapter 2, pp. 32–37), but does Disney really exemplify anything except Disney? These attractions are unique. They have no peers. They rank alongside the world's most spectacular waterfalls and deepest canyons in drawing tourists from all over the globe.

Some places have historical buildings that attract tourists from all over the world. India has the Taj Mahal. Egypt has the pyramids. London has its tower, the Houses of Parliament, Westminster Abbey, and so on. Las Vegas also has a special attraction, and in recent years other cities have discovered that gambling attracts visitors and persuades them to part with loads of money. In 2001, Blackpool received (with interest) a proposal to build a set of Vegas-type casino hotels. If Britain's gambling laws were ever relaxed so as to make this possible, and if this plan went ahead in Blackpool and nowhere else in Britain, it is odds-on that the resort would recover its earlier glory (see Cavill, 2002). However, gambling is ceasing to be a special attraction as more and more places emulate Las Vegas and Monte Carlo.

Another way of boosting visitors is to host a temporary attraction, like a sports or cultural event. These are always intended to benefit the local economy (see Chapter 7). There is always a net cost to public funds, but far more money usually flows in. Is this always good business? Gratton and Taylor (2000) estimate that Euro 96 (the European soccer tournament) added 0.1 per cent to Britain's gross domestic product (GDP) during

April–June 1996. A host city or country can hope to derive long-term bene-fits from the facilities that are built and the publicity received, but these benefits are difficult to measure. There are always too many intervening variables. Rather than a one-off mega-event, a recurrent mini-event, like an annual arts festival, could be a better investment. Calculating the costs and benefits of different sports and arts events is now a subsidiary branch of the tourist industry (see Gratton et al., 2001; Gratton and Henry, 2001).

However, the natural environment can be an exceptionally good attrac-tion. Nothing man-made can truly match the Swiss Alps or the Grand Canyon. Australia has discovered that Ayers Rock (see Box 5.4), situated in a desolate, inhospitable region, is probably its best single asset (superior even to Sydney Opera House; see Box 8.3, p. 184) for attracting international visitors. North America's landscapes, especially the US national parks, are the country's big tourist attractions. America was the pioneer of national parks and also, much later on, of theme parks (Becker, 2013).

The cultural dimension

In recent years, researchers who specialise in the field have been highlight-ing tourism's cultural dimension (see, for example, Aitchison et al., 2000; Crouch, 1999). This is not confined to so-called cultural tourism, which has boomed throughout Europe (see Lyons and Wearing, 2007; Rath, 2007; Richards, 2001). Everything has a cultural dimension. Appadurai (1986, 1996) argues (correctly) that all 'things', including things from the past, are always given their meanings in their present contexts. So 'traditions' are always modern inventions. The sociological gaze has been redirected by the so-called cultural and postmodern 'turns' in academia, and also by the huge efforts and sums of money that destinations and holiday companies now spend on constructing appealing images. The actual built and natural environments may or may not be modified. Locals (certainly those who are paid to work in tourism-related businesses) are trained to enact scripts that tourists are led to expect. The visitors' gaze is pre-focused by all the pub-licity (they know what to look for), and the hosts know what to lay on. Sociologists have drawn attention to how the present-day tourist industry creates identities for places and peoples – their national characteristics and sexual inclinations, for example. 'More and more, local identities become associated with the significance places have for people from elsewhere' (Lengkeek, 2000, p. 11). Visitors are invited to enact reciprocal parts, and all the parties may internalise the identities that have been constructed for them (see Morgan and Pritchard, 1998; Urry, 1990). The construction of place images that are designed to attract tourists can provoke local controversy. For example, Memphis (USA) has not only been culturally reconstructed but partly rebuilt physically for the purpose of boosting its appeal to tourists. The collective memories of huge (mainly non-white) sections of the local population have been excluded from the new product (Silk, 2007). Visitors are believed to seek 'authenticity', but tourism itself inevitably affects what is observed and experienced (see Martin, 2010).

Some astounding claims have been made for the cultural impact of international tourism. It is not only (some) sociologists who claim that cross-national understanding and friendship are strengthened, but it could surely only be in ivory towers that commentators would imagine that our 'pilgrimages' to each other's places, where 'sacred' objects are 'worshipped', might unify all humankind (MacCannell, 1976). Writers on tourism sometimes contrast an older 'traveller' with the modern tourist. For the latter, everything is said to be prepackaged, especially laid on. Maybe, but surely all concerned realise this. Locals in particular surely know the difference between what their places are really like and the images and displays that are presented to tourists.

Various typologies of tourists have been proposed (see Murphy, 1985; Smith, 1995). The Cohen (1979) typology is still among those more frequently cited. Cohen distinguishes five kinds of tourists:

- Recreational tourists who are seeking entertainment.
- Diversionary tourists who are hoping to 'recharge their batteries'.
- Experiential tourists who are in search of authentic and rich experience.
- Experimental tourists who are trying to discover their own true selves.
- Existential tourists who are looking for a better world.

Maybe tourists do not divide neatly into these five particular groups, but the typology alerts us to the fact that tourists differ in their cultural sensitivity.

Sociologists are unwise to ignore the 'basics' of holidaymaking, or to leave the obvious to economists. First and foremost, tourists are going away. 'Where to' can be less important than just going away – from work and home, probably to somewhere warm and sunny. There are scores of acceptable, largely interchangeable, destinations for many tourists. From the brochures or Internet sites, these people seek packages that offer value for money. The tourist trade is price-sensitive. Cultural analysis risks obscuring what is often a blander reality. The most powerful cultural meanings of tourism are surely within the tourists' normal home-based social networks. The holidays that we take do indeed signify who we are. By virtue of the frequency with which we go away, and how far we go (the further the better), we tell others something about ourselves. The 20 per cent of the UK population that does not go away, and those who 'only' go somewhere within their own country, are among those affected (culturally) by international tourism.

MANAGING PRESENT-DAY TOURISM

Only public agencies can manage tourism. Hotels, hotel chains, restaurants, entertainments and attractions promote themselves. Airlines do likewise in competing to fly passengers to destinations that the latter choose. Tour companies create packages of places, accommodation and transport which, they hope, will prove more appealing than competitors' packages. Cruise lines compete on the basis of their vessels, routes, ports of call and on-board catering and entertainment. All these businesses manage tourists. All need managers who are experts in their particular niches of the tourist industry, but they do not manage tourism. It is only the Disney parks (which have on-site hotels) that can claim to be managing tourism, marketing a total holiday experience. The government is normally a country's main tourist sales force. This is normally the job of public agencies who must market a country, region or city. They must persuade tourists to use the hotels, entertainments and attractions that are 'here' rather than somewhere else. Only governments can guarantee all the permissions and protections that make a destination attractive to tourists.

There is one big exception to governments playing the lead role in promoting inward tourism. This is the United States, where the context has been a historically deep-rooted suspicion of all federal government intervention and spending. In the United States, tourism promotion is left to individual states and cities, plus the national parks and theme parks. The outcome has been that the US share in the global tourism market has declined. Visitor numbers little more than flatlined throughout the second half of the 20th century. Then, after 9/11, there were more restrictions and more hassle for inward tourists. Things eased somewhat during the Obama administrations, but the United States continues to punch far beneath its weight in the global tourism business (Becker, 2013). This is despite the fact that the United States remains far and away the world leader in earnings from tourism (see p. 97).

Other governments try their best, but in the 21st century, capturing the tourist trade has become more difficult and simultaneously more important than ever, given the economic value of tourism and its contributions to financial flows into and out of countries, regions and cities. The importance of tourism has been magnified since 2008 because tourism has been among the few major industries that has continued to grow. This applies most of all in the southern European countries where general unemployment has risen above 20 per cent and youth (16–24-year-olds) unemployment above 50 per cent. These are countries where tourism became a major industry from the mid-20th century, when northern Europeans began to fly south for their main holidays. Unfortunately for Europe's Mediterranean countries, this is not one of the tourist flows that is currently expanding. This is a situation that local tourism management must confront.

Nowadays, all countries, regions and cities try to manage tourism but they cannot all be successful even in an expanding economic sector because their task is to outperform the competition and it is impossible for everyone to win. Such is the economic importance of tourism that, at central and local government levels, tourism management has typically migrated away from other leisure services and into economic and business ministries and departments for economic development and regeneration. However, whether today's global tourist flows can be sustained, let alone allowed to continue to grow, is debatable. Travel is fossil fuel-dependent. It contributes to climate change. Can the world allow tourism to continue to grow (see Hayden, 2007)?

Only public agencies have a vital interest in sustainable, ecologically sound tourism: ensuring that visitors do not degrade and devalue whatever attracts them to a place. Only public agencies are sensitive to the importance of balanced economic development so that a country or city does not become over-dependent on tourism. Public authorities are aware nowadays of the dangers of tourist regions becoming locked in subordinate positions in economic dependency relationships (Davis, 1978; Turner and Ash, 1975). Most public authorities, therefore, aim for balanced economic development in which tourism does not become the sole base of the local economy. They know that over-dependence on tourism means lots of low-level, seasonal jobs, and high unemployment out of season.

Governments have to decide whether they want this business and how much they are prepared to pay for it. If they want tourists, then they need to invest in infrastructure and promotion. There are rarely any sound reasons, business apart, for governments to invest in tourism. Whether to invest and, if so, how much are best treated as straightforward business matters. Thereafter, central and local governments should realise that inbound tourism is revenue boosting rather than budget draining. Promoting tourism need not be at the expense of public leisure provisions with social and cultural goals, and for the local population. Rather, the ability of governments to cater for locals' leisure will normally be enhanced by a successful tourist industry.

Managing tourism is more akin to managing economic development than running a public health service or publicly owned leisure facilities. This is because tourism is driven by commerce – by profit-seeking hotels, air, rail and shipping lines, entertainments and tour package companies. It is these players that engage directly with tourists and that are most likely to know what they want and what attracts them to a place. Managing tourism successfully requires commerce to be left in command in the engine room, though not in the driver's seat. Selling a country has been likened to acting as head of an octopus (Becker, 2013). It is not public agencies but commerce that has created the 19th, 20th and 21st centuries' most successful tourist products – the seaside holiday, holiday camps/villages, the overseas package and the ICT systems that enable customers to pick and mix and build their own packages.

Commerce has promoted tourism so successfully that it has become the major item in many households' leisure spending, especially richer households in richer countries. Why are holidays so important to consumers? There are senses in which the holiday is the purest form of leisure that people can experience; it is 'the ultimate change' (Hill, 2002). People may enjoy the Friday PM feeling at the end of the workweek. This feeling is intensified when people go away entirely, for a full week or longer, and get away not just from work but also from their homes and all familiar faces (except their travel companions). The holiday is a total break. It can be hard work in its own way. We may return shattered rather than with batteries recharged. We may actually look forward to returning home at the end of the break. But the holiday is an exceptional opportunity to get away from everything. People can leave their everyday selves behind and, among strangers, adopt holiday persona – jocular, flirtatious, adventurous – irrespective of their reputations back home. Whether it is the first drink in the airport departure lounge, or (for Britons) the first Gallic coffee on the cross-channel ferry, it symbolises liberation. Commerce succeeds by giving people what they want.

Activities that become the base of specialist holidays are usually pioneered by groups of enthusiasts who form themselves into clubs, but it is always through the entrepreneurialism of some of the enthusiasts that the activities become part of the tourist industry. Voluntary associations can add to a local tourist offer. These may be local societies that are interested in the local heritage, art collections and flora and fauna, and which are keen to present these to visitors. Performers of local arts and producers of local crafts can also contribute to the local tourist offer, but in these cases it is tourism that is strengthening the local voluntary societies as much as vice versa.

Public agencies need to use market signals from commerce – the businesses that are in day-to-day contact with tourists and persuade them to part with their money. However, only a public agency can speak for a country, region or city and decide what makes it especially attractive and should be highlighted in the publicity. The actual publicising can be outsourced, but what to publicise is a political decision. Then it is necessary to decide 'whom' to attract. There are very few places apart from Paris and London that can hope to be attractive to virtually everyone. In which countries or world regions should a destination concentrate on promoting itself? There are some destinations such as the Swiss Alps, London and Paris where attracting 'enough' tourists is not a problem. They have to decide which tourists they want to be the majority. This is likely to depend on who spends the most money per day. This is why, in Europe, it used to be Americans but today it is the Japanese, the Chinese and South Koreans who are especially welcome. Destinations must decide whether they are most likely to appeal to young singles and childless couples, or seniors who are less likely to feel at ease amid blaring music 24/7. Alternatively, a destination may promote itself for family holidays (parents with children).

Local politicians and public officials may have their own views, but these will not necessarily correspond with what makes a destination appealing to outsiders. The best signals will always be from commerce, not politicians' and their officials' own hunches. Features that make a destination especially attractive can be made central in place imaging and in profiling the tourists who are most likely to be tempted. Public agencies must also calculate the size of tourist inflows that will be compatible with sustainability, with the local infrastructure and amenities and with basic services such as electricity and water, especially in places where these are scarce commodities.

CONCLUSIONS

One hundred and fifty years ago, it did not appear inevitable that tourism would develop as a primarily commercial leisure industry. It appeared at least as likely that holidaymaking would be organised mainly by voluntary associations, as has remained the case with sport (see next chapter). Commerce quickly became dominant in tourism because it developed the products with the strongest appeal to the majority of holidaymakers.

Commercial businesses have been innovative and remain so. Tourism is a truly dynamic part of the present-day business of leisure.

Tourism is an outstanding leisure industry in its consistently strong growth which has continued through the most recent recession with just a minor blip in 2008–09. Such is the scale of the flows of money that tourism generates that today virtually all countries, regions and cities are seeking to expand inward tourism. It has become an increasingly diverse industry in terms of tourists' countries of origin, their destinations and the variety of holidays from which they can select. It is a highly competitive leisure industry in which it is impossible for every place to be a winner. We have seen that Europe's original seaside holiday resorts declined during the later part of the 20th century as opportunities to travel further away widened. It is possible that the Mediterranean sea, sand and sun resorts, which benefited from this earlier trend, now face decline. Not only there is more competition, but the strongest growth in outward tourism is now from the emerging market economies, whose tourists are unlikely to head for southern Europe's coastal resorts.

The challenge for all countries, regions and cities is to manage tourism so as to derive maximum benefit. Only public agencies can act on behalf of destinations. They must manage an industry in which very few airlines, hotels and entertainments and only some attractions are publicly owned and managed.

Chapter 6

Sport

INTRODUCTION

Sport has become a global multi-billion-dollar business. Cities and countries spend millions of dollars simply bidding to host major events. Major professional sports clubs are targeted by international investors. Top players are now among the world's best paid entertainers. These layers of sport are publicised daily and earn much of their revenue from the media. This gives these layers of sport a high profile, which makes it all the more important to stress that only the top layers of the top sports can be described as commercial businesses. Most sport is still non-profit and remains attached to its original grass roots.

Modern sports and tourism had very similar beginnings, and in each case these beginnings were in 19th-century Britain. Sport and tourism were both pioneered in civil society rather than in the market (the home of profit-seeking businesses) or by government action. Both were part of the 19th-century campaign for rational recreation. The first holidays were organised by churches, Sunday schools, progressive employers and individual philanthropists. Sports were invented by enthusiasts who organised themselves into sports clubs. These clubs joined together in associations which agreed rules of play and organised competitions. However, by the beginning of the 20th century, 'holidays away' had become primarily commercial. Sport, unlike tourism, remained mostly non-commercial and was therefore part of the early-20th-century recreation movement. By then, sport had become the home of a powerful amateur ethic (see Allison, 2001). Most members of the sport community believed that it was morally improper and in any case impossible to make money out of sport. There were inevitable exceptions. By the end of the 19th century, payments to professional players in spectator sports which attracted large crowds had been accepted in most of the relevant sports, but until the late-20th century the earnings of most professional players bore more resemblance to workers' wages than the earnings of top entertainers in films, broadcasting and music. Americans had fewer reservations than Europeans about paying players and also about sport promoters who sought profit. Professional boxing and wrestling contests were usually organised by profit-seeking entrepreneurs. However, team sports were always and still are incredibly risky investments, which tempt only those who can afford this exciting leisure activity and who also seek social status and visibility rather than just financial gain. To this day, most sport is still run and played by amateurs.

However, by the end of the 20th century, two 'game changers' had entered sport. First, the value of television broadcasting rights was attracting new (profit-seeking) investors into popular spectator sports and leading to an escalation in the earnings of top players. Second, the scope for commercial leisure had always been governed by people's disposable incomes which remained when necessities had been purchased, and by the late-20th century the spread of prosperity and a general growth in leisure spending were attracting new commercial providers into participant sport. Formerly, public authorities (including state schools and colleges) had provided facilities (mainly playing fields, gyms and swimming pools) while the voluntary sector ran sports themselves. By the late-20th century, commercial health and fitness clubs were entering the participant sports industry. There had been attempts to run tennis, squash and cue sports for profit, but the gyms have proved more durable. Also, some 'lifestyle' sports were being promoted by businesses that could profit from the sale of specialist clothing, footwear and equipment, plus coaching and specialist holidays.

These developments have changed the character of sport as an academic specialty within higher education. Formerly, sport academics (teachers and researchers) addressed future sport teachers and coaches, managers of public and voluntary sector sport facilities and the distributors and recipients of state funds for participant sport. Today's sport academics also address future and current managers of sport businesses – health and fitness gyms, professional spectator sport clubs that are owned by profit-seeking investors, the leagues that receive and distribute income from the sale of broadcasting rights and businesses that produce and market sports goods and sportswear. To repeat, most sport is still played and run by amateurs, but the big question posed by current trends is whether it is possible to commercialise the top layers without, in the long term, changing the rest of sport.

This chapter proceeds by describing how modernised sports were created in the 19th century, and how these sports were popularised as participant and spectator events by people who were motivated purely by enthusiasm. We identify certain values which are linked to sports' voluntary roots (the amateur ethic, for example) which became entrenched in our main sports very early in their history. The chapter continues by considering the relationship between sports and governments: how sports have looked to governments to provide facilities such as playing fields, to promote sports in education, and sometimes more, and how governments have endeavoured to use sport for their own political purposes, be these social inclusion or nation building and boosting national prestige. The chapter concludes with the expanding role of commerce in spectator and participant sports. It argues that spectator sports have always been and remain high risk for serious investors, and that there are better commercial prospects in participant sport but only if sport can be collapsed into all forms of physically active recreation.

THE MODERNISATION OF SPORTS

What is sport?

Until the 19th century, all kinds of recreation were referred to as sports. Hunting was a sport. So was gambling, and so were fights between animals. The term 'sport' acquired its more limited and current meaning when modern sports were invented during the 19th century. The main sites of invention were England's secondary schools (all private at that time) and universities. The development and incorporation of modern sports into the education of young males was part of a wider reform of education which was then under way. Subsequently, sports have been distinguished by the following features:

- First, sports are games which are separated from the rest of life, or at any rate from the more serious parts of life, by some combination of time, place and rules.
- Second, sports require skill. One can improve one's performance by training and practice. Games of chance such as roulette are therefore excluded.
- Third, sports are energetic. Playing well at sport requires stamina and exertion, and performances improve with fitness training.
- Fourth, sports are competitive. Players compete against each other or against the clock or some other yardstick.

Even on a narrow definition – the four tests listed above – all societies appear to have had sports. They have created sports out of humans' ability to run, jump, throw, climb and swim. Sports may or may not involve implements – balls, or wooden or metal objects of various shapes and weights. They may or may not involve animals. There have been thousands of different sports. New sports are constantly being invented. The sports that were invented during the 20th century include stock car racing, tenpin bowling, five-a-side soccer, waterskiing, surfing, windsurfing, skateboarding, snowboarding, snowmobiling, synchronised swimming and tractor racing. Scientific and technological developments which led to the bicycle, the motor car and the aeroplane made it possible to introduce new sports. In more recent times, the voracious appetite of multi-channel television, with 24 hours of 365 days a year of sports coverage, has led to a new raft of sport inventions. However, the key period when our major modern sports were all invented – athletics, swimming and diving and the various games of football, for example – was the second half of the 19th century.

The early inventors

As indicated above, most of the early inventing was done in Britain, the first industrial nation, and within Britain the main invention sites were the independent (non-state) secondary schools and universities. Sports were modernised, that is, made compatible with urban conditions and industrial time schedules, and, in some cases, 'civilised' by outlawing dangerous practices such as hacking in football, and by the Queensbury Rules in boxing. Modernisation also involved confining play to pitches of limited size and limiting the length of contests. So instead of football games rampaging through entire towns and lasting all day, the new rules confined games to compact pitches and allowed matches to be completed in less than two hours.

Tony Collins (2013) locates the beginnings of modern sports in 17th- and 18th-century England, where certain older forms of recreation including cricket and horse racing were developed as spectator events which could be run for profit. This is part of Collins' broader argument which links the development of modern sports to the rise of capitalism. However, the fact is that most of our modern sports were invented during the second half of the 19th century. This was during the rise of industrial capitalism, and also alongside the formation of modern nation states. These developments were part of the context. Yet despite this, most of the sports that were popularised rapidly were not invented or promoted by profit-seeking entrepreneurs and, as we shall see, very few of these sports are suitable for commercialisation either for amateur participants or as spectator events.

At the 19th-century educational institutions where most modern sports were invented (and soon adopted as part of the curriculum in the independent schools), the new modernised sports were regarded as more than just enjoyable forms of recreation. They were valued for developing fitness and health, and, equally if not more important, character. Team sports were considered especially valuable – ideal training for the country's future 'officer class' not just in the armed forces but also in industry, commerce and the Empire. Boys were taught the need for discipline, to subordinate their own contributions to a group, to observe rules, to respect the authority of a referee and, eventually, to exercise leadership. They learnt to win magnanimously and to accept defeat gracefully while vowing to improve and eventually to succeed.

Popularisation

Modern sports spread rapidly from the sites of their invention. They were taken to the working class by schoolteachers, churches and youth organisations. If the 'officers' could enjoy and benefit from sport, then, it was believed, so could 'the ranks'. Sports were promoted as a form of rational recreation – a way of keeping young men out of mischief. The ranks were not difficult to convert. They adopted sports enthusiastically, especially association football, which was to become the people's game the world over (Walvin, 1975). The Football Association (FA) was formed in 1863. By 1871–72, it was able to organise a national competition, the FA Cup. In 1872, the first international match was played between England and Scotland. In 1885, professional football (with paid players) was 'legalised' (it was already happening unofficially – the first reported professional footballers played for Darwen, a Lancashire club, in 1879). The national Football League competition commenced in 1888. All this was within just a single generation.

Modern sports became popular not just throughout Britain. They are among the country's most successful exports: association football, rugby league, rugby union, cricket, tennis, boxing, hockey, netball, golf, polo, bowls, athletics, skiing. By the end of the 19th century, the new sports were being played throughout the British Empire and, indeed, in virtually all the other countries with which Britain had contact. There were many such countries because even before the Industrial Revolution, Britain had been a great trading nation. The one world region which did not just import but invented some of its own modern sports was North America. The United States invented baseball and its own version of football. Later on, ice hockey and basketball were to become major sports in North America. Much thought, and thousands of pages, have been devoted to this instance of American exceptionalism (see Markovits and Hellerman, 2001; Szymanski and Zimbalist, 2005), especially why the sport called football throughout the rest of the world has never taken off in North America. It has been argued that America's own sports appeal to its people largely because the sports are distinctly American (Gardner, 1974). It may also be relevant that having its own makes it unlikely that Americans will not be world champions in their preferred games. It must also be said that, from the very beginning, spectator sports in North America were more commercial than in Europe (see Sandy et al., 2004). America's sport culture has been different, distinctly American, from the outset.

In modern sports, all competitors occupy the same playing fields. The rules of the games and conditions of play are the same for everyone. This standardisation is among modern sports' distinctive features. This enables all classes, nationalities, religions and races to compete on equal terms. However, it must also be said that in Britain, and elsewhere, the upper and middle classes have sometimes gone to extraordinary lengths to avoid the risk of being humbled by the lower orders. At any rate, this has been a consequence of some of their tactics. In some sports, rowing for example, the 19th-century British governing bodies decided that members of the working class should not be allowed to enter the main competitions. The reason given was the unfair advantage that workers would enjoy due to the physical demands of their occupations. This regulation was rescinded long ago, and governing bodies have rarely been so crude. It has been more common for competition to be informally restricted to social equals. So independent schools have played against other independent schools, grammar schools against grammar schools and universities against universities. A division that helped to keep the classes apart for the first century of modern sports was between amateurs and professionals. The upper and middle classes joined amateur clubs which had their own competitions, and left professional competitions, and some entire sports which admitted professional players (association football and rugby league, for example), to the working class. Rugby's great schism – the split between the Rugby League and the entirely amateur Rugby Union in 1895 – was an unusually clear break (see Collins, 2006). Cricket had 'players' and 'gentlemen' until 1963. Even if amateur gentlemen played in the same sides as professionals and the former did not excel on the field of play, the status of the gentlemen was preserved. The well-to-do have often avoided sports which have been taken up by the working class and have adopted less popular sports, sometimes expensive ones such as horse riding where the riders, as well as the animals, are generally well bred. Or the better-off have formed their own clubs where the location or the fees have kept the places exclusive. It seems that little has changed during the last 100 years in this respect. In Belgium (and very likely elsewhere), the higher-socio-economic strata are the most likely to play sports that involve the use of 'sticks' (golf, tennis, squash, skiing, and so on) plus large and ostentatious outlays of money (as in horse riding and yachting, for example). The lower strata dominate in some solitary sports (angling and cycling, for instance) and in sports which require body contact such as boxing and karate (see Scheerder et al., 2002).

Many class-divisive practices have lapsed only since commerce entered sport. The upper and middle classes have abandoned reticence about competing on level terms with their social inferiors, and have decided to risk defeat, when the potential cash rewards have been sufficiently attractive. In 1990, faced with the prospect of huge sums of TV-linked cash, the Rugby Union rapidly abandoned its long-standing principled objections to professionalism. After football's maximum wage was abolished in Britain in 1961, university graduates began to enter the professional game. Later on, in the 1990s, when the cash rewards in top-level football again rose steeply, young men from middle-class families became willing to quit the academic route towards university and take their chances in the top clubs' football academies.

Enduring assumptions

Despite the tensions that have always been present between the rules and cultures of modern sports and the wider modern world, many assumptions – ideas that were linked to modern sports from the outset – have proved remarkably resilient. To begin with, there is the belief that playing sport makes people healthier, improves their characters and turns them into good citizens. In reality, even the health benefits are doubtful (see Roberts and Brodie, 1992). People who play often enough, and vigorously enough, to improve their physiological functioning, risk paying a price in sport-related injuries. Top-level athletes appear to require far more medical attention than the rest of the population. As regards the social benefits, there is still a lack not only of convincing evidence (see Coalter, 2007; Witt and Crompton, 1996) but even of satisfactory evaluative studies (see Shaw, 1999).

Another long-standing conviction is that playing sport is especially beneficial for children and young people. In practice, all the benefits – physical, social and psychological – appear to be age-independent (see Roberts and Brodie, 1992). If anything, sport is probably most beneficial health-wise in late adulthood. Yet the school-age group and those a little older continue to be the principal targets. Sport is a compulsory part of the national school curriculum in Britain and in many other countries. When in education, young (and older) students are well provided with opportunities to play. Then there is a steep dropout during the years after people leave full-time education.

Another entrenched assumption is that sport is masculine: that boys (and men) ought to enjoy sports but that these activities are less appropriate, or wholly inappropriate, for girls and women. Nineteenth-century elementary schools had boys doing drill while girls were in domestic science classes. Physical exertion, sweating and muscularity have been considered unfeminine. Apart from the social aspect, it was once believed that strenuous exercise could damage women's reproductive capability. There have always been some women, and some girls' schools, that have battled against these assumptions, but it is only quite recently (since the 1990s) that the (English) Football Association has recognised the women's game, and until the 1960s there were no endurance events (races longer than 400 metres) for women in the Olympics (see Box 6.1). Many people still feel that women and boxing are unsuited to each other. But nothing is static. Assumptions

---

Box 6.1 Women in sport

There were no women competitors in the first modern Olympics in 1896. In 1900, women were admitted but only for golf, tennis and yachting. Swimming was added in 1912, but it was not until 1928 that women first appeared in track and field. Even then, they were not allowed to run more than 200 metres until 1960. The women's marathon was first run in the 1984 Olympics.

In 1921, the world's oldest football association, the (English) FA, banned women's football, which was in danger of becoming popular, from the grounds of all member clubs. This ban was cancelled only in 1971. The FA became the authority for women's football in 1993. It is only since 1996 that women's football has been an Olympic sport.

change. Women now compete in all the Olympic sports. Commerce is playing a leading role in these changes. Women's sport still receives far less media attention than men's games, but this will not necessarily be so for ever. There are many sports in which, arguably, women's events are the better spectacles: in tennis, for example, and maybe even in top-level soccer, where male play (compared with women's) has become power rather than skill dominated.

The voluntary base

Many of the features sketched above are evidence of modern sports' non-commercial roots. Commerce's expansionist tendencies will always seek to overcome age, gender and social class divisions. It will do this by designing slightly different products, if necessary. However, unlike the modern holiday, the evening out and popular music, our modern sports were not created by the market. Sport as we know it today (in Europe) is a product of voluntary organisation and public sector support. In some sports, these same bodies have remained in charge while participation has reached mass proportions all over the world, while the sports have become global industries with huge turnovers, and have become the livelihoods of thousands of professional players, agents, managers and a variety of ancillary workers.

It is because sports were originally created and run by non-profit organisations that many people came to believe that it was impossible to run sport on a commercial basis. The reality is that sport can be commercial, but not the sports scene that has existed in Europe for the last one-and-a-half centuries. Another belief that became entrenched early in the history of modern sports is that, even if it was possible, it was wrong to make money out of sport – that all concerned should act for love of the games. This ideal was built into the modern Olympic movement. Baron de Coubertin, a Frenchman, was impressed, on the one hand, by the ideals of the original Greek Olympics (see Box 6.2) and, on the other, by the sporting ethos that he observed in

---

Box 6.2 The Ancient Olympic Games

The first Olympics were held in 776 BC at Olympia in Greece. This was a one-day event with just one race, a *stadion* (over 192 metres). Subsequently the games were held every four years, and by the 5th century BC the event had become a major festival which lasted five days with ten classes of contests. These were running (over distances from

192 to 4,608 metres, with some of the races run in full military armour), pentathlon, jumping, discus, javelin, wrestling, boxing, pankration (a blend of boxing and wrestling), chariot racing and horse racing.

The athletics were embedded in a religious festival honouring Zeus, the chief Greek god. Warfare between the city states was always suspended for the duration of an Olympics. During each games, 100 oxen were sacrificed, and the occasions became associated with enduring achievements in architecture, mathematics, sculpture and poetry.

All the games were held at Olympia. Only free men who spoke Greek could compete (not women, slaves or barbarians). Athletes competed for honour, but winners became lifelong heroes in their home cities, which could be from as far away as present-day Spain, Libya and Ukraine. When they returned home, the winners could expect cash rewards and appointment to leadership positions in their cities.

The ancient games were abolished in AD 393 when (within the Roman Empire) the functioning of all idol-worshipping sanctuaries was forbidden.

Sources: www.olympics.org.uk
www.nostos.com/olympics

England's 19th-century independent schools. Maybe the baron misunderstood both, but the modern Olympics aimed to draw them together and to unite humanity through its common ability to enjoy sport, to play for its own sake and to both lose and triumph gracefully.

In Britain, the original birthplace of modern sport, it is only during the last 50 years that, with very few earlier exceptions, any players have made good money out of sport. Even today, it is only the very top players in the most popular sports who are well rewarded financially. Olympic gold does not lead to riches for swimmers, rowers or archers, to name just three sports. Roger Bannister was not paid in 1954 for becoming the first human to run a recorded mile in under four minutes. Top UK rugby union remained basically amateur until the 1990s. Until 1961, top-flight footballers in Britain were decently paid only by a working-class yardstick. Stanley Matthews, Tom Finney and Bobby Charlton were making hardly better livings than they personally could have hoped for in alternative careers. Would they have been better players if they had been paid more? Sport is a challenge to the ideology of the market which claims that no other motivator can rival cash. It is not clear that professional players are always superior. Since the First World War, professional football has certainly been stronger than the amateur game, but prior to accepting payments to players in the 1990s, Rugby Union in the UK was not inferior to Rugby League in the players' fitness or skill levels, or as an entertaining spectacle. Sport is proof that people will push themselves to peaks of performance purely for the intrinsic satisfaction and the esteem which they attract.

SPORT AND THE STATE

The rapid and widespread popularisation of modern sports would have been impossible without strong and continuing support from governments. Generally, throughout the world, voluntary bodies have done most of the organising while governments have provided the facilities for amateur players.

Governments in most countries have been keen to promote sport. Why? Sport is congruent with all the public sector's special capabilities in leisure (see Chapter 4, pp. 87–90). Governments promote sport as a particularly worthwhile leisure activity: playing sport is believed, rightly or wrongly, to benefit both health and character, and it has been possible to make opportunities to play sport into, in effect, rights of citizenship. Governments have also been alert to the possibility of sporting excellence and international success strengthening national identities and prestige. Also, in recent times, governments have become aware that sport is (at least partly) a business and that national (and regional and local) economies stand to benefit if their teams and competitors gain a significant share of the global audience (see Gratton et al., 2005), and if they can host high-profile events such as the Olympic Games and the football World Cup.

Participant sport

There are inter-country differences in exactly how governments support participant sport. In the Netherlands and Germany, and in some other countries of Continental Europe, state support is channelled largely through voluntary sports clubs. So, after school, children go to their clubs to play sport, whereas in Britain and America they have been more likely to stay behind to play sport extra-curricularly. Many Continental schools use clubs' playing fields, whereas in Britain clubs are more likely to use schools' sports halls and other facilities. In Britain, local authorities provide public playing fields, swimming pools and sports centres which can be used by clubs. In the Netherlands and Germany, clubs are helped to acquire and manage these facilities. There are pros and cons in all arrangements. In Britain, there is believed to be a problem of young people dropping out of sport by failing to make the transition from school-based to club-based participation. 'Too many young people are lost for ever to sport because there is not a straightforward and attractive way, through local clubs, to continue playing after age 16' (Department of National Heritage, 1995). However, on the Continent, there is believed to be a problem of young people failing to join sports clubs (Deckers and Gratton, 1995).

Professional sport

In the UK, state support has been directed overwhelmingly to participant sport. Governments have not regarded it as their responsibility to subsidise clubs that pay their players and attract paying spectators. These clubs have been expected to pay their own way. Governments in other countries have taken a rather different view. In US cities, major spectator sports are often played in publicly owned stadiums, which are made available to professional teams at zero or nominal rents (Crompton, 2001). Cities provide these facilities because they believe that there are public benefits in terms of the money and prestige that are attracted. It is different in Britain, where professional football, rugby and cricket clubs have been expected to provide their own grounds. Other countries' governments have not hesitated when building prestigious national stadiums, whereas Twickenham and Wembley have always been privately owned and financed.

Elite amateur sport

Government support, even for elite amateur sport in Britain, was extremely limited until very recently. Before the Second World War, the administration of virtually all sport in Britain was not only non-commercial but also, at governing body level, free of state intervention. At first, this was simply something that did not happen: modern sports were created and developed independently. However, by the 1930s, non-intervention had become more of a positive policy, demonstrating the purity of British sport and how Britain differed from communist and fascist regimes. For all practical purposes at that time, the UK government was indifferent as to whether or not funds could be raised to enable British teams to compete in the Olympics. Until a Sports Council was created in 1965, most UK sport governing bodies prioritised their independence. But by then it was becoming clear (so people believed, at any rate) that competitiveness at top-flight international level was impossible without some measure of state support.

Other countries' governments had already become far more interventionist. Its hands-off sports history was due to Britain having become the first industrial nation, and, to begin with, a *laissez-faire* one. Elsewhere, economic and social modernisation have often been government led, and these governments have often sought international sporting success as a way of boosting the prestige of the countries (and their political regimes). This was the policy of Germany's Nazi government in the 1930s, and its methods of identifying and then nurturing young sporting talent proved extremely successful in terms of medals won at the 1936 Berlin Olympics. This was despite the black US athlete Jesse Owen winning four gold medals. Subsequently, similar systems for pursuing international sporting success to those pioneered in Nazi Germany were adopted by communist countries after they first began to compete in Olympic Games from 1952. Subsequently, the USSR performed consistently well in terms of medals won, and one additional communist country, the German Democratic Republic, was spectacularly successful (see Box 6.3).

Box 6.3 The German Democratic Republic's elite sport system

This had four principal features:

i.   Scientifically organised selection of boys and girls in early childhood.
ii. Best possible facilities and an organised, squad approach to coaching and training.
iii. Support by highly qualified experts from all relevant disciplines. Thousands of scientists, physicians and trainers were involved. Anabolic steroids were used liberally. Athletes who queried this were told that compliance was a patriotic duty.
iv. Efforts were concentrated within a restricted range of (particularly Olympic) sports.

Sport was supposed to nurture a socialist personality: disciplined, honest, imbued with collective spirit and willing to defend the homeland. International success was intended to demonstrate the superiority of the socialist system over capitalism.

In practice, most East Germans did not participate in organised sport, and the events of 1989 showed that the regime was desperately short of loyal citizens. However, the sport system was spectacularly effective in winning Olympic medals. In the 1988 Summer Olympics (the last before the demise of the GDR), the country won 6.0 medals per million population. As a benchmark, in 2000 the UK won 0.5 (slightly more than the United States but slightly fewer than France).

Source: Green and Oakley, 2001.

Table 6.1 All-time Summer Olympic Games medal table - Top ten nations according to official data of the International Olympic Committee

		Number of games in which competed	Gold	Silver	Bronze	Total
1	USA	26	976	758	666	2,400
2	USSR	9	395	319	296	1,010
3	Great Britain	27	236	272	272	780
4	France	27	202	223	246	671
5	China	9	201	144	128	473
6	Italy	26	198	166	185	549
7	Germany	15	174	182	217	573
8	Hungary	25	167	144	165	476
9	East Germany (GDR)	5	153	129	127	409
10	Sweden	26	143	164	176	483

Table 6.1 presents the all-time (summer) Olympic medal league table up to 2012. The table is headed by the United States with 2,400 medals, but this country had competed in 26 Olympics. The USSR, the second-placed country with a much smaller population than the United States throughout its history, won 1,010 medals in just nine Olympics between 1952 and 1988. Great Britain is third with 780 medals and France is fourth with 671, but both countries had competed in all 27 Olympics. China is fourth with 473 medals but from just nine Olympics and is expected to rise rapidly with its huge population as it competes in more events in successive games. The German Democratic Republic (East Germany) achieved a remarkable record for a small country (less than 20 million) with 409 medals from just five Olympics.

Green and Oakley (2001) have noted that since the 1970s, and especially since the demise of communism at the end of the 1980s, many Western governments have adopted their own (usually weaker) versions of the communist elite sports system. Elite sporting success has become increasingly prominent in state sport policies in some countries. These include Australia, France and the UK (but not the United States) (see Green, 2004). Since UK National Lottery money became available from 1994, the UK has developed a network of elite coaching centres and has introduced World Class Performance Programmes (which contribute to talented athletes' training and travel costs). The administration changed in 1999 following the creation of a Scottish parliament and Welsh assembly. Particular sports in which international success appears most likely are targeted for state support. Based on performances at the 2012 London Olympics, Sport UK increased its funding for taekwondo, triathlon, hockey, judo and sailing. Funding for elite performers in other sports (basketball, synchronised swimming, water polo and weightlifting) was withdrawn completely. A side effect in the UK has been to accentuate the over-representation of privately educated athletes in Team GB (Smith et al., 2013). There is no evidence, despite repeated claims to the contrary, that elite sporting success boosts rates of sport participation throughout the wider population (see, for example, Bosscher et al., 2013).

Sport and international development

Ever since their invention in the 19th century, remarkable capabilities have been claimed for modern sports: developing the players' bodies and characters, and strengthening social bonds within schools, firms, neighbourhoods, towns and cities and national societies. In recent years, sport has added international development to its portfolio of claimed capabilities. Funding is partly from governments as an element in their aid budgets, and partly from international and national sports associations whose incomes have been enlarged by the forms of commercialisation that are discussed below. Donors' motives are clearly mixed. Governments can hope to attract goodwill from the recipients, and this is a form of aid which can be delivered directly to poor citizens. Sports associations can hope to widen the appeal of, and eventually to extend the 'markets' for, their products.

Exactly how sport may assist in the development of relatively poor countries has never been crystal clear, but the expectation is always that there will be wider economic and social spin-offs from the capabilities that sports can develop. One consistent finding from evaluative studies is that sport programmes have no difficulty in attracting and retaining participants. The programmes typically comprise coaching and matches arranged by former professional players. The sport most used in these programmes is football, which is inexpensive, can be enjoyed by players with just basic skills and has proved extraordinarily popular in all parts of the world. Assessments of sports' development effects range from the cautiously enthusiastic (see Levermore and Beacon, 2009) to the highly sceptical (see Schulenkorf and

Adair, 2014). Coalter (2013, 2014) is probably spot on in his review of the evidence which finds no generalisable development effects, and concludes that the real role of sport is to act as 'flypaper', attracting and retaining participants on programmes that also have educational and vocational training components. This is consistent with evidence from England which finds that sport is most effective in raising educational attainments among disadvantaged groups of young people when professional football clubs are used as the locations for after-school classes. Here the location is the 'flypaper' (Sharp et al., 1999, 2001).

SPECTATOR SPORT AS A COMMERCIAL BUSINESS

Game changers

There are different senses or degrees to which leisure businesses can be or become commercial. Financial turnover is not the sole arbiter. Tourism is commercial not just on account of the large share of global leisure spending that it commands, but more fundamentally because the consumer spending is income for profit-seeking businesses. Only a tiny slice of spectator sport has become commercial in this sense, but the size of the incomes of some (still a very small minority) of sport clubs and events has made these look attractive to some profit-seeking investors, and has obliged owners who are not profit seeking to become more businesslike in their methods. It is in this way that the top layers of the top spectator sports have become part of the general commercialisation of leisure provision.

Public sector leisure providers and voluntary associations all need money, and usually want more. This has always applied in spectator sports whether the competitors have been teams or individuals, and the incomes of top players and teams have risen steeply in recent years. This is partly due to the wider national societies, and increasingly the global society that these sports can now address, becoming wealthier. Top professional football clubs in Europe have been converting their grounds into all-seated stadiums or increasing the proportions of the crowds that are seated, and have raised ticket prices. They have introduced executive boxes and various hospitality packages aimed at business proprietors and wealthy individual supporters. Crowds have become older. Many younger and lower-income fans feel that they have been priced out. This would have happened if the only changes had been demographic – older, generally wealthier and simultaneously more unequal societies in terms of income distribution.

However, the top clubs in Europe's and North America's top sports have also benefited financially from the rising value of the rights to broadcast live their events. This change has its origins in the media industries (see Kennedy and Hills, 2009). Multi-channel television combined with satellite communication have made the potential audiences global (see Giulianotti and Robertson, 2009), and the willingness of fans to pay subscriptions for access to channels that broadcast live top sport has led to large new flows of income to top clubs in top sports in terms of spectator appeal. Sport offers compelling and rapidly perishable spectacles: fans feel that, if possible, they simply must watch the live events (Hutchins and Rowe, 2012). The key point to note, however, is that most of this income goes to a limited number of top performers and clubs. In 2014, the global value of the rights to televise sport events was $27.82 billion, up 14 per cent on the 2013 figure, and this rate of increase is expected to continue. Out of the total, 46 per cent was spent on European football. Seventy-five per cent of the total went to just ten top leagues – the top football leagues in England, France, Germany, Italy and Spain, the European Champions League, and the top US leagues in ice hockey, baseball, basketball and American football. In Europe, the flow of money into the top football leagues is skewed in favour of the top clubs (see Box 6.4). These clubs are able to scour the world to attract top players because they can offer the top salaries. Regular exposure on global television

---

Box 6.4 England's Premier League

England's top division in the Football League (formed in 1888) broke away and became the Premier League in 1992. The motivation of the top clubs was to retain full control and use of the funds that they could raise from the sale of rights to televise their fixtures and sponsorship. The top clubs claimed that this was necessary if they were to match the resources available to top clubs in other European countries.

The Premier League acts collectively in selling broadcasting rights. Its first sale in 1992 earned £304 million over five years. The 2013–16 deal was worth £2.7 billion. Premier League matches are now broadcast in 212 territories to 643 million homes. The potential TV audience is estimated at 4.7 billion. Already the Premier League is the world's most watched football competition. The value of broadcasting rights is expected to continue to rise as the actual audience rises towards its potential figure. This is anticipated as national television channels throughout the world market the product energetically to more viewers who are able and willing to pay subscriptions.

This is the scenario which makes Premier League clubs attractive to speculative investors.

expands additional income streams – the value of advertising around pitch perimeters and on players' shirts, and opportunities to sell club merchandise to a global fan base. Clubs within countries, and different countries' leagues, compete for shares in this global market (Millward, 2011).

The sheer scale of their income streams has not made European football clubs attractive investments for major financial institutions. Huge incomes do not guarantee profits. Many top clubs lose money and have no profits to distribute. Competition to stay at or to rise to the top obliges clubs to spend the greater part, and sometimes in excess, of their total incomes on player salaries. Investors may hope for capital gains (Millward, 2013). As long as clubs' revenues increase, the capital value of the clubs may (but will not necessarily) continue to grow. However, club ownership remains 'traditional' in that it is not investment banks and investment funds but mainly seriously rich individuals who are willing to risk their own, or preferably someone else's, money by investing in a club that they hope will remain at or rise to the top.

Traditional ownership and management

The people who pioneered Britain's (and the world's) main sports did not expect to make money. This applied even in football, where, very early on in Britain, the private company became the normal base for professional clubs. Other team sports with professional players and which attract large crowds have always (in most cases) operated as members' clubs. This has applied in UK county cricket and rugby union. In football, maybe on account of the game's mainly working-class support, the private company was considered more suitable for raising the capital necessary to build stadiums and to accept responsibility for employing players and paying their wages. In many European countries, which include Spain and Germany, clubs are still owned mainly by their fans, which does not deter wealthy individuals from investing in (and gaining effective day-to-day control of) the clubs. British football (but not most other British sports) has been different in that most professional football clubs have always had private shareholders (but many of the share owners in the early years were just ordinary supporters). Needless to say, the ordinary fans never held controlling interests. There was usually just one or a group of major share owners, though even they were usually fans rather than merely money men. Until 1981, the rules of the Football Association limited dividend payments to 5 per cent of the shares' nominal value. Directors and other major (and minor) shareholders did not expect to

---

Box 6.5 Manchester United

This club was formed as Newton Heath LYR Football Club in 1878. The name was changed to Manchester United in 1902, and the club moved to its present ground at Old Trafford in 1910. The club was originally funded by the Lancashire and Yorkshire Railway Company, and became an independent limited company in 1892 when £1 shares were sold to supporters. In 1902, four local businessmen saved the club from bankruptcy with an investment of £500. In 1931, the club was saved from bankruptcy again when James W. Gibson gained control with an investment of £2,000.

In 1964, another local businessman, Lois Edwards, acquired 54 per cent of the shares and gained control of the club with a total investment of £40,000. In 1989, there was an aborted sale which valued the club at £20 million. In 1998, another aborted takeover bid (by Sky Television) valued the club at £623 million.

In 2005, Malcolm Glazer, an American sports entrepreneur, gained control in a deal which valued Manchester United at £800 million. Financial institutions declared that this was a gross over-valuation but it is Glazer who has been proved right. In 2013, the sale of some shares on the New York Stock Exchange valued the club at £2.3 billion.

---

make money. At best, they hoped not to lose, and they rarely did lose, their investments. The main reward for a substantial investment was a status position and an attractive hobby – access to directors' boxes and lounges, and the opportunity to play fantasy football, usually (and advisedly) alongside a team manager (see Carter, 2006). At that time, the money value of football clubs was modest by present-day standards. In the 1980s, Manchester United could still be bought for £20 million. Its value has subsequently reached £2.3 billion (see Box 6.5). Huge capital gains have been possible. That said, most professional football clubs have still not become tempting investments. In 2001, Chesterfield (which had huge debts) could be bought for less than £10,000.

New owners

The English Premier League, nominally still operating under the auspices of the Football Association, is the only major European football league that allows its clubs to be bought by almost anyone, from any country, and most of the clubs are now owned by foreigners (see Box 6.6). These are seriously rich individuals, products of the present era of global neoliberal capitalism. The clubs that they own can be described as fully commercial. However, the new owners share much in common with the local

---

Box 6.6 Breakaway clubs

There have been two instances in Britain where fans, disgruntled at being dispossessed of their clubs by foreign owners, have formed breakaway clubs.

FC United of Manchester was formed in 2005 by Manchester United fans who were opposed to the Glazer takeover (see Box 6.5). Immediately, the new club received pledges of support from 4,000 people and had £100,000 in the bank.

Up to 2015, FC United played its home fixtures at Gigg Lane, the ground which it shared with Bury AFC, and then moved into its own newly built stadium within Manchester.

During FC United's first season, it achieved what is still its record attendance of 6,032. Attendances have subsequently levelled at around 2,000 per game. The club achieved rapid promotions to the tier of English football just one level beneath the Football League, which is where it has remained.

The new club's underlying problem is that many of its supporters remain Manchester United fans.

AFC Wimbledon has been more successful. This new club was formed in 2002 when the foreign owners of Wimbledon FC were allowed by the Football Association to relocate the club to Milton Keynes and to rename it as the Milton Keynes (MK) Dons.

AFC Wimbledon shares a ground with Kingstonian in Kingston upon Thames but has plans to move to a newly built stadium within Wimbledon.

The new club's first friendly fixture drew a crowd of 4,657. In 2009, this was surpassed by a crowd of 4,722. However, the new club's record attendance was set in 2011, when a crowd of 18,195 saw AFC Wimbledon triumph in a play-off at the City of Manchester Stadium that gave them promotion to the Football League.

The new Wimbledon side has the advantage over FC United that its supporters had their relationship with the original Wimbledon severed by the team's renaming and relocation.

---

businessmen who became major investors in football clubs in the 19th and 20th centuries. The seriously rich will rarely invest more than they can afford to lose. They gain an exciting leisure activity, and the individuals or the brands that they represent gain global exposure (Millward, 2013). There is the prospect of substantial capital gains, but also the risk of substantial losses. Club owners can offload some of these risks onto the clubs themselves. They can make part of their investments into loans to the club, or they can borrow on financial markets to finance their purchase, and then load the debt onto the club, which is a separate legal entity, maybe using the club's ground or the value of future ticket sales as security. In these circumstances, if a club's income and capital value fall dramatically as a result of relegation from a top league or loss of a top spot in the league, the owner will be a loser and the club itself will be bankrupt. Fans will feel unfairly dispossessed. Critics argue that 'the people's game' is being stolen (Morrow, 2003). However, most fans appear content with their new owners as long as the team is winning.

English football clubs whose owners are not profit seeking need to spend on the same scale as competitors if they are to hold on or rise to top positions in the top leagues. In other words, they must act as if they were profit-seeking businesses. Hence the commercialisation of entire top levels of the top sports. Fans who feel dispossessed may exit, though many are too attached to their clubs to countenance this, and a point to bear in mind is that the commercialised end of sport can succeed only if clubs retain or gain the fans who will pay for tickets and pack the grounds, purchase club merchandise and pay subscriptions to the TV channels that enable them to follow their clubs on television. Fans who pack grounds are needed to create the atmosphere that makes the televised events exciting, but the fans must do this in ways that are inoffensive to viewers. Hence the tougher regulation of fan behaviour: for example, no chants that viewers may find offensive. This changes customary behaviour at football matches, which were formerly occasions when fans were at liberty to be offensive towards match officials and opposing players (see Waiton, 2012).

As noted above, most top Continental European sides are not businesses of the English Premier League type. They are still run in something akin to the traditional British way: to boost the profile and prestige of private owners, nowadays local multi-billionaires or multinational businesses rather than local shopkeepers. Most big European sides, despite their massive turnovers, are still not expected to be sources of income or capital gains for their owners.

It is unlikely that even the top levels of the top spectator sports will ever become fully commercial. Sports were not designed to be run for profit. Outcomes of matches, league and cup competitions are too uncertain. This applies even in the United States, where the major leagues are 'closed', thus eliminating the risk of relegation; where owners are able to relocate their 'franchises' to cities which offer superior stadiums or larger potential crowds; where player recruitment and transfers are regulated to ensure that leagues remain competitive; and where payments to players are capped, thereby preventing too much income leaking into players' bank accounts. Even under these conditions, club ownership remains a plaything of the seriously wealthy rather than attractive to serious investors.

Supporters' trusts

These are democratic associations of supporters and have been formed partly as a reaction to commercialisation, but mainly to help prevent smaller clubs going out of existence. The movement began in England with the formation of the Northampton Town Supporters' Trust in 1992. Today, there are over 140 football supporters' trusts in England. They attempt to exercise influence by purchasing shares in their clubs, and have outright or majority control at some Football League clubs (AFC Wimbledon, Exeter City, Wycombe Wanderers and Portsmouth) and at a larger number of non-league clubs.

The plight of small clubs is partly a result of the success of the major football teams. Fans have higher disposable incomes than in the past, more have motor cars and more have been attracted to the big clubs at the expense of smaller, more local sides. There is the additional attraction of being able to follow a big club on television as well as by attending matches in person, regularly or just occasionally.

In 2007, the supporters' trust movement became international with the formation of Supporters Direct Europe (2012). There are now trusts in 20 European countries. In England, the largest trust is the Manchester United Supporters' Trust, which has 163,000 members. However, there is no chance of rank-and-file supporters taking control of Manchester United or any other major European football club. The situation has not changed since the early days of professional football, when the shareholders with a controlling interest were typically local businessmen. Nowadays, it needs someone from the global seriously rich to pay the price to control a major club.

Commercialisation's tendency to suck resources upwards into major clubs and leagues is illustrated most starkly by the contrast between the wealth of England's major clubs and grass-roots football. England has Europe's wealthiest football league in terms of total income, and some of Europe's wealthiest clubs. Meanwhile, grass-roots amateur football is in a parlous state. Pitches are in poor condition. Local authorities are raising charges for the use of these pitches. The number of grass-roots players fell by 100,000 between 2012 and 2014 (Hunter, 2014). There is a Football Foundation which is funded by the FA, the Premier League and the government. Up to 2014, each was investing £12 million annually in grass-roots football. The Premier League's contribution would not have paid a season's wages of just one of its top-paid stars. Leading clubs argue that they need to retain and spend all that they earn in order to keep abreast of competitors.

The winners: top players

Top players are clear winners in sports which draw large live spectator crowds and even larger global television audiences. Some footballers in England's Premier League earn £1 million per month, which is roughly equivalent to the lifetime earnings of a typical worker. Their rewards are in the same league as those of other top international entertainers. Clubs need to pay these salaries in order to attract the world-class talent which enables them to compete at the top of Europe's top leagues. These players can retire from the sport having become seriously wealthy. However, beneath the very top, typical earnings decline rapidly. Players in the lower divisions of the Football League are still well-paid workers during short careers in the sport (see Roderick, 2006).

In individual sports such as tennis, the individual players are the most likely commercial entrepreneurs. Top players need to form themselves into pools or circuits whose members compete wherever they can raise, then share out, the most money from live audiences, the media and sponsors. Circuits need to be open to new talent, otherwise competitor circuits are likely to be formed, which may in fact turn out to be best for all concerned because then there can be lucrative champion-of-champions (major, grand slam, unification) contests. Golf, tennis and snooker are run in this way. Boxing contests are arranged *ad hoc*. In Formula One motor racing, the car constructors are the key entrepreneurs.

Top players, and only the top players, can reap spectacular rewards, but, first of all, this is only in a few sports. Most sports cannot command sufficiently large live and media audiences day to day and week to week. Swimming, archery, pole-vaulting, rowing and bowling are commercial basket cases. Second, and related to this, it is advantageous if the competitors in individual sports can compete almost every day, throughout most of the year. This is possible in tennis and golf, but simply impossible for boxers and marathon runners. Third, audiences need to be 'educated' to support the sports rather than particular players or groups of players. Large daily media audiences have to be attracted by the sports themselves rather than just by particular stars (whose form and appeal can nosedive rapidly). Fourth, even in the sports where high rewards are possible, the pools of well-paid professionals are usually tiny: a few hundred golfers, a few dozen tennis players and motor racing drivers. In boxing, it is usually necessary to become a world champion, preferably at the heavyweight level, in order to make serious money. Fifth, the non-commercial layers are not wiped out in sports where the stars are spectacularly rewarded. They continue in their customary voluntary ways, usually with hierarchies of local, regional, national and international competitions.

Such is the appeal of careers in US professional sport that a third of white and as many as two-thirds of black 13–18-year-old males manage to convince themselves that they will be able to make livings from sport. The top US colleges benefit from this. They act as nurseries for future professional sports players and national amateur squads, and offer sports scholarships to talented (in sport) high school graduates. These colleges' sports players generate around a fifth of the top sports colleges' total incomes. US college sport attracts large live and TV audiences. The cost of the sports scholarships is covered many times over. The casualties are most of the scholarship winners. Very few leave their colleges with academic degrees, and very few become professional sports players. Out of the million or so who are the top high school and college American football players in any year, no more than 150 can expect to play professionally, and only 3 per cent of these can expect their professional careers to last longer than a year (Brooks-Buck and Anderson, 2001).

There is a comparable situation in the 'academies' that are run by the UK's top football clubs. Every year thousands of schoolboy players attend to display their skills. At age 16, handfuls per club are selected to become full-time trainees. Very few are retained beyond age 18. The top clubs fill their teams with experienced, often imported, players.

The winners: international sports associations

All major sports and sports events have benefited financially from television's thirst for top sport, and the willingness of TV companies and their viewers to pay. Until the 1980s, the Olympic Games was a loss leader. There was little competition to host the games. Cities could hope to benefit from the publicity and goodwill which, they hoped, would follow, but it was always difficult to quantify these benefits (see Gold and Gold, 2009). At the end of the 20th century, Montreal was still paying off debts incurred when mounting the 1976 Olympics. Los Angeles in 1984 changed everything. These Olympics were said to have made money (which they certainly did, for some people), largely, though not exclusively, from the sale of television rights. The rights to televise the Summer Olympics were worth about US$1.2 million in 1960, $50 million in 1976, but by the end of the century their value had soared to around $800 million. At the 2012 London Olympics, the broadcasting rights yielded $2.6 billion. Ever since 1984, there has been strong competition to host the Olympics, and likewise the major football tournaments – the World Cup and the UEFA European Championship.

Host cities, and the international federations that run these tournaments, are clear winners from the creation of global markets for televised top sport. The International Olympic Committee (IOC) was founded in 1894 to run the first of the modern Olympics, which were held in Athens in 1896. The IOC's headquarters are in Lausanne (Switzerland). Its main income is now from broadcasting rights and related sponsorship deals for the four-yearly Summer and Winter Olympics, but since 2010 and 2012 the IOC has also run youth summer and winter Olympics.

FIFA, the governing body for world football, was founded in 1904. It also has its headquarters in Switzerland (in Zurich). Its main tournament and source of revenue is the four-yearly World Cup, but there are also U-20 and U-17 world tournaments (all for men), plus a Women's World Cup and a women's U-17 event, a Beach Soccer World Cup, a Futsal World Cup and the FIFA Club World Cup.

The enlarged revenues of these associations enable them to occupy palatial headquarters and, although both are non-profit, they can pay their executives salaries comparable to those in major commercial companies. Executives travel the world in style and expect to be treated, and are in fact treated, as if they were heads of state.

It may seem paradoxical, but the main beneficiaries of the development of spectator sports towards commercial businesses have not been most club owners but some of their employees (the players), and some voluntary (non-profit) sports organisations that are responsible for selling and then distributing some of the proceeds from the sale of broadcasting rights. Media companies are further beneficiaries and feature in a later chapter.

COMMERCIALISATION AND PARTICIPANT SPORT

Nowadays Sport England likes to emphasise its contribution to the country's economy. It claims that sport is responsible for 1.9 per cent of all value added and 2.3 per cent of all employment. These figures include spending on watching as well as playing, television sports channel subscriptions, sports clothing and footwear and sports-related gambling. However, 65 per cent of the 440,000 jobs in sport are said to be due to people playing (Sport England, 2013). Yet participant sport is commercial no-go territory if the territory is sport, strictly defined. The problem is not just competition from state-subsidised facilities. There is a basic incompatibility. In commerce you play if you are willing to pay. In sport you play if you are good enough. Selection for a team, or position on a squash ladder, depends on sporting ability. Now it is true that, in many sports, competition has been formally or informally restricted to social equals, but thereafter sporting criteria have applied. This is no good for commerce. Money has to rule throughout.

However, sport becomes commercial when it is collapsed into physically active recreation. The alleged character forming virtues of team sports can be set aside. The goal of health-related fitness can be stressed alongside the need to tackle an obesity epidemic. Two-thirds of British adults are said to be overweight (body mass index of 25 or higher). Exercise can be commercialised. In the UK and throughout most parts of the world, there has been a boom in commercial health and fitness clubs, which began in the 1990s and has continued throughout the 21st century. In 2002 in the UK, commercial health and fitness clubs were opening at a rate of 100 per year. The industry was worth £600 million per annum in turnover and had 6 million adult members. Fifty multi-site operators were running around 2,500 'clubs', and there was an unknown number of single-site operators (Audit Commission, 2002). By 2010, the UK had 5,885 clubs with 7.4 million members, around 12 per cent of the adult population, and the industry had a turnover of £3.8 billion. By 2014, total membership exceeded 8 million, a 'penetration rate' of 13.2 per cent, and the market value of the industry was estimated at over £4 billion ('Leisure management', 2014, 2). Joining fees have ranged from £40 upwards and monthly subscriptions from £40 upwards. Clubs differ in the range and quality of the fitness equipment that they offer. You get what you pay for. Do you need the services of a personal trainer? It is doubtful whether the clubs' facilities and personal trainers offer more in terms of fitness and health than could be achieved in people's homes, on the streets and in parks, or in local authority sports centres. However, the commercial sector knows that it must keep its facilities smart and up to date. Public sector facilities are more variable in quality, and in most countries their funding has been squeezed year on year since 'the crash'.

The fitness club industry benefits from its membership system. There is a high rate of member turnover in commercial health and fitness clubs. Many join and soon become less regular or lapsed attenders. The clubs could not accommodate more than a fraction of the members if they all used the facilities to the maximum that they have paid for. Sassatelli (1999) offers a plausible explanation for the drop-off: 'the more participants in fitness measure themselves against each other and a fantasized body ideal the less will be their capacity to continue attending the gym regularly. The more the desired objectives are perceived as vital, the more participants will feel inadequate.'

Commerce has created markets for exercise all over the world, and in Britain spending on sport has continued to rise through the post-crash recession while participation in sport (broadly defined to include all forms of physically energetic recreation) has remained flat. Between 2010 and 2013, sport spending grew by 7 per cent overall. In particular segments of the sports business, the growth rate was steeper: 31 per cent on participation charges, 27 per cent on sports footwear, 21 per cent on club membership fees, 12 per cent on sports goods and 10 per cent on both sports clothing and sport-related gambling (Kokosalakis, 2014). Commerce has created a thriving fitness business in the world's richer countries (see Maguire, 2008) but the populations have not become fitter. EuropeActive (formerly the European Health and Fitness Association) represented over 46,000 facilities with over 46 million members in 2014 when it planned to boost membership by a further 25 million by 2025 (www.ehfa.eu.com). This industry now has a 20-year track record of rising membership and revenue figures alongside static levels of participation in physically active recreation and static (at best) fitness throughout the wider population.

It is impossible to fully commercialise competitive team or individual sports. However, both kinds of sports, but especially individual sports, will be promoted by commercial businesses if this will generate demand for suitable clothing, footwear and equipment. German triathletes spend an average of €2,745 per year on their sport (Wicker et al., 2013). Long-established 'lifestyle sports' such as tennis, golf, snooker and related cue sports, skiing, mountain climbing and angling have now been joined by surfing, scuba-diving, windsurfing, paragliding, parachute jumping and skydiving (see Land and Taylor, 2010). 'Extreme sports' can be extremely good business (see Rinehart and Syndor, 2003). Also, commercial businesses benefit from the indoorisation of what were formerly outdoor-only sports. In addition to five-a-side soccer, there are now indoor versions of cricket, rock climbing, bowling, surfing and skiing. These can be promoted as suitable for novices and as local, out-of-season practice for the more experienced (see Bottenburg and Salome, 2010). Socio-demographic trends are favourable. All these activities can be targeted at relatively affluent men and women who are beyond the peak age for participation in team sports. There are also limited commercial markets for sports that can be played by two-, three- and foursomes – squash, tennis and golf, for example – but even in these sports commerce cannot handle serious amateur competitions, and it has absolutely no purchase on large team sports.

The plain fact is that competitive participant sports and commerce are poor bedfellows. Some leisure activities are inherently non-commercial yet can be sustained in perpetuity because leisure provision has alternative 'engines'.

MANAGING SPORT

Managing sport today presents additional challenges to those that were there in the mid-20th century, and most of the changes have occurred or accelerated since the 1990s. There was a time when managers in sport just needed enthusiasm for the games plus administrative and interpersonal skills. To these, nowadays must be added the ability to address markets. 'Which markets?' depends on the sport and the level of the individuals, teams, clubs and leagues with and within which the managers compete. Another new challenge is that all sport managers today need to engage with the media. Again, exactly how depends on the sport, the level, the club, and so on, but without media awareness and presence, any present-day competitor is heading for the living dead.

Top sport has become part of the international entertainment industry, and managers of national sports leagues and other competitions need to sell their products in a global media marketplace where they compete against other countries' leagues and additional competitions in the same sport, other sports and all other competitors in the global entertainment business. Managers (not team coaches) of professional clubs are more likely than in the past to have owners who are seeking capital gains or, at least, to avoid losses. They must compete in capital markets as well as in their sports. Amateur clubs and leagues compete not just in the market for players but also against other forms of physically active recreation that are owned or sponsored by profit-seeking businesses which may be gyms or manufacturers or merchandisers of specialist sports goods and clothing for (usually non-competitive) lifestyle sports. Everyone needs a presence on the World Wide Web, whether this is to sell tickets or simply to advertise a club's existence. Managers in central government departments that distribute funds for and to sport are likely to have targets set by politicians: participation rates to be achieved, international events to be attracted to the homeland and Olympic medals to be won. Managers at local and regional government levels are no longer simply distributing resources across public facilities. They are more likely to be awarding and organising competitive tendering for contracts, seeking best value, and the managers of the businesses that win the contracts and run facilities need to ensure that they deliver value that no competitor can match. Sport markets are segmented, but they enforce a similar business mentality and practices on all sport providers.

This is all very different from times past when managers of sport associations, leagues and other competitions simply had to enact the wishes of member clubs, when the management committees of amateur clubs had to maintain or hire facilities, keep finances in balance, recruit players and then set them on the field of play. It is still necessary, but it is no longer sufficient to love your sport and know your members. Managers need to play markets as well as their sports. They are all in the present-day business of leisure.

CONCLUSIONS

We have seen that most of the sports that were invented by enthusiasts in the 19th century have turned out to be wholly unsuitable for commercial exploitation. As societies have become more prosperous, more money has been spent on leisure activities, and some of this money has flowed into sport. Increased turnovers have pressured all providers to become more businesslike in their methods. In this sense, sport, like every other leisure industry, has become more commercial.

The ability to perform for global television audiences has greatly enlarged the incomes of top players in top clubs in the most popular spectator sports, but even super-rich clubs remain speculative, high-risk investments. Meanwhile, the majority of sports clubs, even those that employ professional players, can remain in business, and will remain in business, as long as some spectators are there to watch and volunteers will gift their time, and in some cases their money, for the good of their clubs, their teams, their sports.

Participant sport is at greater risk from commerce than spectator sports. This happens when sport is absorbed into physically active recreation which is practised for enjoyment and in the hope of looking and feeling fitter, and becoming healthier. These kinds of recreation can be commercialised in gyms, and by promoting sports that require, or where performance can be aided and status enhanced by, the purchase of expensive items of equipment, clothing and footwear. Socio-demographic trends towards older, more prosperous and also more unequal societies favour the promotion of individual exercise and non-competitive 'lifestyle sports' in preference to now-traditional competitive team and individual sports. Competitive amateur sport is threatened not just by the migration of players into gyms and non-competitive forms of physically active recreation and the possible exit of volunteers who run the teams, officiate matches and organise club competitions, but also by the reduction of budgets and the weakening of the public sector partners who have provided the facilities in which competitive amateur sports are played. These facilities are at risk of closure or degradation through lack of investment during what is likely to become a long-term squeeze on public sector leisure budgets, and the apparent need to spend the cash that is available on leisure projects that generate revenue from visitors, preferably overseas tourists, which leads to bidding for the high-profile, revenue-generating events that feature in the following chapter.

Chapter 7

Events

INTRODUCTION

Attractions such as the Disney parks, Ayers Rock and the Eiffel Tower (see Chapter 5) are enduring, permanent fixtures. Events are different; they are discontinuous. They may be recurrent or one-off but they are always out of the ordinary.

Events are not new, but all the indicators suggest that in the 21st century they have become more numerous (see Quinn, 2013) and that their economic role has risen in significance. The growth of the events business has outpaced official classifications and statistics. No one knows how many events are held, or the total numbers employed in events management. Debbie Sadd (2014) claims that in Britain the events industry employs as many as 550,000, but many of these jobs could alternatively be allocated to sport, the arts or hospitality. In market economies and liberal democracies there are no central registers, but there is unlikely to be any organisation, association, town, village, city or country that does not hold at least one annual event, which may have a long history. Both the event and its history will be known mainly to the participants. What is new is the additions to the events calendar, and the new role that has been attached to many older events – attracting visitors and their money. This is what makes the occasions part of the present-day events business. Its growth is indicated by the job recruitment agencies that are seeking event managers and staff, the spread of event management courses and specialist modules in higher education institutions, and the profusion of textbooks on the subject (e.g. Allen et al., 2011; Bowdin et al., 2011; Foley et al., 2012; Getz, 2007; Richards and Palmer, 2010).

Chris Rojek (2014) has observed (critically) a recent tendency for leisure studies and leisure management courses to be folded into events management.

If we exclude the media and informal socialising, most leisure activities can be treated as events – every sport fixture and every theatrical performance. These can all be treated as events that need to be publicised and marketed and have sponsors sought, a programme constructed, transport arrangements checked, and so on. Events management can be treated as the core skill required for employment in leisure. Not all events are leisure events. There are probably far more business meetings, conferences and exhibitions. However, leisure has the really big events – the sports mega-events – for which all the skills involved in events management need to be used. Events management courses tend to focus on these big events, but most cities and even countries can never hope to host a sports mega, and even for those that can it is smaller events that keep the business buoyant throughout the calendar, year in and year out.

In the past, leisure events were usually for the enjoyment of a local population – the church harvest festival, the local athletics championship, the school nativity play, the gardening club's annual display, the village summer carnival. Public authorities provided amenities for these events. Facilitating events has always been within the remit of public leisure authorities. This is still the case, but today drawing in visitors and tourists (and their money) has become a principal reason why many events are staged, and why leisure services departments are keen to host them. Throughout the world, ancient rites are being kept alive and in some cases have been brought back to life, as tourist attractions. Other things have changed. We saw in Chapter 6 that not very long ago the International Olympic Committee and other international sports bodies had to persuade cities and countries to host their events. Montreal lost money that it could not really afford in hosting the 1976 Summer Olympics (Whitson and Horne, 2006). Things are very different today. There is intense competition.

Events are now a major section of the business of cities' and regions' leisure (or economic development) departments. Events have risen up leisure policy agendas. This is because there are more and more events, though, as already admitted, no one knows exactly how many, and regions and cities have become increasingly keen to host events (the reasons for the increase are discussed below). Thus, 'events' have become vehicles for attracting leisure 'business' into a locality. People who attend any event inject money into the local economy in the form of registration fees, payments for accommodation, food and drink and anything else that they buy while in the area. Events are not separate from but boost inward tourism in excess of what would otherwise be its normal level. Sports and the arts (see next chapter) can be the basis for an event, and public leisure authorities are keen to develop events within their sport and arts portfolios. This is because events are good business, and a rapidly expanding business sector. During 2014, the British Council was publicising globally Torquay's Agatha Christie Festival, the Bognor Regis Birdman festival, Broadstairs' Charles Dickens festival and Newquay's Bellyboard festival, among many others.

A public authority may or may not be the actual host of an event, but it will be part of the public authority's business to assist any local sport, cultural or education organisation or business that is to host, or is bidding to host, an event. The leisure, tourism or economic development department is now most likely to contain an events bureau with dedicated staff (Getz, 2007; Whitford, 2009). If a local or regional authority is bidding on its own account, or on behalf of or assisting a local actual or potential event organiser, the public authority will normally have a package of assistance that it can offer. It will have a list of venues that are available for meetings, competitions and exhibitions of various sizes. It will have a list of local hotels and other accommodation, and prices for all the above. There will be a pre-prepared, standard description of the restaurants, entertainment and attractions that the location offers and which could be made available for use by an event – a castle or stately home, for example. There will be similar pre-prepared material on transport to and within the location. Nowadays, a public authority may outsource its event management role to a specialist company, which will also offer its services directly to other local event organisers.

Depending on the volume of spending that will be injected into the local economy, a public authority will offer inducements either in cash (to the event organisers) or in kind – use of civic buildings or a civic reception, for instance. The actual organisation of an event is likely to be contracted to a specialist firm of event organisers which will (if requested) design, plan and market the event, conduct a risk assessment, address legal compliance issues, handle bookings, registrations on-site and tickets for options within or outside the event itself, take care of catering during the event, ensure food safety, and provide staff for information points and otherwise to be available throughout to assist visitors. Attendance at any event, even a single sport fixture, can be boosted if it can be offered as part of a package including travel, accommodation and a ticket to the event itself, and then maybe tickets for other local entertainments and attractions. The importance of events accounts for the rise in popularity of this specialism within leisure studies and leisure management degree programmes. The aim of the public authority is always to maximise the inflow of visitors to and spending within its territory, while attending to the interests and sensitivities of local communities and the environment.

This is why, in this chapter, government leisure policies are again under scrutiny. What comes under scrutiny is the recent international trend towards governments treating leisure primarily as a business and subsidising, protecting or privileging what are basically commercial or voluntary sector ventures (the events) in the expectation that the countries, regions or cities will gain jobs and money. We saw in Chapter 4 that the underlying rationale is sound. Investing in leisure loss leaders is among the public sector's special capabilities. The justification is always that returns will exceed the value of efforts and investments, and that there will be generalised public benefits. The problem is that all countries, regions, cities and villages are competing for a finite volume of business. What applies to tourism in general also applies to events. The crunch questions are always twofold: whether the public investment will pay off, and whether the benefits will flow to all, most or just minority sections of the public (all or most of whom as taxpayers will contribute to the investment).

This chapter proceeds by defining events and categorising them according to their size and the types of activities on which they are based. The chapter then explains the growing importance of events as a result of the expansion of tourism, the globalisation of the media and the awareness of present-day governments of the economic significance of leisure. Finally, the chapter poses its crunch questions. Are events, especially mega-events, really good business for the hosts, and exactly who benefits?

TYPES OF EVENTS

Leisure events can be classified according to the kinds of activity on which they are based. Most can be classified as based on sport, the arts, other entertainments, heritage, or food and/or drink. Business and academic meetings, exhibitions and conferences are further branches of the events industry (see Kim et al., 2011; Rogers, 2003). Events can also be grouped according to their size (usually measured by the number of people who attend). In these terms, the biggest events are the sports megas. The Summer Olympics are the biggest of all the sports megas, and in recent decades each Olympics has been the biggest ever. These games involve all countries and all the sports that are played in most parts of the world. The games attract many thousands of competitors and officials, and far more spectators. Most individual sports have their own major events, and, of course, the biggest sports have the biggest majors. Football's World Cup is second only to the Olympics. World regional contests such as football's European Nations Cup also count as megas. These are not just matches but tournaments which last for a month. Athletics has its own world, European and other world regional championships. Other sports – cricket, rugby union, rugby league, swimming, martial arts, and so on – have equivalents. The bigger the sport is, the bigger the mega. In tennis, the equivalents are the grand slam tournaments and in golf the majors. These are the events that attract all the star players and the most spectators. Obviously, some megas are bigger than others. Where should we draw the line? In practice, the line is blurred. Did the World Student Games, hosted by Sheffield in 1991 (see Critcher, 1992), qualify as a true mega? Are the Commonwealth Games, hosted by Manchester in 2002 and by Glasgow in 2014, a real mega? Manchester won the Commonwealth Games having failed in two bids to become an Olympics host city. Most sports events do not aspire even to become majors, let alone megas. Most Scottish Highland games are still primarily local occasions, though nowadays they are also a part of Scotland's tourist industry (Brewster et al., 2009). Visitors can admire kilted pipers and dancers, caber tossers and hammer throwers. Nowadays, these events usually end with a games disco.

Arts megas are usually in the same place on each occasion – the Edinburgh Festival of the Arts and the Cannes Film Festival, for example. These events are attended by stars and huge crowds, and they generate immense publicity. The Edinburgh festival began in 1947, and ever since then it has been held during the second half of August. It was originally intended, and it is still intended, to be a celebration of the arts, to attract the very best artists in the world and to achieve the highest possible standards, thereby enriching the cultural life of Scotland, Britain and Europe. Since 1996, modern and popular music have been part of this large festival. There are performances of opera, ballet, postmodern dance, drama, classical music, and so on. There is a simultaneous fringe festival which nowadays offers far more performances and involves more artists than the festival proper. Needless to say, as well as being a celebration of the arts, nowadays this festival is a major highlight in Scotland's tourist calendar. Some arts events are partly trade fairs where deals are done: between film-makers and distributors, theatrical groups and television producers, programme-makers and broadcasters. The sports megas are always primarily contests; most 'trade', such as player transfers in football, is done elsewhere.

High culture has its big events, and so does pop music nowadays. The pop industry's biggest events are not mere concerts but festivals which last for several days. Attending a pop festival has become a *rite de passage* in the transition to adulthood. These events date from the 1960s and, over time, they have become more numerous and, in some cases, bigger and bigger. One of the longest-running UK pop festivals is held at Glastonbury (see Box 7.1). However, a UK festival that lives on in the memories of many who attended was held at Knebworth in 1975. Over 70,000 turned up (a huge figure at that time). There were ten-mile traffic queues. Young people travelled in battered cars and camper vans, some hitchhiked, others used public transport, and they came from all over Europe. They brought sleeping bags and tents, and enjoyed the open air, the beer, the joints, and, of course, the music, which was provided by Pink Floyd, Linda Lewis, Monty Python, Steve Miller, Captain Beefheart and the Magic Band and others.

Box 7.1 Glastonbury Festival

This began as a two-day event in 1970 when Marc Bolan, Keith Christmas and others entertained a crowd of 1,500, whose £1 admission fees entitled them to free milk from the farm as well as the entertainment. Admission was free at the 1971 festival when medieval music, poetry, dancing and theatre were added to the rock music, and 12,000 attended. There were no further Glastonburys until 1978, when 500 travellers converged on the site and an impromptu event was held. Then in 1979 a three-day event with Peter Gabriel, Steve Hillage and the Alex Harvey Band attracted 12,000, who paid £5 each.

The early Glastonburys were not really commercial affairs. The 'profits' went to charities: Campaign for Nuclear Disarmament (CND), Greenpeace, Oxfam and others. Also, throughout the 1970s and 1980s, the festivals were arranged despite opposition from the local council and MP.

By 1987, Elvis Costello, Robert Cray, New Order and Van Morrison were attracting 60,000 at £21 a head, and £130,000 was donated to charities.

The 1990 festival is best recalled for ending with confrontations between travellers and security staff, which led to 235 arrests and £50,000 worth of damage.

1997 was the 'Year of Mud': attendance was 90,000 and admission £75.

In 1999, for the first time, the crowd exceeded 100,000.

Tickets for the 2013 event went on sale on 7 October 2012, and all 135,000 tickets, priced at £205.00, sold out within one hour and 40 minutes.

The events are still raising money for charities: around £250,000 per occasion. But with a 'take' in excess of £10 million, the festival has clearly become at least partly commercial. Interestingly, local opposition has now died down.

Sources: www.glastonburyfestivals.co.uk
www.www.mystical-www.co.uk/glastonburyfestival/

However, the all-time biggest (and arguably most successful) pop festival, an inspiration for all that followed, was Woodstock 1969. This event actually took place in Bethel (New York State). It was a three-day event. Tickets were $18 but in practice admission was free because 450,000 turned up and overwhelmed the site organisation. Those who attended recall the mud and empty stomachs, but also the happy smiling people, the peacefulness, the unadulterated freedom and the great music which was provided, among others, by the Grateful Dead, Jefferson Airplane, Jimi Hendrix, the Who, and Janis Joplin. Woodstock was documented on film. There have been revivals, with mixed success (not a patch on the original according to those who were present in 1969), on the 25th and 30th anniversaries of the original Woodstock.

The Munich Oktoberfest (see Box 7.2) is probably the world's best-known drinking event, but there are many more of this type. All such events are simultaneously about tourism and something else – sport, an art form, beer or whatever. Most poetry, song, piano, wine, beer, garden and pop music occasions are aspirant rather than actual majors, or are still basically for local enjoyment, though what most have in common nowadays is that the events have begun to attract, or, at any rate, the organisers hope to attract,

---

Box 7.2 Oktoberfest

This festival began in 1810 in Munich as a celebration of the marriage of Crown Prince Ludwig. The occasion was enjoyed so hugely that it was decided to commemorate the wedding annually. The wedding celebrations were followed by horse races. In 1811, an agricultural fair was added. Entertainers and beer sellers first appeared in 1818.

In 1880, the festival was switched from October to September for the warmer weather. Nowadays, the 'Munich Beer Festival' lasts for 16 days and usually ends on the first Sunday in October.

Horse racing was removed from Oktoberfest in 1960. Nowadays, the beer is the star turn, and each festival is attended by around 6 million thirsty souls from all over the world. There are giant beer tents (*Festhallen*). Bavarian music rocks the air. There are dances, sideshows, roller coasters and other rides. Contests are held to see which waiter or waitress can carry the most full one-litre beer mugs (the record is 21).

Oktoberfest is no longer celebrated only in Munich. There are similar festivals in many other parts of Germany, and in other parts of the world. In the United States, the oldest and largest is the Milwaukee German Fest, first held in 1846, which now draws around 100,000 visitors annually.

Sources: www.bayernservice.de/E-BAYERNSERVICE/E-Oktoberfest.htm
www.beerfestivals.org/archive/bt/munich_strong_beer.htm

large crowds and publicity. Events are definitely part of the present-day tourist industry.

Chess, tiddlywinks and table soccer enthusiasts all hold conventions. These do not compare in scale with Edinburgh and Glastonbury, but the economies of most cities and holiday resorts (especially out of season) would stutter without a stream of such minor events plus business conferences (which usually mix work and leisure). When added together, the minors can be as important as individual megas, not least in creating a constant, year-round, events industry. Most cities and most countries cannot dream of hosting an Olympics, but ever since the 2022 FIFA World Cup was awarded to Qatar in 2010, it has been possible for every country, and therefore every major city in every country, to dream of hosting this event. However, FIFA World Cups and Olympic Games run only once every four years. Planning and bidding for a mega is a waste of time and money for most cities and regions. The minors are the staple stock in trade of the events industry, and they are probably the 'best buy'. They never require facilities to be built specifically for the event, then never fully used again. For most public leisure authorities, the best events policy is to think small. Mega-events get so much attention because their costs and benefits are controversial.

THE RISE OF THE EVENTS INDUSTRY

Mega-events have become the leisure industries' supernovas. The big megas grow ever bigger. There are more of them. Arts and sports organisations, cities and countries, are eager to host them. They all want megas and, indeed, any events. This enthusiasm for events is less than 40 years old. How has it come about?

The expansion of tourism

There are three interacting reasons. First, as explained in Chapter 5, tourism has become one of the world's biggest industries, and it has displayed an ability to grow and grow and grow. Catastrophes and recessions have created no more than stutters. More people are not just willing but eager to travel, and they have the time and money to make this possible. So there are more leisure travellers who can be pulled towards any special attraction be this a site of natural beauty, a theme park or an event. Tens of thousands of sports fans will travel internationally to watch a single match even if the event is being broadcast live on television. Nowadays, football's UEFA Champions

League final is a reliable sell-out. Supporters treat these occasions as mini-holidays. Tournaments rather than just matches can attract fans from scores of countries who will stay for up to a month. Cities, even countries, become packed with tourists. Football's world and European tournaments are no longer played in empty stadiums. Nowadays, tickets sell out well in advance of the events. Ticket allocation has become controversial. It seems that neither locals nor visitors can get enough. Many fans are prepared to travel without tickets simply to be there and to share the atmosphere.

Sport governing bodies are keen to promote megas because these generate revenue and publicity. So nowadays more sports than ever are organising world events. Specific sports are constantly inventing new international competitions. Football's initial Club World Championship was played in Brazil in 2000. Manchester United competed and was allowed to miss that year's FA Cup competition. FIFA, the organiser, hoped at the time that this event would be repeated regularly and that its profile and audience appeal would gradually increase. This event has become part of the annual calendar, but remains low profile. There is room only for a limited number of genuine megas. They compete against one another.

Countries and cities are as keen as sports and arts organisations to host megas and other events. The attraction is the same. Events mean money and publicity. There is always a boost to tourism. Sports events bring players, officials and spectators. They all spend money which flows into the local economy. The hosts may also hope for longer-term benefits. Host cities of megas are publicised worldwide (see Manzenreiter and Horne, 2004). These big events create opportunities for place imaging. If first-time visitors enjoy the experience, they may return. They may recommend a place to their friends. People who watch an event on television may decide that it is a place that they really must visit. Smaller events may be attracted to a place by the publicity associated with a major event. Hosting a mega is a way in which a place can gain a higher profile on the world map (see Roche, 1992, 2000; Street, 1993). Any event presents opportunities for place imaging and marketing to a wider, possibly international, audience (Gripsund et al., 2010). Cities and countries are prepared to invest millions of dollars in bidding for a big mega, and this bidding itself raises the profile of the relevant sports or arts organisations, as well as the bidders (see Sugden and Tomlinson, 1998). London spent £15 million in bidding for the 2012 Summer Olympics (Benneworth and Dauncey, 2010).

All this makes sense only in the context of a booming and maturing tourist industry. More and more people are travelling from and to virtually all countries. Experienced leisure travellers are seeking something 'different' – a variation on the standard sun, sea or mountains. So, as explained in Chapter 5, the tourist industry has been developing a series of specialised market segments – city tourism, activity holidays and sex tourism, for example. Sports and cultural tourism have become part of this menu. There are participant and spectator forms of sports tourism. Enthusiastic players take golf and tennis holidays. Amateur football, cricket and rugby teams arrange international (holiday) tours. In a similar way, fans will travel for a match, and in even greater numbers for a sports tournament. Cultural tourism exists independently of events. People will visit cities with histories and buildings from bygone ages. Florence, Paris and London have art galleries and museums that attract millions of visitors every year. As Chapter 8 will explain, heritage is business nowadays. So are the high-profile performing arts. People flock to Verona every summer to watch the opera. Festivals act as a boost to cultural tourism and operate as magnets, drawing in tourists who might otherwise have gone elsewhere or at a different time.

It is the ability and willingness of the public to travel that makes events viable and commercially attractive. The number of people (and the amount of money) that can be drawn in has made all kinds of events (garden festivals, cup finals and the rest) more commercial than in the past. This applies to Oktoberfests (see Box 7.2) and pop festivals. In the 1960s and 1970s, the cost (to fans) of pop festivals (which were then very infrequent) had to be kept low because few fans could afford to spend expensive weekends away from home. In any case, the ethos of these events (part of the attraction to the fans who went and an inspiration of some organisers) was countercultural (see Box 7.1). Pop and rock have roots in jazz (the music of oppressed black people). The early festivals were often explicitly pro-civil rights, against atomic weapons and against the war (in Vietnam). The counterculture was tolerant of drug use and pro-sexual liberation. Confrontations with authority were part of the pop festival experience. Event organisers had to appear (and often were) sympathetic. Organisation was typically ramshackle. Site perimeters were rarely secure. Free entry was possible. Everyone who attended was prepared to rough it. If the events were profitable (which they certainly were for some people, including most of the performers), appearances had to suggest otherwise. It is different today. Young fans as well as ageing hippies expect to pay and expect to be entertained in safety and in some degree of comfort.

Recurrent annual arts and pop festivals may not have the same pull as the Olympics but the former have the advantage of being annual, so their booster value to tourism is repeated again and again. Different kinds of events attract different types of tourists, and their profiles, and their typical behaviour while visiting, especially their consumer behaviour, can be as important as sheer numbers in determining their value to the hosts. Single sports matches like football games may be of limited economic benefit to local businesses. Fans may simply arrive for the match and quit the area soon afterwards (see Nash and Johnstone, 2001). Visitors are more valuable when they stay overnight and spend money in the local hotels, restaurants and shops. High-culture events are especially appealing (to potential hosts) because of the upmarket visitors who are attracted. These crowds usually behave themselves and spend vigorously. Pop festivals and sports megas bring greater risks. Some sports, notably football, bring supporters who may drink heavily and fight with rival fans (and the local police), leaving damage and ill will in their wake. British groups of young male spectator sport tourists appear to behave in much the same way as when on seaside holidays. They are likely to consume substantial quantities of alcohol and act out their everyday feelings towards foreigners. What is accepted (or tacitly tolerated) in Corfu easily becomes explosive in the context of a high-profile sports contest.

The media

The second engine which has inflated the importance of events, especially mega-events, has been the globalisation and commercialisation of television. Globalisation has been crucial. This enables events to be broadcast live to a global audience. All the world watches simultaneously. Since 2000, at least two-thirds of the global population has watched at least part of a Summer Olympics (Henry and Gratton, 2001). So all the main sports have now become global sports. Film and recorded music already had global markets. Sport has now joined them, and its principal players have the same kind of celebrity (and earnings) as film and pop stars. The commercialisation of broadcasting (see Chapter 8) has also been crucial. In Europe, one of the main world markets, event organisers are no longer faced by cartels of state broadcasters, all with capped budgets. There is intense competition for television rights, and the bidders include broadcasters who can raise money through channel subscriptions, pay per view and selling advertising space at premium rates when the audience is guaranteed to be large with high-spending groups, notably young males, well represented. Event organisers can raise substantial sums from the sale of television rights (see Chapter 6), and, once an event is being televised globally, additional income streams open. Businesses become keen to sponsor (to have their names associated with) the events, specific sports, teams and players. The event organisers and local hosts benefit from all the secondary publicity that sponsors and their advertising generate. Images of the location are broadcast all over the world. The events themselves are publicised, at no cost to the organisers, by the media that are seeking audiences. Additional spectators may thereby be attracted, and there are likely to be (very difficult to quantify) longer-term enduring benefits from all the publicity.

The big breakthroughs for the sports megas occurred during the 1980s. The 1984 Los Angeles Olympics was the first of these events to be declared a huge commercial success. Montreal, the 1976 Olympic host, incurred debts that were finally paid off only in 2006 (Whitson and Horne, 2006). Moscow in 1980 did not really try. Then the Americans demonstrated how. Most subsequent Summer Olympics – Seoul in 1988, Barcelona in 1992, Atlanta in 1996, Beijing in 2008 and London in 2012 – have been declared bonanzas by the organisers. In 2000, Sydney managed only to break even, and in 2004 Athens recorded a loss. The Winter Olympics continue to have a mixed record. Some make money for the hosts while others are run at a net loss. In football's World Cup, Italia '90 was the breakthrough. The 1986 event had been switched from Colombia to Mexico, because the original hosts were unable to provide the facilities that were required. Ever since then, there has been keen competition to host this mega. Would-be organisers have needed to spend millions of dollars on their bids. It used to be different. Previously it was necessary to persuade a country to go to the trouble and expense.

The role of governments

Governments have been the third event driver. City, regional and national governments, virtually all of them, all over the world, are now alert to the economic importance of leisure. Once upon a time, they set about developing their economies by investing, or attracting investment, in steel mills and shipyards. Now they want leisure businesses – dot-com retailers, media companies, shops, hotels and restaurants, even casinos. How are the shops, hotels, restaurants and entertainment businesses to be attracted? One way is to host a mega and/or a stream of minor events which will draw in the people who will fill the hotels, etc. Governments are key players. They alone have the ability to orchestrate all the other interest groups. Governments provide organisation, can speed up planning permissions and, if seeking mega-events, are invariably required to invest public funds. Bidding for megas has become one of the highest-profile roles of the politicians who head leisure services departments. Heads of state and governments lobby for their cities and countries. Since 9/11, American bidders have been seriously handicapped, which has created more space for other countries. President Obama travelled to Copenhagen in 2009 to lobby for his home city, Chicago, in its bid to host the 2016 Summer Olympics. There were four cities on the final shortlist – Madrid, Tokyo and Rio de Janeiro in addition to Chicago, which was the first city to be eliminated (Rio eventually won). Delegates told Obama that they doubted whether all their athletes and other visitors would be allowed into the United States, and that others feared being humiliated by border guards (see Becker, 2013).

There is now fierce competition to host big events. International awarding bodies can be selective and demanding. The public at leisure has become mobile. Every region's cities compete for shoppers and for the evenings-out market. So all cities want to image themselves as lively places which people will want to see, and where they will want to be seen. Countries are in a similar position. Tourism is the top activity in terms of consumer leisure spending, and present-day holidaymakers have a worldwide choice of destinations. At least, this applies to those who can afford to travel. Most of the world's people are not so fortunate, but it is the holidaymakers with the most money whom all countries are the keenest to attract.

A high-profile event will attract visitors to the event itself, and is likely to attract further events and visitors. This is the so-called legacy effect, which is always very difficult to predict and impossible to quantify afterwards (see below). Becoming a European Capital of Culture is a much-sought prize. Athens was the first to hold the title in 1985, since when it has proved so popular that from 2015 it is being awarded to two or three cities every year. Cities that have held the title all feel that it has assisted their economic development (Palmer/Rae Associates, 2004; Quinn, 2010). Glasgow, which held the title in 1990, is paraded as an outstanding example of how it helped to re-image the place from decaying industrial city to vibrant, thriving cultural and consumer centre (Garcia, 2005). Just bidding for the title, even if the bid fails, is seen as a valuable means of place imaging (Gotham, 2005). Local populations usually seem to welcome the attention and the enhancement of their place's identity (Derrett, 2003).

Voluntary sports and arts bodies find themselves in situations whose logic more or less compels them to act as if they were commercial enterprises. If cities, countries and media companies are competing to host and broadcast the events, what can the organisers do other than sell to the highest bidders? Governments are in a similar situation. If they want leisure business, then they need to compete. Failure to do so guarantees that the business and jobs will go elsewhere. Thus governments – national and local – are 'regulated' to act as leisure markets require. It appears that only the United States feels able to resist. In turn, the governments that win big events must regulate their societies so that the events can be accommodated. This means providing facilities, managing the environment and the local population and supplying the workforce so that the events, together with the people who are attracted, can be treated in the manner that all concerned have come to expect. Thus, the voluntary and public sectors become at least partly commercialised and, in turn, oblige their own dependents to act in commercial ways. When governments invest in facilities for business reasons, they expect the managers of the facilities that receive state support to operate in a similar businesslike way. Projects are judged on their business plans rather than the overall public benefits that only state provisions can deliver, especially difficult-to-quantify benefits such as strengthening citizenship, and setting moral and aesthetic standards (see Chapter 4). Public investment has to be channelled into high-profile facilities – sports stadiums such as Cardiff's Millennium, Glasgow's Hampden Park and the stadium in East London that was built for the 2012 Olympics. There are always opportunity costs. The money might otherwise have gone into facilities designed for local users.

DO MEGA EVENTS MAKE MONEY FOR THE HOSTS?

Nowadays, events make an important contribution to the economies of most cities, regions and countries. They boost local, regional and national economies because the mini- and mid-range events that comprise the bulk of the industry can use the same exhibition halls, meeting rooms, hotels and transport over and over again. Events keep holiday destinations busy out of season. Elsewhere, they spread the business year-round. Attracting and running a series of mini- and midi-events – several will be running simultaneously in most places – is the basic work of city events management. It is a competitive business. Places compete on facilities and price.

Mega-events are different. They are likely to require infrastructure that may never be fully used again. Until recently, the price was judged solely against the value of the place boosterism – celebrating achievements and raising the profile of the host city and country (see Roche 1992, 2000). This was Britain's aim when hosting the Great Exhibition in 1851, and the motivation of France in 1889 in hosting an exposition of the country's achievements. Post-apartheid South Africa shared its celebration with the rest of the world when hosting the 2010 FIFA World Cup. Qatar will spend over a decade under the international spotlight having been awarded the 2022 World Cup (it was awarded in 2010).

However, since the 1980s, hosts have also sought and anticipated economic benefits (see Carlsen and Andersson, 2011; Jago and Dwyer, 2006; Jago et al., 2010; Philips, 2004), hence the fierce competition to host mega-events. Emerging market economies now compete with richer cities and countries (Foley et al., 2012). This top rung of the events business has become an economic bubble. One day it will explode, but for 30 years countries have been spending huge amounts (over and under the 'counter') in bidding for big events. They prepare volume upon glossy volume, plus DVDs, describing the superb facilities that they already possess and which they promise to build. Members of the committees that award big events to cities and countries travel the world expecting to be treated, and being treated, like royalty used to be treated. They have outrageous demands accepted, like exemption from all taxes throughout the years preceding and during the event.

This era will not last for ever. Evidence of benefits is disputed. There is now always local opposition to the deflection of public spending to build the expensive facilities that big events require. The preparations for Brazil's FIFA World Cup in 2014 followed by the 2016 Olympic Games in Rio de Janeiro sparked sustained protests. Local populations contrasted the luxury that was being built with the squalor amid which they lived. Also, we have now seen that the international spotlight can draw attention to warts as well as glamour. The 2014 Sochi Winter Olympics reminded the world of Russia's hot/cold wars and terrorist threats from the North Caucasus, as well as the country's anti-gay laws. Since 2010, when its bid to host the 2022 FIFA World Cup was successful, Qatar has been fending criticism of its labour practices that result in endless fatalities among the low-paid immigrant workers from the Far East who have been building the football stadiums, and the workers' quasi-slave status while in Qatar. In any case, there is no guarantee that the world's football fans will flood into a country where alcohol is difficult (and usually illegal) to access, to swelter in stadiums during matches played at temperatures of 30 Celsius plus.

Academics are divided. The literature ranges from the upbeat – go for top events at all costs (e.g. Smith, 2010, 2012) – through the judiciously balanced (e.g. Horne and Manzenreiter, 2006) to indictments of handing sport and cultural festivals to commercial and political elites (e.g. Foley et al., 2012). Debate rages inconclusively because, as John Horne (2007) has explained, much that is known becomes deliberately unknown by those in favour of hosting an event. For example, there has never been a case where mass sport participation has risen as a result of a country hosting a sport mega. Such a legacy from the London 2012 Olympics was not impossible, but it was always highly unlikely (see Charlton, 2010). There are never data that allow event effects to be disentangled from the effects of other policies and changes in surrounding conditions that can affect rates of sport participation (see Veal et al., 2012). However, we know that the facts simply do not match claims that hosting mega-events boosts inward investment (Jakobsen et al., 2013). When this happens, it is an example of 'leveraging' (see Smith, 2010), which has a different meaning in the events business than in financial services, where it means borrowing in order to invest, or pledging future earnings to fund an investment. Public spending on an event can be justified partly in terms of its ability to 'leverage' spending by other parties that would otherwise not have occurred or gone elsewhere. This usually includes building hotels and transport networks as well as any legacy spending that occurs by making a city look attractive or simply bringing it to the attention of potential investors. Demonstrating such long-term legacy benefits is always difficult. It is easy to show, for example, that becoming a European Capital of Culture leads to an increase in the number of cultural events and visitors, as in Liverpool in 2008 (Garcia et al., 2010), but this ignores the opportunity costs (the benefits if the investment in cultural facilities and events had gone to other projects, or to a different place). An example of 'displacement' arose with the World Athletics Championships which boosted visitor numbers in Gothenburg, the host city, in 1995, while the visitor numbers entering the whole of Sweden during that year were depressed (Hultkrantz, 1998). As explained in Box 7.3, London 2012 was another example. The one 'law' of events to which, so far, there has been no exception is that bidders grossly underestimate the costs and exaggerate the probable benefits (see Zimbalist, 2015).

The mega-event that has been studied most intensely, and by most investigators, is the 2012 London Olympics (see Box 7.3), and here the law of underestimating actual costs proved valid. The initial estimate of public spending at the time of the bid in 2005 was £3.0 billion: the actual spend was £9.3 billion.

Box 7.3 The 2012 London Olympics

Whether hosting the 2012 Summer Olympics would be good business for Britain was always disputed, and will remain controversial for ever.

We know precisely how much the Games cost. It was £11.3 billion, of which £2.0 billion was recouped from local sponsors, ticket sales and the International Olympic Committee. The remaining £9.3 billion was paid by UK citizens, mainly directly by central government, but also via the National Lottery, Sport England and London council taxpayers.

Everything spent by the Olympic organisers was someone else's income, and the spending was nearly all within the UK. There was minimal leakage. The largest item of spending was construction – site preparation and then building the venues, and enhancing transport to the main Olympic park. Any 'profit' from the games could only be from additional spending that was induced (leveraged) – on transport, hotels and building houses and business premises close to or within the Olympic park. Accommodation for athletes in 'the village' cost £0.94 billion and should be more than recouped by selling the 3,850 'affordable' housing units into which the village has been converted. The sport venues themselves cannot be sold: there are no buyers.

Profit to the UK is from spending in Britain by visitors. These include the 16,000 athletes, 8,000 officials, 21,000 media staff and 1.2 million spectators from overseas. Tourism did not derive any immediate benefit from the games. Rather, it is estimated that visitor numbers in London during summer 2012 were 30 per cent down on the 2011 figure. Tourists who would otherwise have visited London avoided the anticipated congestion and inflated prices (which never materialised). This loss of normal visitors more than cancelled the economic boost from visitors who came to London for the games. Any profit to the UK will be from any legacy.

Oxford Economics (2012) estimates that between 2005 (when London won the games) and 2017, an additional £16.5 billion will be spent in Britain as a result of London hosting the event. However, 30 per cent of this total is estimated legacy spending on construction (housing and business premises close to or within the Olympic park, and transport). Tourism is expected (by Oxford Economics) to be a long-term beneficiary. An additional 10.8 million visits to Britain are anticipated between 2005 and 2017.

The problem with estimates is that they are really best guesses. It will never be possible to isolate an Olympic effect from other local and global trends and incidents such as wars and natural disasters.

Also, the costs (£11.3 billion) do not include the cost of bidding for the 2012 games, or the costs of unsuccessful bids for previous Olympics.

There is simply no way of knowing whether the £9.3 billion spent by public authorities would have delivered better value if it had been spent on other projects. The benefits would most likely have been better spread throughout the UK. Most of any benefits from the 2012 Olympics stayed in London.

In any case, whatever London won, Paris and other unsuccessful bidders for the 2012 event lost. Events will boost the global economy only if labour productivity is higher than would have been achieved if the investment had gone elsewhere, which is unlikely because events themselves, tourism and construction are all labour-intensive.

Whether an event yields a profit for the host city, region or country is not just a matter of academic interest. Part of the justification for public spending on events today is that there will be general public benefits, which need not be confined to but will include economic benefits. Most events are profitable for the host location. This is because they can use existing infrastructure – exhibition halls, meeting rooms, hotels and transport. Spending by visitors on registration, admissions, hotels, subsistence and entertainment filters throughout a local economy. Britain and other large, relatively rich countries can host most mega-events without any new building. So there will be economic benefits for Britain from the 2014 Commonwealth Games in Glasgow, the 2015 Rugby Union World Cup and the 2017 World Athletics Championships, which will use the stadium that was built for the 2012 Olympics. After 2017, the stadium will be redeveloped as a football arena. Glasgow may have derived more short-term economic benefits from hosting the 2014 Commonwealth Games than accrued to London during the 2012 Summer Olympics. This is because most events in Glasgow could use existing sport facilities, and visitor numbers to the city rose considerably, enabling hotels to raise normal prices by 50 per cent.

Events that require new infrastructure do not necessarily result in a net loss to the public accounts. Oxford Economics (2012) estimates that the 2012 London Olympics will prove a long-term winner for Britain in purely economic terms. Investing large sums of public money in infrastructure for big events is controversial because the costs are spread widely – throughout the entire UK taxpaying population in the case of the £9.3 billion that was spent on the 2012 Olympics, which breaks down to around £250 per adult. Taxpayers may or may not feel that they received good value for what was spent on their behalf. The spending is controversial because big events create big winners. Everyone may win, but not to equal extents. Today, bid winners who bring big events to their cities and countries, especially events which involve substantial capital outlays by the hosts, can expect to encounter organised local opposition (see Hayes and Karamichas, 2011; Lenskyj, 2008).

■ When a major event requires new building, the biggest winners are construction companies. However, there will be general public benefits because building contracts can be won by local firms, and whoever is contracted to build will employ mainly local labour, and their wages will filter as spending throughout the economy. It is estimated that the 2012

London Olympics created 130,000 jobs in addition to the 70,000 unpaid volunteers.

- Hotels and international and domestic transport businesses will normally benefit from a big event. London 2012 was an exception because the normal (huge) inflow of tourists was depressed.
- Local media organisations benefit. Local journalists cover and file reports on all events, and these reports are available to media throughout the world. The BBC broadcast live every event during the 2012 Olympics. Other national broadcasters could purchase content and use their own commentators. All international purchasers of content concentrate on events where their own athletes are performing, especially if they are winning. So every country sees a different, mediated Olympics.
- The (usually) sport associations that host big events receive huge publicity. Their star performers become celebrities whose images have a market value.
- The host's politicians are able to raise their profiles within their own countries and beyond simply by appearing at a major event.

These big winners, especially the media and politicians, ensure that there will always be vocal, high-profile support for bids to host big events. These are the voices with vested interests in underestimating likely costs while exaggerating likely benefits.

Public investment in events does not have to be justified solely in financial terms. Only the public sector will fund loss leaders such as sport venues that will never be fully used again and which cannot be sold. Events activate this, and all the other public sector's unique capabilities in leisure.

- State support indicates that the types of leisure are considered worthwhile, desirable, to be encouraged.
- High-profile events can boost national and local pride, prestige and identity.
- Citizenship can be strengthened if an entire population can feel part of a carnival experience either by attendance or by mediated involvement.

The other clear winners from big events are the awarding bodies, especially FIFA, which awards the football World Cup to countries, and the International Olympic Committee. These non-profit bodies sell global sponsorship (worth approximately £0.7 billion at the 2012 Summer Olympics) and broadcasting rights (worth approximately £2.6 billion). Just £0.7 billion was handed to London towards the cost of hosting the games. The sums retained by these awarding bodies enable them to maintain luxury-class headquarters and to pay top executive salaries commensurate with commercial sector peers.

All the richer and larger European countries, or groups of smaller European countries, could host a football World Cup without building any new stadiums. Yet recent football World Cups have been awarded to South Africa, Brazil, Russia and Qatar, all of which have needed to build stadiums which will rarely, if ever, be fully used again. FIFA claims that it is spreading its sport globally, but, as explained above, there is no history of hosting a major event boosting mass participation in the host country. Football's appeal is spread by the media and by the intrinsic attractions which have made soccer 'the people's game' ever since its invention in the 19th century. The threat to 'the bubble' is local populations' tolerance of spending their money on facilities which stand underused as a visible legacy throughout the following decades.

Summer Olympics always involve a great deal of new building; venues that can accommodate unusually large crowds of spectators at all the Olympic sports. It would be possible, technically, to revert to the 1948 austerity model and to use only existing facilities, but this is unlikely to happen while the International Olympic Committee is able to demand, and countries are willing to host and build. This bubble will pop only if and when governments find that more domestic support is lost by the vacated ghost sport venues than is won by hosting the games. All trends end: only 'when' is unknown. All sports now have their own world championships. These usually manage to use existing venues. Do the Olympics still have a purpose? Yes, certainly for the construction firms, sports associations and top athletes as well as local media, hotels and transport businesses. The volume of applications to volunteer is an indicator of widespread endorsement. The event's current high-spend model is secure at present. Indeed, the number of sport events that require new building continues to expand, as does the number of countries and cities that are willing to build and host. Azerbaijan built a network of Olympic-grade sport facilities in support of its bids to host the 2016 and then the 2020 Summer Olympics. Both bids were unsuccessful. However, Azerbaijan was awarded the first (2015) European Games, a new mega-event, a regional Olympics. This choice of country was peculiar because, in most people's geography, Azerbaijan is not a European country. However, Europe's sports associations have an interest in maximising participation in their events.

CONCLUSIONS

Events have not been just swept along and they have certainly not been swept away: rather, they have risen on the tide of commercialisation that has swept through all the leisure industries. The economic benefits sought (and usually realised) have skewed public leisure spending towards attracting and hosting events, and leisure courses in universities have been skewed towards events management.

All hosts use ICTs to publicise their events, to handle bookings and, if possible, to report from and on, and to broadcast, the event, ideally throughout the world. A happy surprise for all the leisure industries that host events is that the ability to experience a place or event via the media has not diminished the appeal of being there. There are more business meetings and conferences, and academic meetings and conferences despite the increasing range of tele-alternatives. More people than ever seek tickets for sport mega-events despite the entire programmes being broadcast live, worldwide on television. Enthusiastic crowds increase the appeal of the media spectacle, and people are willing to pay to become part of the live crowds that add value to the media rights. It seems to be too good to be true, but in this case it is true.

At first glance, claims that big events that involve building suitable venues are profitable to the hosts look absurd. The 2012 London Olympics cost £11.3 billion to stage. Just £0.6 billion was recouped in ticket sales, £0.7 billion was given to London by the International Olympic Committee from the sale of television broadcast rights and £1.3 billion in local and global sponsorship deals, a total of £2.6 billion. So there appears to have been a net loss of £8.7 billion. Where is the profit? This is estimated by treating spending on construction as income for local businesses and workers in the host territory. Then there are estimates of additional construction that is induced, and a legacy of increased tourism.

Is this voodoo economics, produced by or on behalf of the big winners? It would be possible to obtain the same benefits by constructing homes and business sites in parkland with mega-venues replaced by community sport and cultural amenities, but in all cases there is a danger that business is simply pulled from adjacent areas. Economic regeneration led by public investment is difficult to achieve. Private enterprises will respond to low-risk opportunities to develop new businesses. However, big events' legacy boost to tourism appears genuine. It follows all events, and the higher the profile of the event, the more powerful the boost. Tourism is a global growth industry, and a publicised event shifts the trend up a notch in the host location. Cultural events are as valuable as sport megas. Countries now welcome the opportunity to host the Eurovision Song Contest. Other cultural events may have a lower profile, but they can be repeated annually, using the same facilities, creating repeated boosts to tourist inflows. Tourism is now among the world's biggest industries. It is among the few steadily growing industries, and most events really are good business for the hosts because they enlarge the host location's share of this buoyant market.

Chapter 8

Culture: Heritage, the Arts and Mass Media

INTRODUCTION

Cultural leisure industries are those where the meaning and value of the product or service are primarily symbolic. Everything – including tourism, sport and events – has a cultural dimension, but this dimension is especially prominent, indeed dominant, in the leisure industries that are considered in this chapter. The heritage, arts and mass media are dealt with together also on account of their overlaps and mutual effects. The arts in this chapter are all live performances to an audience. Exhibitions in galleries can be treated as presentations of works of art, and simultaneously, along with exhibits in museums, as part of a heritage which can be defined as objects which tell a story about the past.

The various arts (live performances and gallery exhibitions) have been delivered at different times by commercial, voluntary and public sector organisations. Heritage is sometimes commercial, but it is usually protected and presented by a combination of public and voluntary sector actors. The original mass media – newspapers, radio, recorded music, movies and subsequently television – have always been either commercial or public service. From their inception, newspapers, movies and recorded music were overwhelmingly commercial, whereas in Europe radio and then television broadcasting were originally developed as public services. The rise of the original mass media virtually wiped out segments of the performing arts. Television forced all other mass media to accommodate. We shall see in Chapter 9 that all the old media are now obliged to coexist with newer media, and that they are doing this successfully and are re-emerging as re-mediated major leisure industries.

Sport and events, the leisure industries featured in the two preceding chapters, have always enjoyed mutually beneficial relationships with the mass media. The media have reported on, and thereby helped to publicise, sports and other events, and this content has helped to sell newspapers and attract radio and television audiences. In the current, global, digital media age, these interdependences are being deepened and strengthened, and are pivotal in the assimilation of formerly separate leisure services and industries into a seamless web of business.

Neither the arts nor the heritage industry are challenged by the new ICT-based media. However, all the arts, heritage and broadcasting have been affected by the wave of commercialisation that has been sweeping through the leisure industries since the 1980s. Heritage has been the resilient and is currently the buoyant survivor among the cultural leisure industries, and is benefiting immensely from the long-term growth of domestic and international tourism.

HERITAGE

Nowadays, those in charge of a country's or a city's heritage like to think of themselves, and to be regarded, as running an industry. The heritage is the natural environment and anything man-made from the past which is valued for telling people something about their history. Landscapes, gardens and battlefields; objects which are stored in museums and art galleries; buildings such as castles, palaces and stately homes; and industrial mills also can be heritage objects. Wigan Pier (built to load coal onto canal boats) is now part of England's heritage industry. Heritage is always created, by being defined as heritage, in the present.

At one time it was mainly local people and historians who were interested in relics from a locality's past. Children were taken to local museums as part of their education (and they still are). Nowadays, however, all the world's main heritage sites draw most of their visitors from further afield. They have discovered that some, though not all, tourists are keen to learn about the past as well as the present of the places that they visit. Site owners have welcomed the revenue. Tourist authorities have recognised that heritage sites can be powerful, arguably their most powerful, tourist magnets. Presentation has improved: tourism is a competitive business. Working models, animated displays and multilingual descriptions have become standard in museums.

The heritage industry has made it possible for visitors to do more than just imagine, and to actually experience something akin to life as it used to be. In York (UK), visitors can meander (on a miniature railway) around a Viking village. In Scotland, they can experience life in a Highland croft. In Salford, they can walk down a traditional terrace street and gaze into the local shops. They can do this in Salford's museum or down the road on the television set of *Coronation Street*. Tourism has made it possible for us to experience an evening in a Gypsy camp, or a rail journey across rickety wooden viaducts or in the luxury of the Orient Express. We can experience desert life, or stay in a stately home and sleep in a four-poster. In North Korea, tourists can stay at a traditional Korean 'inn', eating sat on the floor and sleeping on mattresses laid on the floor. This experience is not suitable for tourists who expect five-star comfort.

Some places are heritage-rich. The lands of ancient Greece are superbly endowed. Likewise all the European capitals except those, like Warsaw, where little was standing after the Second World War. The UK has approximately half a million listed heritage buildings, 17,700 scheduled monuments and 850 designated conservation areas. The central government sponsors 17 national art galleries and museums including the British Museum, which is the country's top tourist attraction. The Louvre (see Box 8.1) is the principal tourist attraction in Paris. Australia and America do not have comparable histories. They need to rely more on their natural assets (Ayers Rock

---

Box 8.1 Le Grand Louvre

This is one of the world's most famous buildings, and one of the more easily recognised since the pyramids were added in the late 1980s. The Louvre has been among the world's greatest public museums since 1793. Its present exhibits include the Mona Lisa and the Venus de Milo.

The original building on the site was a fortress, which was replaced during the 16th and 17th centuries by an elegant palace suitable to serve as a residence for the kings of France. During this period, the Louvre became an artistic capital of the world. Hundreds of artists and craftsmen lived there as guests of the king. By the early 1700s, the royal collection contained over 2,400 objects of art.

Since the French Revolution (1789–1793), the art has ceased to be available only to the upper classes and has been accessible by everyone. Opening the Louvre was one of the great symbolic acts of the Revolution. France's heritage was being claimed by the people.

Sources: http://home.speedfactory.net/psmith/Louvre/
www.louvre.fr

and the Grand Canyon, for example), recently built attractions such as the Disney parks and (in some locations) gambling. The ten most visited places in the United States are two Disney resorts (in Florida and California), two shopping malls (in Minnesota and Boston), three urban locations (Times Square in New York, the Las Vegas Strip and Fisherman's Wharf/Golden Gate in San Francisco), two outdoor sites (Niagara Falls and Great Smoky Mountains National Park) and just one built heritage site (the National Mall and Memorial Parks in Washington, DC).

Tales of places inventing appetising histories for the benefit of tourists are usually much exaggerated, but sometimes true (see, for example, Grunewald, 2002). All countries must have bits of history that they would prefer to airbrush – slave trading, for example. It may feel embarrassing, and bad-mannered, to celebrate military victories in the presence of visitors from the defeated country, especially when the battles are within living memory. However, local historians and interest groups are forever vigilant and will not permit blatant distortions, and today's tourists (and hosts) can be thick-skinned. Some Second World War concentration camps have become tourist attractions. Indeed, 'dark tourism' has become a specialty in the present-day tourism industry.

It may seem strange at first that we conserve and maintain objects and memories from our past and restore them to life, yet given the economic importance of present-day tourism it is really anything but, for the benefit of others. It is often people from afar who are the most interested. New Zealand's Maori cultural sites attract far more overseas visitors than domestic tourists; the latter display relatively little interest (Ryan, 2002). In a similar way, natural habitats and wildlife in Africa are preserved and protected because of their value as tourist attractions. As noted above, things are always made into heritage in the present. It is always a current population that decides what is worth conserving, and why.

Interest in the past precedes modernity. The Renaissance – a movement that began in northern Italy in the 13th century and then spread throughout Europe – sparked an interest in the literature, art and architecture of the ancient civilisations of Greece and Rome. However, in the modern, urban world, the preservation of things from the past has become a collective effort. The first initiatives were by individual enthusiasts, and then by the voluntary associations that they formed to preserve buildings from an age that was passing into history. Governments of countries, regions and cities soon lent their support. They recognised that heritage helps to build a collective identity. It constructs a history of a people and helps to build a common identity, and access to a country's heritage can be made into a right of citizenship. This is why visits to local and more occasionally to national heritage sites have become part of most children's education.

Since 1972, UNESCO has designated World Heritage Sites which are thereby claimed as part of the common heritage of humanity, and 190 member countries have ratified this status, meaning that the governments commit to conserving the sites in question. Countries nominate sites for UNESCO recognition. Up to 2014, a total of 981 sites had been given World Heritage status. Italy has 49, more than any other country, followed by China (45), then France and Germany (38 each). Designation as a World Heritage Site means worldwide publicity, which is believed to lead to more visits, especially by international tourists. The United States does not have the same type or depth of heritage sites as Europe, but in addition to the federal national parks, it has National Heritage Areas, which can be administered by state governments, non-profit organisations or private corporations. These areas are landscapes which have some special natural or cultural resonance, and must tell a story about the United States. Some US sites have been given World Heritage status. These include Independence Hall in Philadelphia and the Statue of Liberty, but most are landscapes.

The UK's National Trust (which covers just England, Wales and Northern Ireland while Scotland has its own parallel body) is one of the world's oldest voluntary sector heritage societies. It was created as a non-profit organisation in 1895 by enthusiasts who wished to preserve things, and the way of life that the things represented, that were passing into history. The National Trust was given statutory recognition and powers in 1907, one of the most important being that it has been allowed to accept donations of buildings, their contents, works of art and land in lieu of death duties. The National Trust has specialised in taking over and maintaining country houses which their owners have been unable to keep up. As far as possible, the trust keeps these premises furnished as in their heyday, and adorned with works of art which were donated with or have some association with the property, its former owners or the locality. In some instances, family descendants of the original owners are allowed to continue to occupy the buildings, or just part of them. Similarly, estates may be maintained as working farms. The National Trust is one of Britain's largest landowners. It is believed that the presence of family occupants and working surroundings enhances the visitor experience. Needless to say, the occupants and farmers must accept that the buildings and estates will be open to visitors at agreed times of the day and year. The National Trust's main sources of income are donations and membership fees. It has around 4 million members who are entitled to free admission to National Trust buildings and parklands. Other revenue is raised from gift shops and catering. The trust also has the assistance of around 60,000 volunteers who act as guides, admit visitors and staff gift shops. This has made the National Trust immune to public sector austerity. It is forever widening its portfolio. Since the late-20th century, it has been acquiring properties from the early industrial era. These include a workhouse. It has also acquired the childhood homes of John Lennon and Paul McCartney.

The work of the National Trust is complemented by English Heritage (and equivalents in other UK countries), which since 1983 has been responsible for all the monuments, castles and ruins that were formerly owned and (possibly) maintained by various government departments. English Heritage's portfolio also includes parks, gardens and places of worship of historical interest, plus submerged landscapes and ancient shipwrecks. In total, English Heritage is responsible for around 400 sites, and admission is free at over 250 of these. Seventy per cent of English Heritage's income is from the government. Other income is from donations and membership fees which (as with the National Trust) confer entitlement to free admissions. There are over a million members.

The heritage industry is not embarrassed by being in receipt of taxpayers' money. This is because visiting heritage sites is a normal use of leisure throughout most sections of the UK population: around 70 per cent visit at least one site at least once in a year. The heritage sector is not threatened by any of the trends that are currently challenging other leisure industries. ICT is not a threat. Internet access is more likely to increase the likelihood of people visiting: it is not a substitute. Commercialisation is not a threat because heritage sites attract visitors from within and outside a country. Opening new museums and art galleries has been part of many cities' economic regeneration strategies (see Box 8.2). The heritage industry is benefiting from the growth of international tourism, and heritage sites are believed to be more effective than any other assets in attracting tourists into a country, then into specific regions and cities. Ageing populations tend to generate additional visitors and volunteers for the heritage industry. Wider economic inequalities enable the better-off to visit and travel more frequently. Awareness that heritage has become a business does not appear to deter volunteers. Quite the reverse: they evidently enjoy their association with buildings, landscapes and other objects that are admired by visitors, especially when the visitors have travelled from afar.

Box 8.2 Heritage and economic regeneration

BILBAO'S GUGGENHEIM

This spectacular building was opened in 1997. The Basque authorities provided pol-itical and cultural backing, and the funds for the museum to be built and operated. The Guggenheim Foundation contributes collections of modern and contemporary art, its programme of special exhibitions and its experience in international-level museum administration and management.

The Guggenheim is one of the central ingredients in a plan to redevelop the city of Bilbao and to revitalise the entire region's recession-plagued economy. Within three years of opening, the museum received over 4 million visitors. In 2011 alone, there were 962,358 visitors of whom 62 per cent were from overseas.

Source: www.guggenheim-bilbao.es

THE TATE GALLERY

This houses the UK's main collection of modern art. It is in London's West End, but to display its expanding collection, the Tate has created two offshoots, both in formerly run-down districts.

Tate Liverpool opened in 1988. It houses the UK's largest exhibition (outside London) of modern and contemporary art. It is in a converted warehouse which is part of Liverpool's Albert Dock. This dock was opened in 1846 (by Prince Albert) and closed in 1972. Tate Liverpool is part of a development scheme which also includes the Merseyside Maritime Museum as well as shops, offices, apartments, bars and restaurants.

Tate Modern opened in 2000. It is in the former Bankside Power Station (which closed in 1981). The site is on the south bank of the River Thames, and is now linked to St Paul's Cathedral by the new Millennium footbridge. Tate Modern displays the Tate's collection of international modern art including works by Dali, Picasso, Matisse, Rothko and Warhol. The Tate Modern and the adjacent rebuilt Globe Theatre are helping to regenerate a formerly derelict area. The gallery attracted 5.25 million visitors during its first 12 months, 4 times the volume recorded by Bilbao's Guggenheim in its debut year.

THE BALTIC

This gallery opened in 2002. It is located in Gateshead, on the south bank of the River Tyne. Baltic Flour Mills opened in 1950 to produce flour and animal feed, and closed in 1981. Since then, the entire area has been characterised by industrial decline, deprived housing estates, poverty and crime. The new BALTIC is part of a larger redevelopment project on Gateshead Quays, which also includes the £60 million Sage Gateshead, a multi-screen cinema, restaur-ants, bars, a nightclub, an international hotel, loft-style apartments and the Gateshead Millennium Bridge (for pedestrians and cyclists) which connects with another rejuvenating area (in Newcastle). The BALTIC featured prominently in the Newcastle/Gateshead bid (unsuccessful – Liverpool won) to become European Capital of Culture in 2008.

Sources: www.tate.org.uk
www.balticmill.com

Levels of employment in the heritage sector are subdued because so much use is made of volunteers. Nevertheless, if museums are included, there are around 35,000 paid jobs in England's heritage industry. This has made heritage into a specialism within higher education courses on leisure and tourism, and a source of apprenticeships for young people who do not enter higher education.

THE ARTS

Development

In the 19th and early-20th centuries, the arts underwent that same modernising process as other leisure industries, and distinct though often interdependent commercial, voluntary and public sector providers were formed. As populations became concentrated in cities, it became possible for commercial theatres to open. Some offered programmes composed of a variety of entertaining acts (music hall in Britain, vaudeville in the United States). Others specialised on straight plays and operettas such as, in England, those created by Gilbert and Sullivan. Performing companies usually had a local base but could also tour. Major cities hosted several theatres, usually with one leading facility that could accommodate thousands and stage expensive productions. Holiday resorts invariably had several theatres, some of which opened only during 'the season'. At Christmas, most theatres would stage a pantomime.

Voluntary societies were formed in all parts of America and in the European countries that were becoming urban and industrial by enthusiasts for different kinds of drama, choral and instrumental performances. Some such groups were based in churches, and others in workplaces. It was much the same as with sports. Local authorities provided accommodation for arts groups to perform in community and civic halls, the equivalent of the playing fields that were designated for sports. The 19th century was an age of philanthropy. Private parkland that had been enclosed by urban growth was often donated by the owners and became a public park. Private art collections were donated to municipal galleries. Collectors donated their treasures to public museums.

Elite culture – the classical music, opera and ballet that had been supported by individual wealthy patrons – was preserved by philanthropists, who typically banded together and often obtained support and contributions from city councils to build concert halls and support orchestras and companies to perform these works. National governments began to offer support to art galleries, museums and theatres which had sometimes, earlier on in Europe, relied on royal patronage, whose work was considered of national importance. The 1920s–1960s was a period of revolutionary change for the arts, which were all challenged by the new (at that time) mass media (see Nasaw, 1993). The original mass entertainment media – radio, movies and recorded music, followed by television – wiped out most commercial theatres. Only major theatres in major cities were able to survive, and sometimes they needed financial support from the city authorities. Cultural capitals, usually but not always the countries' political capitals, were exceptions. London retained most of its commercial theatres. Theatre lovers in the provinces needed to travel, possibly to London, in order to enjoy this kind of entertainment. The US equivalent was New York's Broadway. The mass media dealt a double blow to out-of-home entertainment by encouraging the spread of privatised, home-centred lifestyles. This not only drained support from commercial theatres but also thinned out the amateur drama, choral groups and bands of various types. In Britain, there was a dip in the likelihood of people joining voluntary associations between those born before and after 1955. The latter grew up in the age of television, which completed the battery of (original) new media (see McCulloch, 2014). Since then, economic change and restructuring have led to declines in memberships of trade unions and working men's (*sic*) clubs, but otherwise the voluntary sector, including amateur arts associations, has remained resilient (Li et al., 2002).

Elite culture (high culture) was also in dire straits in the mid-20th century. High rates of income tax and death duties were good for the heritage industry in Europe but disastrous for classical music, ballet and opera. Most of Europe's philanthropists vanished: the United States remained different in this respect. At that time, in the years immediately following the Second World War, it was widely agreed in all West European countries and, of course, in the countries that became communist that, just like sport, high culture was basically not commercial yet intrinsically valuable and worth preserving. Thus, national governments stepped in and became major patrons of the classical arts.

There has been no subsequent revolution in the arts, but since the 1980s there have been ever-strengthening challenges from the neoliberal political and economic contexts. The arts are not threatened by new technologies, ageing populations or widening economic inequalities, but they are challenged by pressures to become more businesslike in their operations and to present a business case for state support. Some supporters of the arts resist, while others try to meet the challenge of becoming a business sector that is a national asset (see below). The post-2008 financial crash context, and the seemingly endless public sector austerity that has followed have intensified pressures on the arts to seek alternatives to state funding. Grant aid from central and local governments has typically been slashed. Exhibitions, orchestras, opera, theatre and ballet companies with international reputations, especially those based in political, commercial and cultural capitals, have been able to raise box-office prices and attract sponsorship from well-known businesses which welcome the opportunity to have their names associated with these organisations and productions. Regional theatres find it more difficult to raise ticket prices and attract sponsorship of similar value. In the UK, many arts organisations outside London have lost former support from central government funds, and also grant aid from local authorities, which have been obliged to eliminate spending on optional services. Amateur arts groups have had grant aid reduced or eliminated, and have also faced higher charges for the use of civic halls. Classical arts companies have been able to blur boundaries and offer popular productions. Classical orchestras and opera singers stage classical pops. As well as Shakespeare, the UK's normally serious, highbrow theatre stages productions such as *Les Misérables* and *War Horse*. Ballet could surely act similarly with balletic revivals of popular musicals. Of course, this would not be real ballet. This type of crossover is impossible for mainstream theatres and amateur drama, choral and instrumental groups.

Arts policy interrogated

Central government support for the arts in the UK is channelled through Arts Council England and its equivalents in the other UK countries. Money is from taxpayers and, since 1994, the National Lottery. This dual-income stream applies also to central government funding for the heritage and sport. In addition to the arts as defined in this chapter, the Arts Councils also channel funds to libraries and a few authors, and to some museums and galleries (which are also treated as part of the heritage industry in this book).

At first glance, the arts appear to be funded generously by the central government compared with sport and the heritage. Arts Council England receives around £600 million per year. The combined grants of Sport England and UK Sport amount to just £300 million. English Heritage manages on just £130 million (figures are for 2012–17). A justification for these differences is that the heritage business does not have to create but simply preserves and presents. Sport, it is said, receives more support than the arts through education and local authorities which provide playing fields and sports centres. However, local authorities can and do provide similar facilities for the arts, and education could, though it does not, ensure that all children learn to act, sing, dance and play a musical instrument. It can also be argued that the top layers of sport gain massive revenues from live spectators and media rights, more of which could be distributed to the grass roots. However, top football clubs, for example, counter-argue that they must retain and spend all that they earn in order to remain top clubs.

The manner in which the Arts Councils, especially Arts Council England, distribute their budgets is subject to constant scrutiny and criticism. The main criticisms are that too much is spent on a small number of leading arts organisations, and that too much is spent in London and too little in the rest of the country. Arts Council England can highlight how it has annual funding streams dedicated to touring by its top London-based organisations (£18 million), and 'bridging organisations' (£10 million) which connect schools and local communities to the arts. However, these sums are exceeded by the annual grants given to single, London-based arts organisations: £25 million for the Royal Opera House (which performs ballet as well as opera), £20 million for the Southbank Centre (mainly music) and £18 million for the National Theatre, which always has Shakespeare within its annual programmes. Defenders of this funding argue that certain arts must be done either excellently (and therefore expensively) or not at all. There is no danger that the top layers of either the performing arts or sport could be undermined by neglecting their grass roots. In both cases, potential top talent can be identified in childhood and then nurtured in special squads and schools. Spectator and audience interest can be maintained via the media and socialisation in sports- and arts-loving families.

The arts community has responded in different ways to what appears to be never-ending austerity in public sector spending and neoliberal expectations. Some simply reject commercial criteria when judging artistic merit and value (e.g. McGuigan, 2004). They argue that art is valuable for its own sake, for its intrinsic merits. The judgements of art experts are offered as sufficient justification for state support. Some argue that the arts deliver non-commercial benefits which are impossible to quantify in terms of money, but can nevertheless be shown to be real benefits (see, for example, Scott 2014a, 2014b). However, sport or any other leisure activity is just as able to claim to be an intrinsic good. Engagement with the arts enhances well-being, but so does engagement in any kind of leisure that is active and social.

Some attempted justifications of state support for the arts lack credibility. The arts are not credible as routes to the social inclusion of disadvantaged groups (Woods et al., 2005). The arts have a stronger upward social class skew in their appeal than any other kind of leisure. The cultural dimension of the 2008–12 Olympiad may have taken performances and exhibitions throughout Britain (McGillivray and McPherson, 2012), but far more people will have watched the 'real' (sporting) Olympic Games on television or by attending events, and will have felt involved in the progress of their country's athletes, than were engaged by the Olympics' cultural dimension. The arts look feeble as means of boosting national prestige and strengthening national identity compared with foreign policies backed by military power, the standards of living and ways of life that earn admiration for Scandinavian countries and international success in popular sports at major events.

Other supporters present a business case for the arts. They have two distinct but complementary arguments. One is that the arts boost inward tourism. In recent years, around 10 million of the visitors to Britain, roughly a third of the total, have engaged with the arts and culture during their stays (Centre for Economic and Business Research, 2013). All visitors – tourists and business travellers – are merged together here. However, the really serious problem with these statistics is that they conflate arts and culture. It is not state-supported opera, ballet and classical music that are most likely to engage visitors, though the buildings that house these arts may be tourist attractions (see Box 8.3). In 2012, 7.7 million of Britain's inbound travellers visited a museum, 4.2 million visited an art gallery, 5.8 million visited a castle, 5.0 million visited a historic house and 6.4 million visited a religious building or monument (Deloitte/Oxford Economics, 2013). It is heritage, not the live performing arts, that attracts huge numbers of inward tourists.

In any case, the arts (more narrowly defined) with which visitors engage may not be those that are state supported. In 2013, London had 52 theatres, mostly commercial. These theatres were benefiting from the recession-proof growth in tourism. Audience numbers in 2013 were 4 per cent higher than in 2012. Box-office receipts were up by 11 per cent. The gross box-office take was £585 million, almost as much as the entire central government annual spend on the arts in England. It would be impossible to cram the 10 million visitors who engage with the arts or culture into the auditoriums of England's state-supported performing arts companies.

State-supported arts in England cater for small cultural minorities. Table 8.1 shows that the live music performances that were best attended in 2013–14 were not those that received state support but were those that the government

Table 8.1 Percentages of the population aged 16 and over who attended live music events of different types in England, 2013–14

Musicals	21
Classical concerts	7
Jazz	5
Ballet	4
Opera/operetta	4
Other	32

Source: Department for Culture, Media and Sport

department responsible for the distribution of state support labels 'other'. These comprise the various kinds of popular music (rock, hip hop, rhythm and blues, reggae, country and western, folk, and so on). Just 7 per cent of the population aged 16 and over went to a classical music concert and 4 per cent went to an opera and/or ballet performance.

That said, although unable to pack in more than a tiny proportion of inward tourists at live performances, the buildings occupied by state-supported performing arts companies, alongside heritage buildings, can become tourist attractions in their own right (see Box 8.3).

Box 8.3 The building as the main attraction

THE BOLSHOI THEATRE

After the Kremlin and St Basil's, the Bolshoi is probably Moscow's best-known building. It is situated in the square which is at the very centre of the radial-circular network of Moscow streets. The theatre, with its monumental colonnade and quadriga of bronze horses, stands in the northern part of the square. It was built in 1820–24 and was meant to be the finest theatre building in the world. The original building was partly destroyed by fire in 1855 but was rebuilt preserving the original layout while increasing the height of the theatre with an additional third storey. The five-tier auditorium is famous for its excellent acoustics and rich ornamentation.

Many outstanding artists have performed at the Bolshoi. Fyodor Chaliapin sang there, and Galina Ulanova and Maya Plisetskaya danced on its boards. Today, a new generation of young Russian performers are maintaining the Bolshoi's fame.

Sources: www.bolshoi.ru
http://glasssteelandstone.com/RU/BolshoiTheatre.html

SYDNEY OPERA HOUSE

This must be one of the most recognised images in the modern world. Yet the building was opened only in 1973. It is situated on Bennelong Point, which reaches out into Sydney Harbour.

In the late 1950s, the New South Wales government launched an appeal for funds to construct an opera house and a competition for its design. The Danish architect Jørn Utzon won the competition. As is often the case, his design and his victory were extremely controversial. The opera house cost 102 million Australian dollars (approximately US$50 million), which was a massive amount of money at that time.

The building contains a main auditorium (2,679 seats), a separate opera house, a drama theatre, a smaller playhouse and a smaller still studio. It also has an impressive reception hall and forecourt.

Nowadays, the opera house provides guided tours for approximately 200,000 visitors each year and has a total annual audience of around 2 million at its performances.

Sources: www.sydneyoperahouse.com
www.cultureandrecreation.gov.au/articles/sydneyoperahouse/

ROYAL OPERA HOUSE

London's Royal Opera House is the home of three international performing arts companies: the Royal Opera, the Royal Ballet and the Orchestra of the Royal Opera House.

The first theatre on the site (the Theatre Royal) opened in 1739. It was primarily a playhouse. The first serious music to be performed there was the operas of Handel, who personally gave regular performances up to 1759. The original building was destroyed by fire in 1808, but a replacement opened quickly in 1809 with a performance of *Macbeth*. There was another fire in 1856, and the third and present building opened in 1858. It became known as the Royal Opera House in 1892 but continued with a mixed programme until 1946 (when the Arts Council was established), since when it has been devoted to opera and ballet.

In 1975, the house was given adjacent land to enable it to extend, but the extension, accompanied by a thorough refurbishment and modernisation, had to await National Lottery funds (£78 million) becoming available in the 1990s.

Sources: www.royaloperahouse.org
www.fsz.bme.hu/opera/roh.html

The second part of the business case for the arts is about the formation and attraction of a creative class. These are people whose work creates 'intellectual property rights'. Their presence in a city is supposed to attract sunrise industries which are able to regenerate ailing post-industrial economies (Florida, 2002, 2012). The creatives produce computer software of all types, fashion, advertisements, design and content for the media. They are supposed to prefer to work and live in cities with lively cultural quarters. Research in Germany has found that these creatives relocate mainly for high salaries (Moller and Tubadji, 2008), but their presence does appear to predict economic growth and more general cultural activity in a region, though there is no evidence that the creatives are especially attracted by access to state-funded arts. These arts may nurture creativity, but this would be an argument for strengthening the presence of the arts in general education rather than the protection and privileging of minority tastes.

The classical arts have a special problem because they have never accommodated to the mass media. Radio and recorded music meant redundancy for most singing voices that needed no amplification to fill a large auditorium. The sounds of big bands and full orchestras could not be reproduced on radio or records through a tiny speaker. Smaller instrumental groups, or larger ensembles with fewer instruments playing simultaneously, became more appropriate. Comedians needed new repertoires once a joke had been told or a sketch performed on radio. They adjusted. Popular novels are rewritten as stage plays and then again for film. Stage plays are rewritten for television. Broadway musicals are rewritten for Hollywood. Singers lip-sync on film, but audiences expect the recorded sound to be reproduced live at concerts. Modern popular singers are able to do this. The classical arts have not accommodated to the mass media in a comparable way. Other arts have found ways of making one version of a product stimulate demand for other versions. The classical arts' supporters may argue that any accommodation would debase the culture, hence their need for state support.

Cultural taste and social class

The success of the classical arts in obtaining and retaining state support will be related to the link between cultural tastes and social class. The higher social classes in modern societies are no longer highbrow snobs. They have become cultural omnivores everywhere (see Bennett et al., 2009; Peterson and Kern, 1996). However, the top social class is still distinctive in being far more likely than any other class to retain high culture among its tastes. This phenomenon appears to be global. It applies in Britain (Savage et al., 2013) and also in Russia, where the new rich have ceased to spend ostentatiously (as in the brash 1990s) in favour of culturedness (Schimpfosal, 2014).

The meaning of any taste is derived partly from the typical class positions of those who exhibit the taste in question. Simultaneously, the meaning of belonging to a particular class is constructed partly from its members' distinctive tastes and lifestyles (Bourdieu, 1984; Bourdieu and Darbel, 1997). Cultural differences consolidate the class structure, while the class that is best able to do so uses its economic power and political influence to privilege its distinctive tastes.

The arts are not ailing branches of the cultural leisure industries. They have been able to accommodate to a commercial age. Some arts require and some of these receive state support. Most do not. The commercial theatre flourishes with audiences boosted by tourism in cultural capitals. Elsewhere, decades ago, most theatres were lost to the mass media. Amateur enthusiasts may be fewer in number than in the pre-mass media age, but in any city, town or village there will be enthusiasts who produce stage plays and perform their favoured kinds of music. Writers continue to write, painters paint and sculptors sculpt. A few become rich. A tiny number receive state support. Others do it because the art is their passion which neither technology nor the market can suppress.

MASS MEDIA

These are extremely important leisure industries. They have been extremely important since the 1930s and remain so to this day. They dominate the cultural sector of leisure, and indeed the whole of leisure. Television viewing alone accounts for around two-fifths of all leisure time. All governments have media policies: inevitably so, because the media are such an important part of people's lives and they are also big business. Nowadays, Britain is just one country where it has become impossible to understand the government's media policies except in terms of encouraging further growth in the industry and gaining as large as possible a share of the global market. All over the world, except under communism and fascism, state policy has been to leave the regulation of media primarily to the market, the big exception being broadcasting in European countries, where it was treated, originally, basically as a public service (see Briggs and Burke, 2005). However, in recent times, European broadcasting has undergone extensive commercialisation. Most governments have stood aside or even encouraged commercial 'invaders'. In 1980, around three quarters of all European TV channels were public service (McCullagh, 2002). Today, well over

80 per cent are commercial. Why have governments stood aside? Largely for business reasons. They realise that excluding or fettering commerce could cost trade and jobs.

Beginnings and early development

We speak of mass media when a communicator can reach an audience beyond the scope of 'live' sight and sound. So the mass media are capable of reaching large audiences, and the audiences are created by the media. Audiences are not usually from any specific neighbourhood, social class, church or any other organisation. The media create their own viewer, listener and reader groups. These may be drawn unequally from the various socio-demographic groups, but the audiences are not coterminous with any previously existing formations.

Print was the first medium of mass communication (see Eisenstein, 1983). William Caxton invented the printing press in 1478. Thereafter, it was possible to mass produce books, magazines, pamphlets and newspapers, but the circulations were usually tiny by present-day standards. In Britain, the 'popular' press was created towards the end of the 19th century. The *Daily Mail*, Britain's first popular newspaper, was founded in 1896 followed by the *Daily Mirror* in 1903. These were daily newspapers with national circulations (to all regions) and which were read by people in all social classes (but mainly the working class). By the end of the 19th century, advances in printing technology and the availability of cheap (compared with other types of paper) newsprint had been joined by the telephone and the telegraph, railways and a literate population to make mass-circulation (in the modern sense) newspapers viable (see Williams, 2009). Newspapers have always been regulated primarily by competition. They (the newspaper owners and editors) claim that this gives readers a choice of opinions. To an extent this is true, but by the First World War, competition from the mass-circulation dailies had all but wiped out more radical publications with smaller readerships (Curran, 1977; Lee, 1976).

Sales of gramophones and records began to take off after the First World War (when radio began to develop). By then, discs played on turntables had replaced the revolving cylinders which carried the first recordings (see Box 8.4). The gramophone was among the new range of consumer goods sold by department and mail-order stores from the 1920s onwards. Worldwide sales of recorded music then grew steadily for the remainder of the 20th century.

Box 8.4 Recorded sound

Thomas Edison invented the phonograph in 1877. The sound was reproduced from rotating sheets of tinfoil.

In 1893, Emile Berliner produced the first disc with a recording on just one side, to be played on a hand-driven gramophone.

The double-sided disc was patented in 1904, and by 1923 the gramophones were mechanically driven and all the recording companies were using these technologies. A mass market was created during the 1920s when radio created a mass demand for a new type of popular music.

The original record with one number on each side was joined, after the Second World War, by extended and long-playing discs. Cassette tapes and compact discs (CDs) subsequently became the recorded music industry's main products. The video-tape and subsequently the digital videodisc (DVD) made it possible to add pictures to the sound, and these also became alternative ways of distributing films.

Sources: Steffen, 2005
http://memory.loc.gov/ammem/berlhtml/berlhome.html
www.ovationtv.com/artszone/programs/bigbangs/berliner.html

From the start, films (see Box 8.5) and recorded music, like the press, developed as commercial leisure industries. Broadcasting developed rather differently in Britain and most other European countries (see Wheen, 1985). From the outset, it was subject to much tighter state regulation. The British Broadcasting Company was formed in 1922 by a group of radio manufacturers who had decided that the way to make money out of radio was to sell receivers to households, and to broadcast programmes that would create a demand for the equipment. Almost immediately, the British Broadcasting Company was granted monopoly rights and subjected to state regulation.

Box 8.5 Moving pictures

In 1888, W. K. L. Dickson, assistant to Thomas Edison, created the Kinetograph, which made short pictures. These were intended to be shown peep show style in a Kinetoscope. However, the French were the first to lay on a theatrical performance of a moving picture. This was in Paris in 1895. The French had developed a superior and lighter camera, the *cinematographe*. Edison followed quickly and displayed a film to a New York audience in 1896. Up until the First World War, European film-makers were every bit as inventive and successful as their American counterparts. In 1907, London's first film theatre opened, and by 1910 London had around 300. This new leisure industry was then expanding rapidly.

America established a decisive lead only during the war when Europe was preoccu-
pied with other things. Before the end of the war, America was producing 'full length'
feature movies, which were attracting large audiences to picture houses. Soon after the
war, Los Angeles became the main US centre of moving picture production. Its attractions were the sun and the varied landscape.
   The first feature-length sound picture was *The Jazz Singer* (1927).

Sources: Robinson, 1996
         www.thomasedison.com
         www.precinemahistory.net

It was nationalised in 1927 and became the British Broadcasting Corporation.
Radio was regarded as a natural monopoly because airspace was limited
and, in any case, governments at that time were concerned about the likely
power of the new medium. They believed that broadcasters, by speaking
directly into all the nation's homes, would be able to shape people's tastes
and opinions. The use of radio (and other media) by the totalitarian governments in Nazi Germany and Stalin's Soviet Union in the 1930s appeared to
endorse these concerns. Broadcasting, it was believed, would be dangerous
if left in private hands, or if broadcasters were under the pressure of market
competition. There were fears that broadcasters would pander to a 'lowest
common denominator'. The UK's BBC was to be a more responsible 'pater-
nalist', but politically neutral, broadcaster. John (Lord) Reith, the BBC's
first director-general, wanted broadcasting to educate, inform and enter-
tain the whole nation free from both political interference and commercial
pressures.

   Broadcasting developed differently in America, where there was less fear
of the market and deeper reservations about anything that looked socialist
than in Europe. In any case, the sheer size of the United States meant that
there was no danger of a single broadcaster being able to command the
entire population. Thus, from the outset, in America broadcasting was a
commercial business, funded by advertising. There have always been public
service slots within the US commercial channels, public service programme-
makers and even entire public service radio and TV channels funded by
non-profit organisations and state sources, but in America these have always
been within a basically commercial industry. In most European countries,
in the early years of broadcasting, this situation was reversed. Commerce
had wedges within what was basically a public service. 'Light' commercial-
type entertainment was not allowed to dominate the airwaves. However, the

radio did enable its star entertainers to become household names throughout their countries, and rich (by the standards of the time).

Radio broadcasting quickly became a huge success all over the world. Take-up was rapid in the economically advanced countries. Over a million 50-pence radio licences had already been sold prior to broadcasting commencing in Britain in 1922. During the 1930s in Britain, the wireless became standard domestic equipment. This was the age of radio. In Britain, television broadcasting (by the BBC) commenced in 1936, was suspended during the Second World War and then resumed afterwards, and the television set rapidly replaced the radio as the staple source of family entertainment (and news also). We were then into the age of television, which has lasted up to the present day.

The age of television

Throughout their development, all the mass media have adapted to and influenced one another. During the second half of the 20th century, all pre-existing media were obliged to accommodate to the dominant position of television. Other cultural industries had already been squeezed by radio and the cinema. Theatre audiences had declined. Television added to the pressure and squeezed the size of crowds at spectator sports, but playing sport was unaffected, and tourism likewise. Households were acquiring motor cars which enabled them to take more days out, which led to more visits to attractions and heritage sites. Even so, television became dominant. Radio lost its truly mass audience and adapted by filling niches that television could not or was failing to fill: in-car entertainment, local news and gossip and continuous music, for example. The cinema, like the radio, lost most of its earlier mass audience to television. In Britain, there were 1.35 billion cinema admissions in 1951, which had declined to just 53 million in 1984 (the low point up to now). Newspaper sales have declined throughout the 'age of television', and as we shall see in Chapter 9, they are now further threatened by the new media. However, sales of recorded music continued to rise throughout the second half of the 20th century.

Revolution begins in the original mass media

The mass media had become the dominant cultural leisure industries by the mid-20th century and have retained this position to the present day while undergoing major changes. The reasons are as follows:

■ The spread of prosperity has enabled people to spend more, which has led to an expansion of advertising. This could have filled more newspaper pages but in practice the advertising has gone first to television and radio, and then more recently to the new media (see Chapter 9).

- Also, more prosperous consumers have also been able and willing to pay more for media content.
- New technologies have created space for more radio and television channels and broadcasters, and enabled smaller companies to operate radio stations and to record and market music.
- The triumph of neoliberalism in economics and politics has discouraged state regulation and other kinds of state intervention in what has become a commercialised media marketplace.

This has transformed broadcasting in Europe, where it was originally treated differently than the other media. The limited airspace at that time (the 1920s) made competition inappropriate (or so it was believed). Also, as noted above, there were fears (maybe exaggerated) of the power of the spoken word being broadcast directly and simultaneously into all of a nation's homes, and there were also fears about the influence of broadcasting on public taste. The outcome was that broadcasting developed within a regulatory framework, which produced a distinctive type of public service broadcasting (see Burns, 1977). This had three key features, all of which soon became hallmarks of the UK's BBC:

- Political neutrality.
- Balanced programming: broadcasters were not permitted to pack the schedules with the most popular programmes measured in terms of listening and viewing figures.
- Accessibility to all sections of the (home) population.

All these features of public service broadcasting became at risk during the second half of the 20th century, and have now become things of the past. European governments have been losing their ability to operate broadcasting as a public service. This is partly because, as the European Union, they have collectively decided to follow America in adopting competition as the best regulatory framework (Collins, 1999).

In the UK, the weakening of state control began with the birth of commercial television in 1955. BBC Radio already had limited competition from overseas commercial stations (mainly Luxembourg), which was joined in the 1960s by so-called pirate stations broadcasting from vessels just outside UK territorial waters. Luxembourg and the pirates specialised in popular music: at that time, the BBC was refusing to dedicate an entire channel to the hit parade.

Commercial television was introduced into the UK in 1955 under pressure from would-be broadcasters and advertisers. The Conservative government at that time was sympathetic to these demands, and by the 1950s it was known that other countries (notably the United States) had lived with commercial broadcasting without either democracy or levels of popular taste collapsing. So in 1955 the BBC and ITV began to compete for audience share, but this competition was within a public service framework which remained in place when additional channels were launched – BBC2 in 1964, then the advertising-funded Channel 4 (in 1982) and Channel 5 (in 1997). Advances in broadcasting technology and the rising demand for advertising space had made additional channels viable. This was also the context in which commercial radio broadcasting began in 1973 and then steadily expanded.

Subsequently, satellite and cable broadcasting, coupled with digital technology, have probably dealt a death blow to public service broadcasting as known up to now. Satellite broadcasting in Britain (by Sky) began in 1989, and Sky commenced digital broadcasting in 1998. Viewers with digital receivers and 'boxes', or satellite or cable connections now have access to hundreds of television channels. One outcome has been a massive expansion of the broadcasting industry. There are now many more companies making many more programmes. Another outcome of the wider choice of channels is that broadcasters have less influence over what people actually view or listen to. Audiences have more choice. They can do their own scheduling. Even 'balanced' programming on all channels would not ensure that viewers' diets were balanced. By the 1980s, the video recorder was adding to viewers' ability to watch what they wanted, when they wanted.

Broadcasters have lost influence over what people view, and public authorities, which answer to governments, have been losing control over what is broadcast. Satellite, cable and other broadcasts to subscribers are not subject to the same public service requirements as the UK's 'traditional' channels. It is difficult, probably impossible, to set standards of taste and decency for material that is beamed in by satellite (or, as is now possible, transmitted via the Internet). With cable and satellite broadcasters able to extend the limits and to concentrate on the most popular types of programmes, the 'traditional' channels have demanded similar freedom in order to protect their shares of the audience. So 'unpopular' news programmes have been pushed beyond, or to the fringes of, peak viewing hours, and documentaries now concentrate on issues with viewer appeal, especially sex.

Another outcome is that more of what is available for people to view is of foreign origin. More and more people throughout the world are able to watch the CNN, NBC or BBC versions of world events rather than their own countries' news. In a similar way, they are able to watch the Premier (football) League or the Spanish or Italian leagues, rather than their domestic football competitions. However, the fact that people are able to do something does not mean that they will necessarily do it. In all countries, the most popular TV programmes are produced locally (Hesmondhalgh, 2013). The United States has a larger slice of the global film market than any other producer, but the American share is well under 50 per cent. India actually produces more films per year than the United States. Cultural imperialism has become more difficult to achieve as more and more countries have developed their own broadcasting industries. There are new exporters. For example, Latin America exports *telenovelas*. Australia is now the source of some soaps that are watched all over the world (*Neighbours*, for example).

The old public service principles are being quietly sidelined (see Born, 2004). Since 2012, all UK households have been obliged to go digital if they have wished to continue to receive television signals. This has enabled the government to auction off the analogue wavebands to other commercial businesses (telephone companies). The BBC, as we have known it up to now, is certain to become a casualty. We have already lost broadcasting as a pillar of citizenship – everyone having access to all broadcasts. In the new commercial world of broadcasting, viewers get what they pay for. However, there is nothing to stop governments maintaining free-to-air channels carrying a full range of programmes (though these would not include the most popular programmes, which would be sold to commercial channels), or assisting the poorer sections of the population to pay channel subscriptions. We may be losing broadcasting's ability to create a common culture – programmes that virtually everyone watches and which then become the currency of small talk and political debate. Maybe, there will be no repeats of *Dallas* and *Cathy Come Home*. Or maybe there will still be programmes with mass appeal. In any event, here we see again that the voluntary, public and commercial sectors are not just alternative delivery mechanisms. The media provide further examples of how the sectors differ in what is provided. Commercial broadcasting is not just a different way of delivering the same content as broadcasting as a public service.

CONCLUSIONS

There have been three eras in the development of the modern cultural leisure industries:

■ The first began in the 19th century with the formation of commercial, voluntary and public sector providers, and the different, sometimes competing, sometimes complementary services that they offered.
■ The second era began with the rise of the original mass media from the 1920s onwards. Demand for live entertainment was reduced. Most theatres were among the casualties. Performers – actors, instrumental musicians and vocalists – needed to seek careers in films, radio or recorded music, and subsequently there was television. Musicians ceased to move from live concerts to the media. They needed to win fans through the media before they could command audiences for live performances. Amateur arts production also declined as television encouraged a trend towards privatised, home-centred lifestyles.
■ The third era has been marked by an intensification of competition among the media for market shares. This has spread commercialisation throughout all the media. There may still be publicly owned broadcasting platforms, but these are now obliged to operate as businesses rather than services for the general public. We shall see in Chapter 9 that this competition for market shares that began in the 20th century rendered the old media fit to compete alongside the newer media, which are now creating entirely new kinds of leisure businesses.

One view is that we are now entering another era, a fourth era, created by the new digital media. It is claimed that these are not only adding new options, intensifying commercialisation and competition, but re-figuring the entire media landscape. New media break down the old division, the hierarchical relationship, between producers and audiences. Anyone can 'post' content. Communication can be lateral as well as vertical. What once applied only face to face, by land mail and by telephone now applies to all media. It is argued that television is having to reposition itself in a post-broadcasting era, the traditional broadcast being from a central communicator to a dispersed audience (see Andrejevic, 2009; Turner and Tay, 2009). Moreover, 'the box' in the living room has lost its privileged position. Viewing can be on a personal computer (PC) or an on-the-move device (Goggin, 2011). Merrin (2014) claims that these developments are outdating media studies as taught in higher education up to now. Chapter 9 considers the impact of the emerging, new digital media-based leisure businesses.

Heritage has been the great survivor among the cultural leisure industries. It has prospered as families have taken more days out and as tourism has grown. Heritage survived alongside the original mass media and is proving equally immune from ill effects from the latest new media leisure industries.

Another thing has not changed: producing cultural products commercially has always been high risk. Most revenue is generated by a relatively small number of hits. This applies to stage shows, films, radio and TV programmes, music and books. Production costs tend to be high relative to reproduction costs, so really big hits are extraordinarily profitable (Hesmondhalgh, 2013). Chapter 9 explains that the new media have greatly enlarged the number of producers, most of whom become losers, while greatly enhancing the rewards available for a small number of winners.

Chapter 9

New Leisure Industries

INTRODUCTION

Change has been constant throughout the history of modern leisure industries. There have been repeated outbreaks of fashion, especially among young people. Teddy Boys appeared in the 1950s. Punk became fashionable in the 1970s. Other innovations have endured – the long-playing record/CD and new television channels, for example, though these examples of enduring products have been affected by the latest technologies. What were once new television channels have become old and now face more competition, but can compete for larger and wider audiences. The vinyl music record has been eclipsed by the CD, and the album is now challenged by the ability of listeners to download single tracks.

Over the longer term, we can identify two long-running waves of change. The first, discussed in Chapter 1, was the development of leisure as a social service. This movement began in the 19th century, became more coordinated during the first half of the 20th century and continued up to the 1950s. The main drivers were voluntary associations, acting in partnership with, and with the support of, public agencies, and over time increasingly with financial support from governments. The second long wave has been commercialisation, which really took off in the 1950s when the birth of 'affluent societies' was being announced throughout the Western world. Commercialisation accelerated from the 1970s as governments all over the world began to adopt neoliberal (free market) economic policies. Government responses in the aftermath of the 2008–09 financial crash have added to the momentum.

Within these long waves, there have been shorter periods during which entirely new leisure products have been invented which have transformed people's uses of leisure time and money. The first outburst of inventive-ness was in the 19th century, when the initial modern leisure industries were created. These included our modern sports and the modern holiday. Simultaneously, the three main types of leisure providers – commercial, voluntary associations and the public sector – were formed. The second outburst was the advent of the original mass media between the 1920s and 1950s. Today, we may be amid a comparable outburst which will re-pattern people's uses of leisure and restructure all the leisure industries. The cata-lyst has been digital ICTs. These technologies have been incorporated into all kinds of businesses, including leisure businesses. They have led to the invention of wholly new leisure products and the formation of a new batch of leisure industries. The long-term significance of these changes, and whether these will be comparable to the impact of the first generation of mass media, is still uncertain, and is unlikely to become clear until the mid-21st century.

The new technology industries have been developed alongside the spread of Internet use: more specifically the proportions of households that have broadband connections, and the proportions of individuals who are broadband users, originally via a PC but now alternatively from a mobile device. The United States has led the world in broadband take-up. The percentage of households with broadband connections rose from 0 in the late 1990s to 70 per cent in 2013. By then, 86 per cent of US house-holds had Internet connections via broadband or dial-up. The rapidity of this spread has been comparable to radio and movie-going between the World Wars, and television after 1945. By 2014, 90 per cent of UK adults (age 16 and over) were Internet users and were spending an average of 20 hours per week online. It was 27 hours a week among 16–24-year-old Internet users (Ofcom, 2015). In the developed world, the digital divide is closing rapidly, just as it was soon eliminated during the spread of televi-sion. At present (but for how long?), there is a stark digital divide between the developed and developing worlds: in the latter in 2014 only 31 per cent of people were Internet users. That said, there are already far more people in developing than in the developed countries. The total numbers who are part of the digital marketplace are already skewed towards the developing countries or, as they are now called, the emerging market economies.

We have seen in previous chapters that all the older leisure industries have been affected and have needed to adapt or adjust to the challenge of new digital technologies. Rising proportions of all retail purchases are online (see Chapter 2, pp. 30–31). The ability to order online for home delivery is reducing footfall at drive-to supermarkets. One response by the malls has been to develop retailing into retailtainment. Holidays are now bookable online and customers are able to build their own packages. Digital media have made it possible to follow sports in entirely new ways. Gambling is a leisure industry that is expanding as people become able to place bets from a PC, Tablet or smartphone while a match is in progress. The box in the living room is now just one way in which people can watch television.

In this chapter, we deal with how older leisure industries have been challenged, how some have suffered while others have adapted and thrived, but mainly with new kinds of leisure businesses that have been moved from science fiction into people's daily lives by broadband and digital information technologies. Most pioneers who have developed new leisure products using digital technologies have been (or have rapidly become) commercial entrepreneurs. That said, we should note that Tim Berners-Lee, who invented the World Wide Web (www) in 1989, did not patent anything and has drawn no royalties. We must also note that many new media businesses have been started as hobbies. These include Facebook, which was created by Mark Zuckerberg and fellow Harvard students in the early 2000s. Also, Wikipedia is owned by a non-profit foundation. Most leisure-related websites are run as hobbies and never attract sufficient visitors to be developed commercially. However, this latest wave of new technologies has been developed, and the uses of the technologies have been pioneered, in a neoliberal era, and the new emerging leisure industries have amplified the ongoing commercialisation of leisure. The zeitgeist has been to 'go for it' if an innovation has shown commercial potential. Perhaps surprisingly, we shall see below that amid all the innovation older media have not been eliminated. Rather, they have been re-mediated and have adapted to the new media environment. Radio, television, recorded music and films are re-emerging as major leisure industries that have adapted to the digital age.

The types of business that are discussed in this chapter could be allocated to 'new media' or 'creative industries' rather than the leisure sector. This is another illustration of the blurring of boundaries. The hobbyists who developed the original computer games and social media sites could hardly have imagined how quickly and how many people would devote their leisure time (and money as well in the case of computer games) to these products. For the handful of inventors whose hobbies have become industries, this has been more of a happy accident than intentional.

In 2008, Matt Mason likened new media spaces to a Wild West: territory with no rules which was being contested by hackers, bloggers, file sharers, major corporations and punk capitalists. Today the territory is more settled. The main types of new or emerging leisure industries have become distinct. The leading businesses in most leisure market segments remain to be established. Maybe there will never be securely established market leaders, but the divisions between different types of new media leisure businesses are now clear and will probably endure. However, the ICT-based leisure sector is likely to remain territory where it is possible to become very rich very quickly. This is because it is unnecessary to create large manufacturing and distribution operations (as applied with radio, films and music records). Thomas Edison and his assistant who were the first to produce recorded music (in 1877) and moving pictures with their Kinetograph (in 1888) could not immediately build multi-million-dollar businesses on the basis of these inventions. It is different in the digital age. Small start-ups now have rapid and low-cost access to a huge market of potential customers who are already equipped with computers and broadband.

COMPUTER GAMES

Up to now, these have been the big commercial winners among the new leisure industries that have been created in the era of digital ICTs. Today, the games can be played on a general-purpose PC, a dedicated console that uses a television set as a monitor, an arcade machine or a handheld device – an iPad or some other Tablet or a smartphone which can access the Internet and operate apps (see below). The computer games market predates the Internet and first took off in the 1970s. Since then, the products and the market have been transformed, growth has accelerated and the industry is still growing having absorbed and adapted to digital technologies. Most American adults (as well as children) are now game players (but note that they may now play using on-the-move devices rather than sat in front of a PC or console plus TV screen). The computer games market is worth around $80 billion globally in annual sales, greater than books, the global cinema box office and global TV sports rights (Dyer-Witheford and Peuter, 2009; Harambam et al., 2011).

The first games were invented by computer scientists for their own amusement in the 1950s and were played on mainframe machines. One of the earliest games, created in 1958, was *Tennis for Two*. Then, during the 1970s, there were two developments which transformed a hobby into an industry. First, games were developed that could be played on first-generation home PCs such as the ZX Spectrum. These games used a television set as monitor and most were variations on *Tennis for Two*, that is, simulated games of tennis or squash. *Pong* was the generic template. At that time, games were still being developed by hobbyists who also wrote for and produced gaming magazines. Second, in the 1970s, the Japanese companies Sega and Nintendo developed coin-operated arcade machines which offered more exciting experiences than pinball. Many of these new arcade games were based on shooting, but they also offered a Grand Prix racing car experience. Then came *Space Invaders* in 1978. This game became the industry's first blockbuster (Kent, 2001).

During the 1980s, advances in computer technology led to the marketing of consoles (computers designed for game play) which could be connected to a household television. From 1983, Nintendo marketed console games featuring *Game Boy*, *Pokémon* and *Super Mario*. Sega, another Japanese company, entered the console market in 1985. Its successful games included *Sonic the Hedgehog* and *Total War*. Sega ceased producing consoles in 2001 following the market failure of its Dreamcast console. The (then) American company Atari entered the console market in 1986, since when the company has experienced several changes of ownership but successive owners have been unable to match the competition in the console business. All the early consoles offered versions of the popular *Space Invaders*. Nintendo marketed versions of *Game Boy* which could be played on a dedicated handheld device from 1989, and successive versions have sold over 120 million units worldwide. Sony, another Japanese company, entered the console market with its first version of PlayStation in 1994, and Microsoft launched the Xbox in 2001. Nintendo launched its first version of Wii in 2006.

Computer games now have a history of 50-plus years, so their inclusion in a chapter on new leisure industries might be questioned. The justification is that computer games are still emerging: the scale and character of this industry and its products have been transformed by digital technologies and broadband, and computer games belong alongside other new media leisure businesses.

Consoles are bought already loaded with suites of games to which additional games and more advanced versions of those already loaded can be purchased. The market for simpler versions of console games, and original games that can be played on a handheld device, has expanded with the marketing of smartphones and Tablets such as iPads. On-the-move time is now filled with texting, emailing, listening to recorded music through headphones, watching films and playing computer games. The best-selling genre among the computer games is 'action', which is followed by 'shooting', with 'sport' in third place (Crawford, 2008). *Grand Theft Auto* has been a huge success. The first version of the game was marketed in 1997, and by 2012 successive versions had sold 125 million units. There have been the same public controversies that accompanied the development of earlier leisure industries – fears that players will learn and copy violent acts, and become addicted to gameplay.

New games are typically produced and developed by hundreds of small companies and a small number of giants such as Electronic Arts, Inc. (see Box 9.1). The console producers outsource development work on existing and projected games. As with other cultural products (books, films and music records), most of the games that are developed do not sell. Small firms become successful by creating what become industry blockbusters, which make the business owners rich for life. Games that small businesses and hobbyists create can be sold to one or more of the console manufacturers, a major games company or marketed independently as DVDs in versions

---

Box 9.1 Electronic Arts (EA), Inc.

This firm, based in Redwood City, California, has been a pioneer and is now a leader among businesses that specialise in designing, developing, publishing and distributing computer games.

The business was founded in 1982 by Trip Hawkins, who was formerly an Apple employee. Early on, the business took three decisions that made the firm distinctive and proved crucial to its success:

- Its games are platform neutral, meaning that they can be adapted for any console.
- It deals directly with retailers.
- It regards its products as art forms, and its staff as artists who are credited on product labels.

EA has a suite of sports titles which include the *FIFA* and *Madden NFL* series. Its other better-known games include *Battlefield*, *Need for Speed*, *Dead Space*, *Star Wars* and the *Harry Potter* series.

Like other major new technology businesses, Electronic Arts constantly acquires smaller businesses that are becoming actual or potential competitors.

There are around 600 staff at the Redwood base, but a total of over 9,000 work in 'studios' located all over the world.

Total revenue was $3.7 billion in 2013.

Source: www.ea.com

suitable for the various consoles. Alternatively, simpler games can be made available online or activated by an app (see below) on a PC, smartphone or Tablet. In 2014, King, a British company that had marketed a smartphone (app) puzzle game called *Candy Crush*, floated on the New York Stock Exchange at a value of £7 billion.

The spread of broadband during the 21st century has led to the development of games that can be played online – mass multiplayer games – but these are best grouped with other virtual worlds (see below). These are not games which end with a winner and loser, or where the player has a score. The games are ongoing, like life, never ending.

VIRTUAL WORLDS

These are a type of game but there are no winners and losers, and no end. A player simply leads a parallel life in a virtual world. Broadband has made these games possible. A game player needs a console or PC with an Internet connection.

One of the best-known virtual worlds is *Second Life*. Players become residents in a territory that covers 700 square miles. A player is represented by an avatar (see below) which interacts with other residents. In *Second Life*, residents can spend a virtual currency which can be converted into US$. The competitors of *Second Life* include *EVE Online*, *Habbo* and the popular *World of Warcraft*.

One becomes a player in these parallel worlds by paying a subscription for a month or year. Initial visits may be free. This funding model results in a high turnover of players. *Second Life* claims that its virtual world has around a million residents at any time with 400,000 new residents (and presumably a similar number of lapses) each month. At any time, the inflow of new residents could shrink to a trickle and the virtual world's population would enter a downward spiral. This is why virtual worlds remain in the ownership of small companies. There have been no big money purchases or stock market floats. However, in 2014, Oculus was bought by Facebook for $2 billion before Oculus had begun selling its product. Oculus had developed a three-dimensional (3-D) virtual world through which goggles-wearing players could navigate using handheld devices. This could, but will not necessarily, be the future of virtual world play. If so, Facebook will have made an inspired investment. If not, Facebook stood to lose only $2 billion out of its own $134 billion stock market valuation.

SUBSIDIARY BUSINESSES

These are not confined to, but are usually subsidiary to, the computer games and virtual worlds industries.

Avatars

This term was introduced into computing (adopted and adapted from Hinduism) by Chip Morningstar in designing his role-playing game *Habitat*. The characters in the game were called avatars, representing the players.

These representations have various uses in computing. Avatars can be used in Internet forums such as blog sites where a symbol or a distinctive image replaces a (less interesting and memorable) username. Electronically created characters (avatars) can guide visitors around websites. However, avatars are now associated most of all with computer games. The early games had fixed characters, but later versions have allowed players to customise a template – to select clothing, hairstyle, facial and other physical characteristics. Depending on the game, a player may be an alien, a monster, a medieval knight, or a present-day soldier. Recent versions of console games – Nintendo's Wii, Sony's PS3 and later versions and the Microsoft Xbox – have avatar market places where players can select the characters who will represent them in the games. Multiplayer online games will offer a new player a basic avatar, which the player can then customise. A cottage/bedroom industry has emerged in which avatars are developed (mainly in Asia) for sale to richer players (mainly in North America) (see Yu-Hao Lee and Holin Lin, 2011). Some avatars become famous offline and are marketed as toys and incorporated as characters in films and in print.

Apps

App stands for application software which commands a computer to perform a task. One of the best-known apps is Internet Explorer. Apps may be bundled into a computer's system software before it is purchased, and Internet Explorer is included as one among many apps that are produced by Microsoft for its Windows system. Other apps that come with most computers give access to entertainment, mostly games of various types. Apps may be downloaded from an online store, probably the App Store, which is developed and marketed by Apple and was opened in 2008. By 2013, it contained over a million apps and had over 400,000 account holders who were downloading 60 billion apps annually.

An app may be free or paid for. Free apps typically provide Internet access to a basic version of a game to which enhancements can be bought. Apple keeps 30 per cent of the revenue from purchases from its store, and the remainder goes to whoever uploaded the app. Up to 2013, the top revenue-generating app had been *Angry Birds*, which was created in 2009 by the Finnish company Rovio Entertainment. By the end of 2010, there had already been 2 billion downloads, vastly more than the bestselling games designed for consoles. Subsequently, the *Angry Birds* game has become the basis of a television series, a movie and even a theme park.

WhatsApp has been another major success. This is an instant messaging service that can be operated from a PC or mobile device and can transmit text, still images, video and audio. The app was created by two Americans who were formerly employees of Yahoo, Brian Acton and Jan Koum. The site was handling 10 billion messages each day by August 2012 and 27 billion by June 2013. Later that year, it had 400 million users and was adding another million users every day. It was expected to have a billion users by the end of 2014. Google made an unsuccessful $1 billion bid for the business in 2013. Then in 2014 WhatsApp was bought by Facebook for $19 billion. At that time, WhatsApp had less than 100 employees, who all became rich as a result of their shares being bought by Facebook, and a handful, including WhatsApp's creators, became very, very rich.

Throughout the world, there are thousands of small businesses and bedroom entrepreneurs who are creating games and other kinds of software that can be activated by an app. As has been the case with older cultural industries (films, music records and books), most software products flop while a few make fortunes for their developers. We should also note that, like all other emerging Web-based leisure businesses, even the most successful app creators have very few employees.

SOCIAL MEDIA

This batch of emerging industries is still in its infancy compared with computer games. Social media have been created in the age of broadband, which is younger than the Internet. At the beginning of the 21st century, less than 5 per cent of American households had broadband connections and America was the world leader. Social media sites allow users to share information with other members of a community or network, and now account for more online time than any other use, including pornography, which was the 'market leader' for many years. The best-known social media sites will be known to readers of this book. They are likely to be users. However, most sites are developed by small groups of friends or colleagues, members of a club or people who share a particular interest. The site constructors may have prior experience in the computer industry, or they may have acquired sufficient know-how from friends. Most of the sites (which were originally called chat rooms) are used solely by members of a specific club or supporters of a sport team, for example, and expenses are covered by the users. However, some sites attract, and may be designed to attract, very large numbers of visitors.

If and when such sites need to employ staff and import additional expertise, they may sell a share of the ownership to investors – wealthy venture capital-ists or numerous small investors through crowdsourcing (see Howe, 2008). Internet sites such as Kickstarter enable small investors and new media (and other) entrepreneurs to contact one another. Computer game development can be funded in this way. Employees who are taken on by small businesses are likely to be paid modest salaries and offered slivers of stock in the com-pany. This can be, but will probably not be, a route to immense wealth. There are several kinds of social media.

Social networks

Facebook is currently the best-known social networking site and has squeezed competitors into crevices of cyberspace. Facebook was formed in 2004 by a group of Harvard students which included Mark Zuckerberg (see Kirkpatrick, 2011). By the end of 2013, Facebook had 1.2 billion users and employed 3,500 worldwide. It became a publicly listed company in 2012 with a market value of $134 billion. Facebook and other sites with massive numbers of users raise revenue from advertising. The more visitors a site receives, and the more information it collects about its users (which can be used to target adverts), the higher the rates that can be charged to advertisers.

Dating websites are specialised social networking sites. Users market themselves and shop for partners. Dating services may aim for the largest possible memberships, or specialise on graduates, professionals or gym club members, for example. Some sites specialise in facilitating cross-national relationships (Ukrainian brides for grooms in Western countries, for instance). These sites are typically funded by user fees, which are usually tiered by time limits.

Blogs

There are thousands of blogs on the Internet (see Barlow, 2008; Rettberg, 2008), but by far the best-known site is Twitter. This was launched in 2006. Registered users can make short entries. By 2012, the site had 500 million registered users and was receiving 340 million tweets and 6 billion searches per day. By then the site had 2,300 employees. Towards the end of 2013, Twitter became a publicly listed company valued at $32.76 billion. The founders, and even employees with just slivers of stock, became wealthy.

Collaborative projects

These are sites where the users collaborate to create a product. The most famous example is Wikipedia. This is now the world's largest encyclopaedia. It was co-launched in 2001 by Jimmy Wales, and by 2012 contained over 30 million articles in 287 languages. There were 4.5 million articles in English. Anyone can register with Wikipedia, write and then post an article. Any registered user can edit an existing article. All this labour is donated freely.

Wikipedia is hosted by the non-profit Wikipedia Foundation. The online encyclopaedia does not carry advertising. Its income is from public donations and it receives around $45 million each year. The site attracts around 500 million unique visitors per month. In 2012, it was being run by just 142 employees, but editing is by volunteers. The site would be worth billions of dollars if it was for sale, but the foundation's articles forbid this. Collaborative projects in which users come together to pursue a common interest are usually non-profit because they attract far too few users to have a market value. Wikipedia is the extraordinary exception.

Content communities

These sites specialise in a particular kind of content. YouTube is the market leader (see Burgess and Green, 2009). This site was created in 2005 by three former PayPal employees. By 2012, 100 hours of video were being uploaded every minute, and the site was attracting a billion unique visitors per month. This site's revenue is wholly from advertising: 45 per cent is retained by YouTube and 55 per cent goes to the uploaders, split according to the number of views that their content attracts.

YouTube was sold to Google for $1.65 billion in 2006. If the owners had delayed, the price could have been higher. Facebook was valued at £134 billion when the stock was first traded in 2014. However, it is possible that within 10 years, Facebook's users will have drifted away. If so, they will probably drift to other social media sites. Social networking spread initially among, but is no longer confined to, young people. By 2014, 72 per cent of UK Internet users had social media profiles (Ofcom, 2015). Specific sites may blossom and then fade, but basic divisions between the emerging leisure businesses are now likely to remain stable: sites specialising in particular kinds of content, collaborative projects, social networking, and so on. Meanwhile, the ability of specific sites to grow rapidly in use and then decline just as quickly may be a long-term feature of these businesses.

YouTube's main competitor is Dailymotion, which was formed in France in 2005 by six individuals who pooled €6,000 to start the site. Additional funds were raised from private investors in 2006, and subsequently there was a further investment by the French government's Strategic Investment Fund. In 2008 the site went international (it ceased to be wholly French language), and in 2013 it was bought by Orange for $120 million. At the end of 2012, the site was attracting 116 million unique visitors each month, far beneath YouTube's billion.

NICHE OPERATORS

Nearly all the emerging types of businesses described above have been commercial. The big exception is Wikipedia. One wonders whether Jimmy Wales and his partner would have gifted this to a non-profit foundation had they envisaged correctly how many contributors, editors and users their invention would attract. Would they have donated so much content to a for-profit encyclopaedia? The commercial character of the businesses does not appear to diminish the flow of material to YouTube or users of Facebook. These new businesses have been developed in a commercial age. Computer games are still created by hobbyists. Facebook was not launched with the aim of making its founders into billionaires. However, as previously noted, the spirit of the neoliberal age is that if a venture can be made profitable, then why not go for it? The contributors and site visitors do not appear to be deterred.

The point that must be stressed is that most collaborative projects are the work of small groups of enthusiasts for a hobby, a sport, a type of music or some other special interest. They do not expect or even hope that their sites will make money. Digital ICTs have facilitated the formation of thousands of communities of interest, and a by-product has been the creation of micro-markets serving geographically dispersed enthusiasts. The spirit of Tim Berners-Lee lives on, and the voluntary sector is represented in cyberspace, but these are niche residents. The big players are commercial (with the exception of Wikipedia). Other enthusiasts have developed their hobbies into mini-businesses. The Internet has made it easier to attract the numbers that make specialist holidays commercially viable. Other enthusiasts become not just customers but also an unpaid workforce who provide content. Is this the latest form of capitalist exploitation (see Scholz, 2012)? The speciality may be an outdoor activity such as desert trekking or Arctic exploration, or a specialist holiday within the green or ecotourism niche markets. It may be a sexual taste such as S&M (sadomasochism) or the broader category of 'fetishes'. It may be child pornography. A feature of Facebook that has assisted its expansion is the ease with which specialist communities of interest can be formed among its members. This feature attracts users and simultaneously makes the site more valuable to advertisers.

An overall effect of digital technology has been to fragment older mass markets. There are more kinds of music available for purchase than ever before. Western and more specifically American cultural domination are being undermined. The global trend is towards listening to recorded music produced within the listener's country (Bekuis et al., 2014; Ferreira and Wadfogel, 2010). New dimensions have been added to older leisure activities. People now 'window-shop' online as well as by visiting retail parks and high streets. There is now the option of online gambling from a PC or while on the move via a smartphone or Tablet. Digital technology creates new niches for non-profit communities and commercial businesses alike.

EMPLOYMENT IN THE EMERGING LEISURE INDUSTRIES

A striking feature of cyber-leisure businesses is the small size of their payrolls compared with the companies' user volumes and market value. Facebook employs around 3,500 worldwide. Twitter employs around 2,300. Wikipedia has fewer than 150 employees, and WhatsApp employed fewer than 100 when it was acquired by Facebook in 2014. These businesses are never going to rival car makers, retail banks, health care and education in the number of jobs that they create.

Social media and collaborative projects are able to keep staff costs low because users supply free content. Wikipedia's users edit and correct each other's contributions. The normal source of revenue for the new cyber-businesses is advertising. They suck advertising from older media, especially newspapers. Social media are attractive to advertisers because users supply so much information about themselves: not just age, sex and place of residence, but also (maybe) likes and dislikes, where they spend their holidays and political orientations. This information is invaluable for targeted advertising.

There are alternative funding models. Wikipedia and WikiLeaks (which are not related) rely on donations. Some sites charge users. In 2014, Whisper was a fast-expanding site which allowed users to send and post text messages anonymously. Users were being charged $5.99 per month, and the service was building a large user base among US college students and in Silicon Valley.

Computer games businesses have more employees. The companies themselves may not create the games that they market, but they must make the software fit for the marketplace, and they must also produce non-virtual goods (consoles and DVDs). In 2014, Nintendo had just over 5,000 direct employees. Others (around 2,000) were employed indirectly by Nintendo, mainly in distribution and hardware production. It is impossible to separate Xbox and PlayStation employees from the general payrolls of Microsoft and Sony, respectively. However, games companies need to exercise quality control. In contrast, social media typically disclaim responsibility for content which may be plain wrong, libellous or offensive. They will act on complaints, but do not have the staff that would be required to monitor input routinely.

Cyberspace leisure businesses offer extreme examples of new technology, Silicon Valley-type employment profiles. A few entrepreneurs become extremely rich. Core workforces are well paid by successful companies. Salaries are modest in start-ups, where employees are likely to be offered slivers of stock, which will make them rich if the businesses flourish and are bought by venture capital firms or in stock market floats. All the businesses are fragile. MySpace was launched in 2003 and sold to News Corporation in 2005 for $580 million. Bebo was launched in 2005 and was bought by America Online for $850 million in 2008. These have been among the worst buys of the 21st century. Both firms shrank dramatically in user numbers and value during Facebook's rise to dominance. Facebook and Twitter could experience the same trajectory. Facebook's and other market leaders' strategy for averting this threat has been to buy new emerging stars of cyber-leisure. Facebook did this in 2012 by purchasing Instagram, a photo-sharing smartphone app, for $1 billion, and Face.com, which had developed facial recognition software, followed in 2014 by purchases of WhatsApp and Oculus, which had developed solar-powered high-altitude drones which could remain airborne for five years and could possibly become a replacement for satellites. Only time will tell whether this strategy works for Facebook. Its management obviously realises that Facebook must become more than just a social media site in order to face a reasonably secure future.

Cyber-leisure businesses are perpetually vulnerable to new start-ups. So core staffs are kept as small as possible. Other employees are on temporary contracts linked to specific projects. Or the work is subcontracted to smaller companies. There was a brief time window when demand for ICT skills and know-how exceeded supply, but this imbalance was soon reversed. Silicon Valley employment had ceased to be well paid by the end of the 20th century. By then, skilled professionals could expect to spend repeated periods between projects during which they had to keep their skills and knowledge up to date and maintain the social networks through which further work could be obtained (see Benner, 2002; McKinlay and Smith, 2009).

Between 2001 and 2004, Carrie Lane (2011) interviewed workers in the high-tech sector in Dallas, another hub of America's sunrise economy. These employees were slipping into and then out of jobs, but they were generally accepting, even evangelistic, about their precarious employment. They identified as self-marketers with bundles of valuable skills to offer. Follow-up interviews during the recession that followed the financial crash of 2008–09 found the employees seeking ways of coping and coming to terms with careers that had not turned out as they had hoped and expected. They had been forever changing gear rather than driving forward.

This new career model is spreading into older media (see below). There are few long-term career jobs in television today. Programme-making is outsourced by broadcasters to smaller companies which take on staff to complete specific contracts (see Hesmondhalgh and Baker, 2010; Siebert and Wilson, 2013). Most computer games are initially created and developed by small businesses. Most struggle, then fail (see Box 9.2). A lucky few are responsible for blockbusters such as *Space Invaders* and *Grand Theft Auto*. There are blurred boundaries between hobbyists, entrepreneurs and 'consultants' who live off successive time-limited contracts and projects.

Many features of employment in cyber-leisure are not only shared with other new technology sectors but also with older leisure industries, but in cyber-leisure the relevant features are accentuated. The emerging leisure industries are not upgrading jobs in leisure which, despite their glamorous appearances and therefore appeal, have always had a downside. In professional sport, one of the older leisure industries, a few players become

---

Box 9.2 Game-makers

Birgitta Bergvall-Kareborn and Debra Howcroft (2013) questioned 60 app developers from Sweden, the United States and the UK. They were all developing apps for Apple or Google (Android) platforms. Some were wholly self-employed while others were self-employed alongside employment with another company.

Their publishing experience ranged from just one app to 45. Some published apps had never been downloaded. The most successful had over a million downloads. Total revenues ranged from $50 to $150,000.

These app developers knew that their careers were precarious but

- they wanted to work with leading-edge technology,
- they derived enjoyment from mastering a technical conundrum and
- they all wanted to become rich.

---

exceptionally rich and famous, but most have modestly paid short careers in which their jobs are experienced as hard work (the training and lifestyle demands rather than match play) (see Roderick, 2006). Most musicians who are paid for their work are semi-professional. Full-time careers are usually brief. Jobs in gyms and tourism have always been fragile. Demand has been seasonal, and hours of work have been 'unsocial'. In retail and hospitality, employees' appearances and personalities are expected to be offered as part of the service (see Warhurst and Nickson, 2007). Niche leisure businesses in surfing, go-karting and paragliding expect employees to be living advertisements for the products (see Land and Taylor, 2010).

This matters because leisure has become an increasingly important source of jobs in post-industrial societies. The profile of employment in the emerging leisure industries is an extreme version of employment in the older leisure industries that they are joining. A very small number of workers become incredibly wealthy. A larger number can build long-term decently paid careers. Most become part of the precariat – often a well-qualified section with degrees in media studies, sport studies, tourism and computing.

CYBER-LEISURE BUSINESSES IN CONTEXT

Only the leading games console businesses (Microsoft, Sony and Nintendo) and game developers and publishers such as Electronic Arts can be described as giants of the sunrise economy. Even Facebook is nowhere near the size of Apple, Google or Microsoft (which has the Xbox among its many products).

Businesses that specialise in cyber-leisure are at the small to medium end, and in one of the most fragile segments of the new-technology economy, where even the major players look perpetually insecure. Microsoft, Apple and Google are the current giants in the digital technology sector. Facebook's development strategy implies a desire to challenge the big three. These businesses are currently engaged in a 'digital war' for domination in cyberspace (see Arthur, 2012; Goldsmith and Wu, 2006).

Since the 1980s, Microsoft has been the big-name, dominant presence in computer software. The business was famously founded in 1975 by Bill Gates and Paul Allen, and has specialised in the development of software for desktop and laptop computers (see Manes and Andrews, 2013). It developed MS-DOS, which operated most of the world's computers throughout the 1980s and into the 1990s. Most computers still use Microsoft's Windows system and Microsoft's Office Suite, which includes Word, Excel and PowerPoint, plus Outlook webmail and Internet Explorer. The business was valued (by the stock market) at around $340 billion in 2014 and had around 100,000 employees worldwide. Even Microsoft has begun to look vulnerable, specifically to declining sales of computers and the growing popularity of Tablets (especially the iPad) and smartphones (like the iPhone). Microsoft has responded by developing versions of Windows (starting with Windows 8) that are suitable for installation in these products. In 2013, it acquired Nokia, once the world's leading mobile phone manufacturer. The Xbox has also been part of the diversification strategy. Microsoft constantly purchases smaller companies and incorporates their technological innovations into its own products. One day an emerging competitor will decline Microsoft's takeover offer.

Apple was founded by Steve Jobs and two partners in 1976. Its original products were computers, and Apple still produces the Mac(intosh) series. However, the business expanded rapidly from the late 1990s by developing the iPod, the iPhone, the iPad and the iTunes and App stores. By 2014, Apple had 408 retail outlets in 14 countries and employed 75,000 worldwide. It was valued by the stock market at around $450 billion. Almost all Apple's manufacturing is outsourced (to Asia), and product development is outsourced to much smaller companies and independent operators such as those studied by Bergvall-Kareborn and Howcroft (see Box 9.2). Like Microsoft, Apple constantly buys smaller companies in order to acquire and use their technologies in its own products. This is how these leading firms try to ensure that they remain market leaders. In 2014, a major question mark over Apple's future was still whether the firm's technological inventiveness would survive the death of Steve Jobs in 2011 (see Kane, 2014).

Google was founded by two PhD students in 1998. Its main product was and still is an Internet search engine. This is despite developing Gmail, its own office suite and the Android smartphone operating system. In 2014, over 90 per cent of Google's revenue was still from advertising. By then, Google had around 48,000 employees and 70 offices in 40 countries.

All these leading sunrise companies are famous for their flat organisations, informality in dress and workplace relationships. Apple describes its headquarters as a campus. The businesses are also renowned for their tax avoidance behaviour, taking profits in low-tax countries rather than where they earn their revenues.

Sony and Nintendo are giants. Even Facebook is in a lower league but could catch up through diversification. Most governments would love their countries to produce the next Microsoft, Apple or Facebook, but even if this became the future of one of their start-ups (all countries have these), the jobs created would not necessarily be in, and taxes would not necessarily be paid in, the business' country of origin.

THE RE-MEDIATION OF OLDER MEDIA

The big winners among the new ICT-based leisure industries (up to now) have been computer games in terms of the value of retail sales, and social media in terms of number of users and time spent on the sites. However, perhaps surprisingly, the biggest of all winners in the new media age have been the older media which have re-mediated themselves successfully. The exception is print, more specifically paid-for newspapers. Other older media – films, recorded music, radio and television – are flourishing. When these now-older media were new, which was in the early- and mid-20th century, they did not kill off or even diminish the appeal of existing leisure industries such as sport and tourism. The exceptions at that time were sales of alcohol and visits to premises (pubs) which specialised in alcohol sales and consumption, and the variety theatre/music hall. However, alcohol recovered after 1945 as part of a sustained growth in the hospitality industry, and concerts which last for just an evening, or continue throughout a day or longer (festivals), have revived live popular entertainment. Sport has embraced new ways of marketing its spectacles in the era of ICTs (see Hutchins and Rowe, 2012). Tourism continues to flourish: the virtual experience is clearly not a substitute. Similarly, events continue to increase and become ever larger despite the various alternative types of meeting at a distance that become available.

Print

Paid-for newspapers are the big casualties in the old plus new media environment. By the Second World War, radio was rivalling newspapers as the public's main source of news. Then television became dominant. Newspapers reacted in different ways that made tabloids and broadsheets (as they are now described) more distinct. Tabloids devoted less space to political and business news, and more to news about sport and other forms of entertainment. These newspapers began to fill pages with reports on other media – television programmes (recent and forthcoming), recorded music, films and the lives of their stars. Broadsheets offered more in-depth coverage of politics and business than was available on radio and television.

The tabloids' problem in the ICT era is that news about entertainment is available online. The broadsheets' big problem is that their in-depth coverage of news is available online, and much of the advertising that they used to carry has also drifted online. Newspapers themselves are now available online, but few, which are specialist products such as the *Financial Times*, have found a formula to make this pay. If the content is behind a paywall, readers and advertising revenue drop. If content is free, advertising alone does not replace revenues from earlier sales of hard copies and the advertising that the hard copies used to attract.

However, the number of free, hard-copy newspapers is growing, sometimes with several updated editions during each day. These newspapers either are distributed free at points where people congregate on their journeys to and from work, or are delivered to all households in a district. The circulations of these newspapers make them attractive to advertisers. Paid-for local newspapers have difficulty in surviving alongside the challenge of free equivalents, which can rapidly build larger circulations, attract more advertising and contain more pages than paid-for competitors. All newspapers are having to adapt to the new media environment in one way or another, and so far the freesheet solution has proved the most successful.

Other printed media are comfortable, at least. The number of books published and sold continues to increase. Readers have had the option of e-editions since Amazon marketed the first Kindle in 2007. Meanwhile, magazines aimed at specialist audiences – people with a keen interest in cars, football, fashion or gossip about sport, screen and television stars – are coexisting with the new media. It is the traditional daily national and weekly local newspapers that were once purchased in large quantities at bookstalls and newsagents and delivered to households that are in crisis and may not survive for much longer in the 21st century.

Television

This has been the major winner in the new media era. Today broadcasting can be via 'traditional' airwaves, cable or satellite. Digital technology gives viewers access to hundreds of channels: some free to view, others requiring a subscription. A wide choice of channels is available 24/7 every day of the year. Most people watch only a limited number of all the channels that they can access. Their choices depend on whether they are particularly interested in sport, history, films, news or the arts or prefer channels with mixtures of popular entertainment. Many programmes are streamed and can be viewed on a PC or an on-the-move device. High-definition, large-screen television sets may have increased the popularity of viewing at home. Catch-up options have enlarged the audiences for many programmes. Overall, people are spending more time watching television than ever before. Television is still far and away the top leisure activity in time accounted for. It is still the normal default option in most households: people watch or at least switch on when they are not doing anything else. However, for some sections of the population, the default options have long been radio or recorded music, and in the new media age these may have been joined by computer games and social media, but none can match time spent watching television across the entire population. Hutchins and Rowe (2012) have argued that sport has now entered an age 'beyond television'. They are correct. Sport can now be accessed on a laptop, a Tablet or a smartphone, but this has not diminished television audiences for live sport. The value of sports broadcasting rights continues to rise. People will pay for the superior quality of the spectacle on a traditional television set. This is why most football fans remain law abiding even when they have the option of low or zero-cost unofficially streamed alternatives (see Birmingham and David, 2011).

However, the television audience has fragmented. No programmes today can command the number of viewers that was possible when people were restricted to a small number of channels transmitted across the airwaves using analogue signals. Traditional European public service broadcasting – meaning all broadcasting treated basically as a public service – cannot survive in the new market for audience shares. The old public service broadcasters may still be operating, but no longer within what is basically a public service. Before long these channels are likely to follow the industry trend towards funding by advertising, viewer subscriptions for specific channels or a mixture of the two.

Radio

Radio and films (see below) have slid smoothly into the new media age because by the 1980s they had learnt how to coexist alongside television. Radio did this by specialising on content that it could do better – music and talk. Digital technology has permitted a vast expansion in the number of (mainly local) radio channels. Most are financed through advertising. Radio caters for lots of special tastes, and is available to listeners at home and while travelling in motor cars, and also via handheld devices such as smartphones or Tablets with headphones attached.

Film

Cinemas can no longer pack in the huge audiences that flocked to picture palaces from the 1930s up to the 1950s, by when audiences were being lost to television. However, by the 1980s, cinema audiences were growing again. This was achieved by film distributors building multi-screen facilities, which gave visitors a wide choice of films.

Equally important, by the 1980s, the industry had developed a marketing sequence which began with cinema release, subsequently or simultaneously offering films for sale on a video cassette and later on a digital videodisc (DVD). Then a film would be made available through television, nowadays first of all on pay-per-view premium channels, followed by general subscription channels and finally via free-to-air channels. The number of television channels that need content 24/7 has enlarged the demand for old and new films, so the studios remain as busy as ever. There are now markets for films that never reach cinema screens.

Renting as well as selling video cassettes of films began in the 1970s. Shops were soon complemented by video cassettes and videodiscs available by mail to purchase or rent for brief periods of time. Then with Internet broadband it became possible to stream films on demand from huge libraries. Netflix and its competitors have now become major businesses in the film market. Users pay a subscription which gives unlimited access for a stipulated time period, or pay per download.

Recorded music

Publishers and artists of recorded music have learnt how to prosper in the new media age. In the early-21st century, they claimed (rightly or wrongly) that they faced disaster. Their enemy was peer-to-peer file sharing, which, music publishers claimed, was depressing sales of music and undermining the industry. Napster, launched in 1999, was the best known among the file-sharing servers at that time. The industry's response was to have file sharing criminalised. Napster closed in 2001, but the industry has been unable to prevent successors being formed and then quickly disappearing. As Matthew David (2010) has argued, it is impossible, in practice, to make sharing something that you own into a criminal offence (see also Cammaerts, 2011; Gillespie, 2007). In any case, opinion was always divided on whether sales were being depressed, stimulated or unaffected by the spread of free file sharing. This enabled listeners to sample a wider range of music than they would have purchased, thus possibly leading to purchases of the music of artists and genres that they had not previously bought or even heard.

The recorded music industry has not just survived but thrived in the new media environment not so much by outlawing its supposed enemy as by developing new ways of marketing its products. Apple released the first iPod in 2001. This rapidly became the Walkman of the 21st century. The Sony Walkman was first marketed in 1979 and made it possible to listen to music cassettes through headphones while on the move. The iPod is a much smaller memory pack which can store large quantities of music and (depending on the model and its storage capacity) video also. The music can be listened to through headphones attached to a PC or a much smaller dedicated device than the original Walkman.

The industry has also introduced online stores from which music (and other digital products) can be bought and downloaded. Apple opened its iTunes Store in 2003. Spotify, a Sweden-based music streaming service, was launched in 2008. These libraries contain thousands of items which can be browsed by artist, record label and musical genre. A purchase may be a single track, an entire album or open access throughout a time window. The casualties have been high-street record shops and disc manufacturers. There are no marginal production costs per number of downloads, and distribution costs are minimal, so the price of recorded music has fallen while publishers have been able to maintain their profits, and artists and composers have continued to receive royalties.

The availability of recorded music has never threatened the viability of live concerts. There are now more than ever. Ageing artists whose music remains available in online libraries have been able to maintain or revive their appeal without preventing newcomers building fan bases.

Most names of today's major music publishers are survivors from the pre-digital age – Sony and Universal, for example. These firms are now multi-media 'empires' as are News Corp and Vivendi, which have interests in music, film, television and sometimes radio and print also. All the old media (except newspapers), and some of the most successful leisure businesses of the pre-digital era, have re-mediated themselves and are thriving.

CONCLUSIONS

New media leisure businesses have joined rather than replaced most of the older media. Indeed, most of the older media have been reinvigorated. The effects were similar when the original mass media joined the earlier leisure industries. Lethal damage or even severe injuries have been exceptions: the variety theatre/music hall in the mid-20th century, and printed newspapers from the late-20th century and continuing in the 21st century.

Since 'the crash' of 2008–09, UK citizens have been taking fewer holidays abroad (still beneath their 2007 peak in 2013). However, they have been taking more holidays within Britain, and visiting heritage sites and other domestic attractions more frequently. The other main 21st-century trend in Britain has been towards spending fewer evenings drinking in pubs. The British pub appears to be the main victim of people spending more time being entertained at home by old and new media (see Roberts, 2013). Visits to pubs and spending on alcohol began to decline several years before 'the crash', so the appeal of old and new media options is the most likely cause. Holidays are different. Overseas travel by UK residents will most likely recover, reach and then surpass its former heights when household incomes recover their post-2008 losses. Trends in other countries may be different, but there is no country where the new media leisure businesses have wreaked havoc across older leisure industries.

It seems possible that people today are managing to do more with their leisure than in the past. If so, how has this been possible? Households have been able to spend more on leisure, because over the long term, incomes have risen and this has enabled more to be spent on non-essentials. In other words, or looking at this trend from a different perspective, there has been more money to be earned by the leisure industries. As regards leisure time, hours of work contracted in first-wave industrial countries up to the 1970s. Since then, (paid) work-free time has continued to increase, but the gains have gone mainly to groups outside the working-age population – mainly to the young who have been staying longer in education, and the retired who are now living for longer than ever before. Despite higher rates of unemployment since the 1970s than in the 30 years that followed the Second World War, employment rates within working-age populations have risen due to increased labour force participation by women. Overall, there has been more money available for leisure spending, and more leisure time (though the gains in time and money tend to have gone to different sections of the population). However, a complementary explanation of people's ability to do more is the compression of literally spare time which used to be spent 'doing nothing', just hanging about at home or in the streets, contemplating contentedly, or plain bored. Maybe more people are doing more multitasking: not just watching television while doing housework but also attending to social media while listening to recorded music. Many of the new options are free or have very low marginal cost. This is because producers' reproduction and distribution costs are so low, which makes it possible for a music track to be available for $1 and a simple version of a game for $5. A million downloads means $5 million in revenue.

More leisure choices must be a benefit, in principle, for leisure consumers. They have a wider range of options. Overall, new media leisure businesses have added to the number of jobs in leisure, which, again in principle, must be good news for workers. However, very few of the new media jobs are secure career jobs, and employment in the older media has been destabilised. The heroes of new media leisure businesses may be exceptionally talented or just lucky, but they register success with rapid and spectacular capital gains rather than building solid firms which provide secure jobs for large workforces.

The new media have created a new public sphere in which civil society associations can form and function. The voluntary leisure sector has gained a new dimension. The Internet has the potential to bind humanity into a global network that is able to speak truly for 'the people'. In practice, however, Internet communities operate in many different languages. Most of the communities are small. Members speak mainly to the like-minded. Simultaneously, new spaces have become available for creating victims such as targets of cyberbullying and leakages of information that its owners intended to be kept within the walls of their own organisations – businesses, governments or voluntary associations. Site operators are able, in practice, to disclaim responsibility for content unless the content antagonises their own government, or the government of another powerful country.

The new media have intensified competition for market shares across the whole of leisure. Tourist destinations and tour operators, event hosts and businesses that manage events do so in intensely competitive business environments. Comparison sites that assist purchasers to select destinations, travel and accommodation are funded by the businesses that are being compared on these sites. The businesses feel that they cannot afford not to purchase advertising space. Different sports, and different competitions within the same sports, compete for shares of a global audience.

Governments know that they cannot stop history, but they can decide whether to be swept along and oblige public leisure services to become more commercial, more businesslike, more competitive in their aims and methods. Governments have to decide whether any leisure opportunities, and if so which, should be protected as rights of citizenship, and whether national, regional and local prestige and identity building through leisure provisions have an intrinsic value that justifies the costs.

Section III

Conclusions

Chapter 10

Policies, Employment, Education

INTRODUCTION

'There is no money for leisure' is likely to be the public sector's 'bottom line' for the foreseeable future. At any rate, there will be no new money. The likelihood is year-on-year cuts in central and local governments' leisure budgets, a perpetual drive for savings from 'administration' and from facilities that remain under public sector management and reduced grant aid for all recipients. The post 2008–09 context has not created a wholly new scenario but has simply accelerated and added urgency to pre-crash trends.

Yet suddenly there is new money. From somewhere, the UK government found over £9 billion for the 2012 Olympics – over 20 times the combined annual budgets of Sport England and Sport UK. The eventual costs were underestimated (deliberately or accidentally?) at just £3 billion when London bid for the games in 2005. Politicians, sports organisations and the media seem to be caught on waves of exuberance when bidding for sports mega-events – the kind of exuberance that creates bubbles in stock markets. Somehow Britain found the resources to do whatever it took to run an event that the world would admire. At the time it seemed churlish to object, and the games were certainly a great fun event for Britain in the summer of 2012. No one of consequence complained at the time. Was it worth it in economic or any other longer terms? These will remain questions for perpetual debate. It is never possible to disentangle event effects from other causes in forever-changing contexts.

Leisure spending by the public, not by governments but by private consumers, is likely to continue to grow. The spending will be mainly by the better-off in societies where economic inequalities remain huge and may continue to widen, and by relatively affluent young childless adults and better-off seniors.

Most of the future growth will be in the emerging market economies, which now account for rising proportions of all international tourists. These are the mobile spenders whom all destinations now compete to attract.

There will be greater scope for commerce to commercialise, and also for voluntary associations to cooperatise provisions that were formerly managed within the public sector. In the process, the products – the leisure services and experiences themselves – will change. Commerce turns everything into a commodity with a price tag. It caters for consumers. It seeks the business of all consumers – whoever has money to spend whether they are locals or international tourists, male or female, whatever their ages and whatever their tastes, provided these can be met profitably. The voluntary sector serves members and clients, and often fuses the production and enjoyment of its services. Well, that is how voluntary associations used to operate before they were under pressure to become more commercial. Public, that is government-provided, services are for citizens and can uniquely offer a citizenship experience. They can bolster national prestige, and boost citizens' pride in their national identities. That said, loss leaders which leverage other spending on infrastructure and facilities that attract leisure business (which may mean tourists, the countries' own residents on their days and evenings out or media companies) have risen and will continue to rise in importance in distributing public leisure spending. Public agencies are most likely to continue, whenever possible, to treat their leisure spending as investment. In public discourse, the 2012 London Olympics were always referred to in this manner rather than as a fun splurge. There was to be an upward step change in tourist inflows. Spending on the infrastructure required to host the games would leverage additional investment. Visitors would spot new investment opportunities in Britain, and, of course, there would be a legacy of increased sport participation, which would create a healthier and happier population. We now know that none of this happened except possibly increased tourist inflows, where it is impossible to separate any Olympic legacy from other trends that have continued to boost international tourism.

However, governments can at least hope for financial returns (and sometimes a profit) from their spending on big events. The sources of income are the same as those that are likely to accrue from more modest levels of government spending on leisure, but with big events the stakes are higher. There will be income from admission and user charges, plus the tax revenues from the earnings of workers in the jobs that government spending on big leisure events supports, which is mainly on the construction of facilities, and from sales taxes when the workers spend their earnings. Big events can attract additional revenue from sponsorships and broadcasting rights. Leisure spending is regarded as particularly valuable, and really is especially valuable to a country when the spenders are inbound tourists because they inject new money into an economy. Leisure spending, whether by governments, domestic residents or tourists, spreads economic benefits throughout a population by creating new business opportunities and jobs. It is the latter – jobs – that spread the benefits of spending on, or investing in, leisure most widely.

National and local governments have always been willing to fund leisure loss leaders when they have anticipated a payback for the national or local economies. It makes sense for this aim of government leisure spending to become a priority in societies where the leisure industries have grown into major business sectors, and where the provision of leisure goods and services is among the few sources of new jobs. This does not mean that the rest of the public sector's unique capabilities in leisure must be set aside. Spending that makes sense in economic terms can simultaneously boost national prestige, strengthen national identities and extend citizenship. If not, some of the revenues that accrue from governments' investments in income-generating leisure projects can be used to fund community leisure services. It is a win-win, not an either-or situation. However, the competition for the mobile $, € and £ is zero-sum. One city's, region's or country's gain is another's loss. Leisure spending could boost the global economy only if productivity in leisure businesses was higher than elsewhere, which is simply not the case. In a neoliberal age with markets making the decisions, countries either compete by investing in infrastructure and seeking big, medium-size and small events, or the business goes elsewhere.

All spending on leisure goods and services, whether the spenders are governments, local residents or inbound tourists, ripples with a multiplier effect throughout an economy as the staff employed in leisure jobs spend their earnings, thereby creating employment elsewhere. Hence the policy relevance, insofar as government leisure spending is intended to be an investment which boosts the economy and spreads prosperity, of identifying exactly which leisure-related sectors are currently the main job creators. The numbers employed in different kinds of leisure businesses have been cited in earlier chapters. Here we need to draw this evidence together and compare the performances of different kinds of leisure business in spreading wealth by creating jobs. We have seen that all leisure industries have a tendency to overestimate the number of jobs that they are responsible for and their contributions to the national economy. Nevertheless, the approximate numbers employed in different leisure sectors are known, and there is no dispute about which leisure industries are the main job creators today. The statistics cited below are for the UK. All the data are published by the Office for National Statistics (www.ons.gov.uk). The numbers will be different in other countries, but other national 'league tables' are unlikely to reorder the different kinds of leisure businesses in terms of their ability to generate employment.

This chapter therefore proceeds by locating leisure jobs. It then considers the implications for how the public sector can best use its special capabilities in leisure provision, including investment in loss leaders, and concludes with the implications for education in leisure-related subjects.

EMPLOYMENT

Going out

Jobs supported by tourism, in what are described as tourism-related or tourism-characteristic industries, are best subsumed under 'going out'. The going out may or may not involve one or more overnight stays. Those concerned may be from within or outside the country. They may be on business or leisure or a mixture of the two. They support jobs in food and beverages (out-of-home eating and drinking), accommodation, transport and entertainment. Among these, the largest employer in the UK is food and beverages (around 1.5 million jobs) followed by transport (around 600,000 jobs plus approximately 36,000 employed by travel agents), then accommodation (around 430,000 jobs) and creative arts and entertainment (roughly 90,000 jobs). Altogether, 'going out' supports around 2.7 million jobs (all figures are for the post-2011 period). These businesses are far and away the main sources of leisure-related employment, and conveniently they are the main types of jobs that are supported by tourism. This means that public investment which attracts inward tourists and persuades the domestic population to 'go out' without leaving the country is the type of government leisure spending that will be most effective in dispersing the economic benefits throughout a population via the jobs that are created.

Media

The old media employ approximately 630,000 in the UK. There are around 500,000 jobs in print, which is still far and away the main source of media-based jobs. Employment in films, radio, television and recorded music totals around 130,000. Collectively, the media follow going out in the league table of leisure-related jobs. Governments can maximise media-related employment by ensuring that domestic conditions for creating media content are as attractive as in competitor countries. Public service broadcasting, which draws revenues from all tax or licence fee payers, and creates large domestic audiences for free-to-air programmes, is one way of doing this. However, this alone will not ensure that content is locally sourced. For this, countries need dynamic creative industries and content creators (scriptwriters, music composers, songwriters, programme producers, and so on). As yet, there is no proven recipe for success. Education in the arts is one possibility. Another is the development of city cultural quarters which are attractive to the 'creative class' (Florida, 2002, 2012).

The key point to note here is that the new media make minor contributions to the media-related leisure jobs' total. These are not the businesses to target if the goal is to maximise media-related employment. Only around 1,000 persons are developing computer games in the UK. Social media sites are employment-light. Governments are ill advised to fund start-ups. Entrepreneurs will self-start in bedrooms and garages. Those whose products show potential will be backed through crowdsourcing, or by wealthy individual investors or investment/hedge funds. These businesses produce goods where the reproduction and distribution costs are negligible, usually downloads activated by an app. Winning in this kind of business makes a few people extremely rich but does not generate huge payrolls. If the UK (or any other country) became the base of the next Microsoft, Apple or Google, most production and development work would be outsourced and probably offshored, and profits would be taken in low-tax havens.

In the UK, there are over half a million jobs in computer programming and related occupations. Computer games and social media are not among the giant employers in the new technology sector. The old media are still the big leisure-related media employers, they are currently employing more rather than fewer staff than in the past and print still employs far more than all other media combined. Today's leisure scholars and students will surely be persuaded that leisure is now a business. They should then realise that 'going out' is where most employment-generating leisure business is done, followed by the media, among which print, the oldest of the mass media, is still far and away the largest employer.

Sport

This is the source of between 300,000 and 430,000 UK jobs, depending on how broadly or narrowly sport is defined. The core sport jobs are in management and administration in professional sport clubs, similar jobs in central and local government departments with responsibilities for sport and in participant sport facilities (playing fields, sport and swimming centres, and fitness gyms), where, in addition to administration and management, staff also work as teachers/coaches, in health, safety and security and in site and facility supervision and maintenance. Finally, there is a relatively small number of professional players. Employment in sport can be maximised (but not increased indefinitely) by providing land and indoor facilities for people to play and for spectators to be entertained. However, facilities will be underused in the absence of demand from the public. There are actions that governments can take to make a country, region or city more attractive to tourists, and which generate more visits by the home populations. It proves far more difficult to persuade the public to pay to watch or play more sport.

It is even more difficult to attract visitors from outside a country to visit in order to play or watch sport. These really are niche leisure markets. Sport mega-events attract large numbers of visitors but are not repeatable year-round or even annually in any country. Domestic spectator sports can be marketed to global audiences, but the greater part of the audience is always home based. The English Premier League is the world leader in exporting its product, but half of its broadcasting rights revenue is from the domestic audience. The rest is in far smaller sums from other countries all over the world.

Events

Commercial events management companies are a new kind of part-leisure business. Official statistics in the UK have yet to catch up with the formation of an events sector. Up to now, staff have moved, and still move into events from careers in sport, the arts and hospitality or general leisure management in local authorities. Events may be run by sport or arts organisations or hotels, or by any other business. Alternatively, nowadays, the management of an event may be contracted to a specialist event management company.

We saw in Chapter 7 that there are many types of events. There are mega-events such as the Olympic Games, but the events industry will also organise a business breakfast for just ten people, wedding and birthday parties, the conference of an academic society or the meeting and exhibition of a business federation or a single company. Event management businesses specialise in marketing the product (the event) by advertising, posted mail and using available email lists. They may be responsible for attracting exhibitors, handling the booking and on-site registration of those who attend and arranging catering, and will probably offer those who attend travel, accommodation and entertainment options. The venue for an event may be preselected, or the event management company may be asked to identify alternative possible locations. It may have to address light, sound and safety issues, and plan everything around an event agenda. Total employment in events is unknown. Estimates range up to 550,000, but these jobs are difficult to separate from employment in sports, the arts and hospitality. Organising events may be just part of a current job, or a job performed for a finite period within a longer career in sports, the arts, hospitality or general leisure management.

Events are not necessarily leisure related, but all the indicators suggest that leisure events are becoming more numerous and larger. Event management is now recognised as a distinct field by employment agencies, and it has become a popular option within most higher education courses in leisure, sports and tourism. Events have been claimed by the study of leisure because the facilities that are used and the skills that are required in events management are those needed in the management of sport and tourism, and sport has the biggest events. Cities, regions and countries can make themselves attractive locations for events by developing menus of meeting places, types of accommodation and infrastructure (mainly transport), plus entertainment and catering options for visitors. Place imaging and promotion can only be undertaken by public authorities.

Member clubs

These employ around 240,000 in the UK. Some of these jobs could be allocated to sports or the creative arts, but the voluntary sector also includes churches, professional associations, trade unions and charities, plus hobby groups. Voluntary associations which have national and sometimes worldwide memberships will need paid staff. There are no specific requirements for employment in this sector. Enthusiasm for the activity and membership of the association are usually the essential qualifications. Nevertheless, it is important to bear in mind that the public's uses of leisure do not lead to people being employed and create jobs solely in the public and commercial sectors. The voluntary sector has many paid employees as well as volunteers.

Other

Gambling employs around 100,000 in the UK. The rest of the population's leisure spending creates jobs in telephony (over 200,000), the production, repair and maintenance of motor vehicles, home improvements, gardening, hardware such as furniture, televisions and computers, fashion and cosmetics and other kinds of body adornment. Retail employs over half a million. Much leisure-related employment is not in what would normally be regarded as leisure industries. The leisure/not-leisure boundary is blurred on the supply side. It is throughout many kinds of business that a society of leisure has been growing.

PUBLIC SECTOR CAPABILITIES

We have seen that 'going out' is far ahead of the rest in terms of generating leisure-related employment. This spending is especially valuable to a country when the spenders have 'gone away' from their home states. The jobs that are created by going out are mainly in food and beverages, accommodation and transport, but people are unlikely to go to a particular place for the experience of the travel, the hotel or guest house experience or the catering. What attracts them to a given destination? There are clues in the places and sites that are the most visited. The Louvre in Paris was the world's most visited site in 2013 (9,334,435 visitors). It was followed at some distance by the British Museum in London (6,701,036 visitors). The world's top ten most visited sites included three in Paris and three in London. All the sites in the world's top ten were galleries or museums.

All 'most visited' league tables must be interpreted cautiously. There are many places with more footfall than Paris's Louvre. Many airports are far ahead: Atlanta with 96 million passengers in 2014, Beijing with 86 million and London's Heathrow with 73 million. Some rail terminals (Union Station in Washington, DC, and the Grand Central Terminal in New York City) are far ahead of the Louvre in footfall, but people are unlikely to travel in order to visit an air or rail terminal. Some shopping malls attract more visitors than the Louvre, but should these be set alongside tourist destinations? Many 'places' such as New York's Times Square and the Las Vegas Strip have more visitors than the Louvre, but the Louvre's true comparators would be sites within Las Vegas, and the sites within New York towards which people who pass through Times Square are heading. Disney sites also outrank the Louvre, but these are really 'resorts' whose proper comparators are other resorts such as the UK's Blackpool. The sites where visitors are 'counted in' are outranked by some outdoor spaces: some of the US national parks, Niagara Falls and Beijing's Forbidden City, which is a space, that is more like a park than a gallery or museum. However, a feature shared by nearly all the 'most visited' sites and places is that they are supported by public funds though they may be under voluntary sector or commercial management. These are the types of infrastructure in which governments can invest and thereby make their cities and countries more attractive to actual and potential visitors. Unlike big events, these sites will attract visitors indefinitely. They can be operated from year to year without new investment on the scale required to host mega-events.

Most major tourist destinations are attractive to visitors on account of the combinations and conglomerations of sites that can be visited. Britain's main attraction is in fact London with its numerous heritage sites, galleries and museums, plus the entertainment that is available. Britain is not exceptional in the appeal of its heritage. It is the number of sites, not any one, that makes cities such as Paris and London attractive tourist destinations. Commerce provides entertainment – theatres and 'attractions' in or close to cities such as London and Paris.

Merlin's portfolio of attractions (see Box 10.1) is a commercial equivalent to the heritage sites that are usually maintained and managed by the public and voluntary sectors. Merlin's UK sites add to the country's tourist offer and attract the home population for days out and short stays, and being headquartered in Britain means that the country hosts most of the Merlin group's management and administrative jobs. Merlin's stock market value is a fraction of that of Facebook, but Merlin employs 6 times as many staff.

Box 10.1 Merlin Entertainments

This business is based in Poole (UK), and was valued at $5 billion when it floated on the stock market in 2013, when Facebook was valued at $134 billion.

Merlin operates in 23 different countries, where it runs around 100 attractions, ten hotels and three holiday villages.

Merlin's better-known attractions include the following:

- Legoland parks in the UK, Denmark, Germany, Florida, California and Malaysia
- Madame Tussauds
- The London Eye
- Sea Life Aquarium parks
- Alton Towers (England)
- Warwick Castle (England)

Merlin's next venture will be a set of Shrek attractions.

The group's sites attract around 60 million visitors a year, and the total payroll is around 22,000 (many of whom are seasonal).

European countries (and many others) have a wealth of man-made heritage plus their natural environments. What is most likely to persuade residents of a country to do their going out without going abroad? Cost is obviously one consideration. It was among the reasons why, from the 1950s onwards, UK holidaymakers began deserting domestic seaside resorts for the Mediterranean, where the other attraction was that the sun was more reliable. The other attractions for residents to go out in their own country (and maybe stay overnight) are the same as for inward tourists – heritage sites and landscapes plus commercial entertainment as offered in London's West End theatreland and commercial attractions such as the Merlin facilities. Heritage is cheap to provide. Landscapes are gifts of nature. The construction costs of what are now relics, surviving castles, monuments and old churches were borne long ago. Conservation is relatively cheap. The labour forces in heritage, galleries and museums are tiny compared with the numbers employed in transport, accommodation and food and beverages. Much of the labour required at heritage sites is offered by volunteers. It makes sense for national, regional and city governments to protect, conserve and place-market themselves on the basis of their heritage sites, landscapes and entertainment. The public sector needs only to provide museums and galleries and protect the heritage (natural and man-made). Commerce will do the rest. It will offer all types and grades of accommodation, places to eat and drink, transport, entertainment and attractions.

Some traditional holiday resorts still attract more visitors than even the most visited heritage sites. Blackpool still has more annual visits than the British Museum. However, inward tourists to Britain do not head for Blackpool. In France, they do not head for Deauville. In the United States, they do not head for Coney. Visitors to the UK are most likely to head for London. In France, they are most likely to head for Paris. In London and Paris, they are then most likely to visit the heritage sites, galleries and museums and theatres.

Events can add to the number of visitors to a city, region or country, but even the sport mega-events attract only a fraction of the total annual numbers of the top heritage sites. A city's, region's and country's heritage sites are the assets that governments need to cherish in exercising one of the public sector's unique capabilities in leisure of funding loss leaders when there will be net gains in spending and jobs.

Old and new media can be left to take care of their (mainly commercial) selves. Communications via cable, satellite and the airwaves need to be regulated, but users will cover the costs. Public service media programmes and channels, accessible by all citizens, can be retained if this is considered desirable. These programmes and channels can be funded with hypothecated taxes (television licence fees and maybe, as in many countries, licence fees for radio receivers and Internet connections).

Professional sport can fund itself. Participant sport, the voluntary sector more generally, and the events industry are major employers (though well behind 'going out'). The public sector needs to ensure that the amenities that these industries need are available. The relevant amenities are playing fields (though often nowadays with artificial surfaces), indoor centres and swimming pools for sport, and meeting and exhibition rooms and halls of various sizes for voluntary clubs and events. Management of these facilities can be outsourced, and costs may be fully recouped from user charges, but only governments can ensure the availability of amenities plus the maintenance and protection of public outdoor spaces, including green spaces. 'Spaces' have no costs of production, but there are opportunity costs to be foregone – income that would accrue from selling land and amenity sites for redevelopment as retail parks, car parks, business and residential accommodation. Before 'selling any family silver', politicians should realise that any revenue will be one-off, and that they are depriving future generations of the enjoyment of leisure assets that were preserved, and sometimes bought or donated, by earlier generations.

Funding loss leaders for the economic benefits that accrue indirectly to governments via tax revenues, and to the wider populations in the form of increased business opportunities, employment and hence consumption, is just one of the public sector's special capabilities in leisure. The others are extending citizenship rights by making certain leisure opportunities available to all citizens, strengthening a city's, region's and country's prestige and the collective identities of the citizens and signalling that particular tastes and activities are considered especially worthy (by the state, speaking and acting on behalf of the wider population).

We must bear in mind that national prestige and identity, and citizenship, do not depend exclusively or evenly mainly on leisure. International prestige will depend more on diplomatic and military strength, and a country's standard of living and way of life. The basic rights of citizenship in modern societies are the protection of the law, the right to vote and thereby elect and dismiss rulers and rights to education, to health care and, according to prevailing standards, to a minimum income and decent housing. That said, heritage, galleries and museums 'tick all the boxes', and amenities meet the citizenship criterion, provided, in all these cases, any user or admission charges do not deter any section of the population.

Performing arts and top sport cannot meet the citizenship or prestige and identity-building criteria. There can only be one best country, so no formula can work universally. Top-level athletes have alternative sources of support. They can be paid for performances and sometimes just for appearances, they can obtain sponsorship and sport governing bodies could use more of their income from broadcasting rights to promote their sports and provide more and better facilities for all amateur players. State funding for specific arts and top-level sport may be justified for signalling worthiness. It is up to politicians to make this judgement. High culture is probably safe, given that it is the culture of the ruling class (see Chapter 8, pp. 185–186).

Even if the money has run out or, at any rate, there will be less than in the past, and despite rampant commercialisation, it remains possible for the public sector to exercise all its unique capabilities in leisure provision. It may not be able to do as much as in the past, but it can still do enough. The basic requirement is for politicians to recognise their special capabilities, and then act accordingly.

EDUCATION

Leisure and its kindred subjects – sport, media, tourism and events – have become popular student choices in higher education in recent years. Leisure studies began in North America, spread into Britain, then into other modern, English-speaking countries, and as more countries modernise, the study of leisure in general and specific kinds of leisure is becoming global.

The popularity of these subjects among students is easy to explain. There are rarely any specific academic prerequisites. Students can start these subjects afresh, from scratch, on entering higher education. Students will usually be interested in the subjects that they choose – sport, media, tourism or leisure in general. Equally important, they are likely to know that these can be sources of employment and that more jobs are being created in these fields.

Higher education systems in countries where these subjects have become popular student choices produce far too many graduates for them all to gain employment in the fields, but this is equally true in most social sciences, arts and humanities. Most students do not study for degrees in the social sciences, arts and humanities in the expectation that they will be employed in such occupations. They study the subjects in order to enter general graduate labour markets. Graduates in leisure-related subjects are equally able to seek employment in many additional fields. Most sports studies graduates in Britain do not progress into careers in sport (Minten, 2010), but this does not mean that their academic backgrounds will have no value in their employment. It is an asset in all businesses to know the customers, and when the customers are from the general public, knowledge of their typical tastes and lifestyles will be an advantage. Graduates in leisure and related subjects progress into many different occupations, and in most of these occupations, their knowledge about the public's leisure and the different tastes, opportunities and constraints on how various socio-demographic groups can spend their time and money will be an asset. The blurring of boundaries makes the case for the study of leisure to feature in most arts, humanities and social science disciplines rather than to be confined in the ghetto, where the study of leisure has been nurtured. The time is right for leisure studies to spread its messages more widely.

Government departments with leisure responsibilities need staff who understand the capabilities and limitations of commerce, the roles, strengths and limitations of the voluntary sector and what the public sector can realistically aim to achieve when there is no money for new ventures and less for what has been supported in the past. This knowledge need not be acquired in first-degree studies. Given the varied career destinations of graduates in leisure-related subjects, and the varied routes that remain open into careers in all types of leisure provision, the expert knowledge that is required is probably best gained in postgraduate, often post-career entry courses. In any case, it is only the media where the majority of jobs are at levels traditionally associated with a university degree. Sport- and tourism-related jobs are usually 'intermediate' at best in their locations in the occupational class structure. Higher education qualifications are not required in most jobs in sport, transport, food and beverages and hospitality. Most jobs in these business sectors require vocational education and training rather than higher education. The anomaly of training in classical high culture having become firmly embedded in higher education requires a class explanation.

FINAL CONCLUSIONS

Commercialisation, and more widespread uses and constant innovations in the latest digital technologies, cannot be resisted by public leisure policies. In this respect, they are like ageing populations and widening economic inequalities. These are simply new realities that all leisure providers confront. Any country that tried to opt out would have to become a fortress economy, controlling all inward and outward movements of goods, people and capital. Current member countries would have to leave the European Union, whose social agenda has been subordinated to the hope of using market forces to become the world's most competitive economy with the world's best-educated and most highly skilled and productive workforce. The European Union itself could become a fortress economy, but this would require a centralisation of political power that is still decades ahead even if the trend towards an 'ever-closer union' continues.

The good news for all leisure providers is that neither commercialisation nor new technologies can eliminate anything that previously existed provided existing provisions are sufficiently valued by consumers, citizens (whose wishes must be represented by politicians) and members of voluntary associations. Twentieth- and 21st-century history shows that commercialisation and new technologies usually add to the public's leisure options. When older leisure goods and services suffer, this is the result of people's choices.

The voluntary sector is not threatened. Indeed, there are new opportunities to use new technologies to deepen contact with and to recruit new members and users. There are also new opportunities to take over the management of leisure services that were formerly run directly by central and local governments. That said, there is no compulsion. Provided there are members with sufficient enthusiasm for their sports, arts, hobbies and crafts, voluntary associations can continue in their habitual preferred ways.

Finally, the public sector may have less money to spend, and governments' priority, given prevailing labour market conditions and modest (if any) economic growth rates in first-wave industrial countries, may now be to use leisure spending as investment to trigger wider economic regeneration. Even so, governments can still exercise all their special capabilities in leisure provision. These do not depend on central or local governments' acting as direct providers. They do depend on not frittering resources on projects whose aims are beyond the public sector's capabilities in leisure, like the social inclusion of otherwise disadvantaged groups, and trying to change people's lifestyles in a preferred way. In a snap phrase, the public sector will be most effective and strong by getting 'back to basics'. The basic message is to cherish heritage. The pay-off will be attracting 'going out' spending and the employment that this creates. The secondary message is to provide or ensure the availability of amenities – spaces and places of all types which include rail and air terminals, city precincts and places to meet, to play and to be entertained. Commerce and the voluntary sector will do the rest.

Bibliography

Aall, C., Klepp, I. G., Engeset, A. B., Skuland, S. E., and Stoa, E. (2011), 'Leisure and sustainable development in Norway: part of the solution and the problem', *Leisure Studies*, 30, 453–476.

Aitchison, C., Macleod, N. E., and Shaw, S. J. (2000), *Leisure and Tourism Landscapes: Social and Cultural Geographies*, Routledge, London.

Albemarle Report. (1960), *The Youth Service in England and Wales*, HMSO, London.

Alexandris, K. (2008), 'Performance management and leisure management', *Managing Leisure*, 13, 137–138.

Allan, G., and Crow, G. (1991), 'Privatisation, home-centredness and leisure', *Leisure Studies*, 10, 19–32.

Allen, J., O'Toole, W., Harris, R., and McDonnell, I. (2011), *Festivals and Special Event Management*. Wiley, London.

Allison, L. (2001), *Amateurism in Sport*, Frank Cass, London.

Andrejevic, M. (2009), 'The twenty-first century telescreen', in Turner, G., and Tay, J., eds., *Television Studies after TV: Understanding Television in the Post-broadcast Era*, Routledge, London.

Anheier, H. (n.d.), 'Voluntary associations'. http://fathom.lse.ac.uk/Features/122550/.

Appadurai, A. (1986), *The Social Life of Things: Commodities in Cultural Perspective*, Cambridge University Press, Cambridge.

Appadurai, A. (1996), *Modernity at Large: Cultural Dimensions of Globalization*, University of Minnesota Press, Minneapolis.

Arthur, C. (2012), *Digital Wars: Apple, Google, Microsoft and the Battle for the Internet*, Kogan Page, London.

Audit Commission. (1989), *Sport for Whom?*, HMSO, London.

Audit Commission. (2002), *Sport and Recreation*, Audit Commission, London.

Bacon, W. (1997), 'The rise of the German and the demise of the English spa industry: a critical analysis of business success and failure', *Leisure Studies*, 16, 173–187.

Bailey, P. (1978), *Leisure and Class in Victorian England*, Routledge, London.

Bailey, P., ed. (1986), *Music Hall: The Business of Pleasure*, Open University Press, Milton Keynes.

Bandyopadhyay, P. (1973), 'The holiday camp', in Smith, M. A., Parker, S., and Smith, C. S., eds., *Leisure and Society in Britain*, Allen Lane, London.

Bang, H. (2009), 'The direct and indirect influences of sporting event organization's reputation on volunteer commitment', *Event Management*, 13, 139–152.

Barlow, A. (2008), *Blogging America: The New Public Sphere*, Praeger, Westport.

Becker, E. (2013), *Overbooked: The Exploding Business of Travel and Tourism*, Simon and Schuster, New York.

Bekuis, H., Lubbers, M., and Ultee, W. (2014), 'A macro-sociological study into the changes in the popularity of domestic, European, and American pop music in Western countries', *European Sociological Review*, 30, 180–193.

Benner, C. (2002), *Work in the New Economy: Flexible Labor Markets in Silicon Valley*, Blackwell, Oxford.

Bennett, T., Savage, M., Silva, E., Warde, A., Gayo-Cal, M., and Wright, D. (2009), *Culture, Class, Distinction*, Routledge, London.

Benneworth, P., and Dauncey, H. (2010), 'International urban festivals as a catalyst for governance capacity building', *Environment and Planning: Government and Policy*, 28, 1083–1100.

Bergvall-Kareborn, B., and Howcroft, D. (2013), ' "The future's bright, the future's mobile": a study of Apple and Google mobile application developers', *Work, Employment and Society*, 27, 964–981.

Berrett, T., Burton, T. L., and Slack, T. (1993), 'Quality products, quality service: factors leading to entrepreneurial success in the sport and leisure industry', *Leisure Studies*, 12, 93–106.

Bianchini, F., and Parkinson, M., eds. (1993), *Cultural Policy and Urban Regeneration*, Manchester University Press, Manchester.

Birmingham, J., and David, M. (2011), 'Live-streaming: will football fans continue to be more law abiding than music fans?', *Sport in Society*, 14, 69–80.

Bishop, J., and Hoggett, P. (1986), *Organising around Enthusiasms*, Comedia, London.

Bliers, H. (2003), *Communities in Control: Public Services and Local Socialism*, Fabian Society, London.

Born, G. (2004), *Uncertain Vision: Birt, Dyke and the Reinvention of the BBC*, Vintage, London.

Bosscher, V. de, Sotiriadou, P., and van Bottenburg, M. (2013), 'Scrutinizing the sport pyramid: an examination of the relationship between elite success and mass participation in Flanders', *International Journal of Sport Policy and Politics*, 5, 319–339.

Bottenburg, M. van, and Salome, L. (2010), 'The indoorisation of outdoor sports: an exploration of the rise of lifestyle sports in artificial settings', *Leisure Studies*, 29, 143–160.

Botterill, J. (2010), *Consumer Culture and Personal Finance: Money Goes to Market*, Palgrave Macmillan, Basingstoke.

Bourdieu, P. (1984), *Distinction: A Social Critique of the Judgement of Taste*, Routledge, London.

Bourdieu, P., and Darbel, A. (1997), *The Love of Art*, Polity Press, Oxford.

Bowden, S. (1994), 'The new consumerism', in Johnson, P., ed., *Twentieth Century Britain*, Longman, London.

Bowdin, G. A. J., Allen, J., O'Toole, W., Harris, B., and McDonnell, I. (2011), *Events Management*, Elsevier Butter-Heinemann, Oxford.

Brewster, M., Connell, J., and Page, S. J. (2009), 'The Scottish Highland Games: evolution, development and role as a community event', *Current Issues in Tourism*, 12, 271–293.

Briggs, A., and Burke, P. (2005), *A Social History of the Media*, Polity, Cambridge.

Brooks-Buck, J., and Anderson, E. L. (2001), 'African American access to higher education through sports: following a dream or perpetuating a stereotype?', *Widening Participation and Lifelong Learning*, 3, 26–31.

Bryman, A. (1995), *Disney and His Worlds*, Routledge, London.

Burgess, J., and Green, J. (2009), *YouTube: Online Video and Participatory Culture*, Polity, Cambridge.

Burls, A. P. (2010), 'The multifunctional values of therapeutic green spaces', http://www.hphpcentral.com/wp-content/uploads/2010/09/5000-paper-by-Ambra-burls.pdf.

Burnett, J. (2000), *Riot, Revelry and Rout: Sport in Lowland Scotland before 1860*, Tuckwell Press, East Linton.

Burns, T. (1977), *The BBC*, Macmillan, London.

Butler, K. N. (1978), 'Roles of the commercial provider in leisure', in Talbot, M. A., and Vickerman, R. W., eds., *Social and Economic Costs and Benefits of Leisure*, Leisure Studies Association, Leeds.

Calhoun, C., and Derluguian, G., eds. (2011), *Business as Usual: The Roots of the Global Financial Meltdown*, New York University Press, New York.

Cammaerts, B. (2011), 'The hegemonic copyright regime vs the sharing copyright users of music?', *Media, Culture and Society*, 33, 491–502.

Carlsen, J., and Andersson, T. D. (2011), 'Strategic SWOT analysis of public, private and not-for-profit festival organisations', *International Journal of Event and Festival Management*, 2, 83–97.

Carlsen, J., Andersson, T. D., Ali-Knight, J., Jaeger, K., and Taylor, R. (2010), 'Festival management innovation and failure', *International Journal of Event and Festival Management*, 1, 120–131.

Carter, N. (2006), *The Football Manager: A History*, Routledge, London.

Castells, M., Caraca, J., and Cardoso, G. (2012), 'The cultures of the economic crisis: an introduction', in Castells, M., Caraca, J., and Cardoso, G., eds., *Aftermath: The Cultures of the Economic Crisis*, Oxford University Press, Oxford, pp. 1–14.

Cavill, A. (2002), 'Repositioning Blackpool to become Las Vegas of the UK', presentation at Leisure Studies Association Conference, Preston.

Centre for Economic and Business Research. (2013), *The Contribution of the Arts and Culture to the National Economy*, Centre for Economics and Business Research, London.

Centre for Leisure and Sport Research. (2002), *Count Me In: The Dimensions of Social Inclusion through Culture and Sport*, Leeds Metropolitan University, Leeds.

Charlton, T. (2010), 'Grow and sustain: the role of community sports provision in promoting a participation legacy for the 2012 Olympic Games', *International Journal of Sports Policy and Politics*, 2, 347–366.

Chorafas, D. N. (2012), *Basel III: The Devil and Global Banking*, Palgrave Macmillan, Basingstoke.

Clarke, J., and Critcher, C. (1985), *The Devil Makes Work*, Macmillan, London.

Coalter, F. (1990), 'The politics of professionalism: consumers or citizens', *Leisure Studies*, 9, 107–119.

Coalter, F. (2007), *A Wider Role for Sport: Who's Keeping the Score*, Routledge, London.

Coalter, F. (2013), *Sport-for-development: What Game Are We Playing?*, Routledge, London.

Coalter, F. (2014), 'Sport-for-development: pessimism of the intellect, optimism of the will', in Schulenkorf, N., and Adair, D., eds., *Global Sport-for-development: Critical Perspectives*, Palgrave Macmillan, Basingstoke, pp. 62–78.

Cohen, E. (1979), 'A phenomenology of tourist experiences', *Sociology*, 13, 179–201.

Cohen, S. (1991), *Rock Culture in Liverpool*, Oxford University Press, Oxford.

Cole, S. (2006), 'Information and empowerment: the keys to achieving sustainable tourism', *Journal of Sustainable Tourism*, 14, 629–644.

Collins, R. (1999), 'European Union media and communication', in Stokes, J., and Reading, A., eds., *The Media in Britain: Current Debates and Developments*, Macmillan, Basingstoke.

Collins, T. (2006), *Rugby's Great Split: Class, Culture and the Origins of Rugby League Football*, Routledge, London.

Collins, T. (2013), *Sport in Capitalist Society: A Short History*, Routledge, Abingdon.

Crawford, G. (2008), '"It's in the game": sports fans, film and digital gaming', *Sport in Society*, 11, 130–145.

Critcher, C. (1992), 'Sporting civic pride: Sheffield and the World Student Games of 1991', in Sugden, J., and Knox, C., eds., *Leisure in the 1990s*, Leisure Studies Association, Eastbourne.

Crompton, J. L. (2000), 'Repositioning leisure services', *Managing Leisure*, 5, 65–75.

Crompton, J. L. (2001), 'Public subsidies to professional sport team facilities in the USA', in Gratton, C., and Henry, I., eds., *Sport in the City: The Role of Sport in Economic and Social Regeneration*, Routledge, London, pp. 15–34.

Crompton, J. L. (2007), 'The role of the proximate principle in the emergence of urban parks in the United Kingdom and the United States', *Leisure Studies*, 26, 213–234.

Crompton, J. L. (2008), 'Evolution and implications of a paradigm shift in the marketing of leisure services in the USA', *Leisure Studies*, 27, 181–206.

Crompton, J. L. (2013), 'The health rationale for urban parks in the nineteenth century in the USA', *World Leisure Journal*, 55, 333–346.

Cross, G. (1993), *Time and Money: The Making of Consumer Culture*, Routledge, London.

Crouch, D., ed. (1999), *Leisure/Tourism Geographies: Practices and Geographical Knowledge*, Routledge, London.

Crowhurst, A. (2001), 'The portly grabbers of 75 per cent: capital investment in the British entertainment industry, 1885–1914', *Leisure Studies*, 20, 107–123.

Curran, J. (1977), 'Capitalism and control of the press', in Curran, J., Gurevitch, M., and Woollacott, J., eds., *Mass Communication and Society*, Edward Arnold, London.

David, M. (2010), *Peer to Peer and the Music Industry: The Criminalization of Sharing*, Sage, London.

Davis, D. E. (1978), 'Development and the tourist industry in Third World countries', *Society and Leisure*, 1, 301–324.

Davis, S. I. (2009), *Banking in Turmoil*, Palgrave Macmillan, Basingstoke.

Deckers, P., and Gratton, C. (1995), 'Participation in sport and membership of traditional sports clubs: a case study of gymnastics in the Netherlands', *Leisure Studies*, 14, 117–131.

DeLisle, L. J. (2004), 'Leisure and tolerance – a historical perspective', *World Leisure Journal*, 46, 2, 55–63.

Deloitte/Oxford Economics. (2013), *Tourism: Jobs and Growth. The Economic Contribution of the Tourism Economy in the UK*, Deloitte, London.

Department of National Heritage. (1995), *Sport: Raising the Game*, Department of National Heritage, London.

Derrett, R. (2003), 'Making sense of how festivals demonstrate a community's sense of place', *Event Management*, 8, 49–58.

Devine, F. (1992), *Affluent Workers Revisited: Privatism and the Working Class*, Edinburgh University Press, Edinburgh.

Dixon, R. M. (1991), *Black Arts, Policy and the Issue of Equity*, Race and Social Policy Unit, University of Liverpool, Liverpool.

Doherty, A. (2009), 'The volunteer legacy of a major sport event', *Journal of Policy Research in Tourism, Leisure and Events*, 1, 185–207.

Donohoe, H. M., and Needham, R. D. (2006), 'Ecotourism: the evolving contemporary definition', *Journal of Ecotourism*, 5, 190–210.

Driver, B. L., Brown, P., and Peterson, G. (1991), *Benefits of Leisure*, Venture Publishing, Pennsylvania.

Dyer-Witheford, N., and de Peuter, G. (2009), *Games of Empire: Global Capitalism and Video Games*, University of Minnesota Press, Minneapolis.

Eisenstein, E. L. (1983), *The Printing Revolution in Early Modern Europe*, Cambridge University Press, Cambridge.

European Commission, Directorate-general for Employment and Social Affairs. (2003), *The New Actors of Employment*, Office for Official Publications of the European Communities, Luxembourg.

Featherstone, M. (1991), *Consumer Culture and Post-modernism*, Sage, London.

Ferreira, F., and Wadfogel, J. (2010), *Pop Internationalism: Has Half a Century of Music Trade Displaced Local Culture?*, NBER Working Paper 15964, National Bureau of Economic Research, Cambridge, MA.

Finnegan, R. (1989), *The Hidden Musicians*, Cambridge University Press, Cambridge.

Florida, R. (2002), *The Rise of the Creative Class: And How It's Transforming Work, Leisure, Community and Everyday Life*, Basic Books, New York.

Florida, R. (2012), *The Rise of the Creative Class: Revisited*, Basic Books, New York.

Foley, M., McGillivray, D., and McPherson, G. (2012), *Event Policy: From Theory to Strategy*, Routledge, Abingdon.

Franzen, A. (2000), 'Does the Internet make us lonely?', *European Sociological Review*, 16, 427–438.

Garcia, B. (2005), 'De-constructing the city of culture: the long-term cultural legacies of Glasgow 1990', *Urban Studies*, 42, 1–28.

Garcia, B., Melville, R., and Cox, T. (2010), *Creating an Impact: Liverpool's Experience as European Capital of Culture*, University of Liverpool, Liverpool.

Gardner, P. (1974), *Nice Guys Finish Last: Sport and American Life*, Allen Lane, London.

Getz, D. (2007), *Event Studies: Theory, Research and Policy for Planned Events*, Butterworth-Heinemann, Oxford.

Gillespie, D. L., Leffler, A., and Lerner, E. (2002), 'If it weren't for my hobby, I'd have a life: dog sports, serious leisure and boundary negotiations', *Leisure Studies*, 21, 285–304.

Gillespie, T. (2007), *Wired Shut: Copyright and the Shape of Digital Culture*, MIT Press, Cambridge, MA.

Giulianotti, R., and Robertson, R. (2009), *Globalization and Football*, Sage, London.

Glyptis, S. (1989), *Leisure and Unemployment*, Open University Press, Milton Keynes.

Godbey, G. (1997), *Leisure and Leisure Services in the 21st Century*, Venture Publishing, Penn State.

Godbey, G., and Parker, S. (1976), *Leisure Studies and Services: An Overview*, Saunders, Philadelphia.

Goggin, G. (2011), *Global Mobile Media*, Routledge, London.

Gold, J., and Gold, M. (2009), *Olympic Cities: City Agendas, Planning and the World Games, 1896–2016*, Routledge, London.

Goldsmith, J., and Wu, T. (2006), *Who Controls the Internet?*, Oxford University Press, Oxford.

Gotham, F. K. (2005), 'Tourism from above and below: globalization, localization and New Orleans' Mardi Gras', *International Journal of Urban and Regional Research*, 29, 309–326.

Gration, D., Raciti, M., and Arcodia, C. (2011), 'The role of consumer self-concept in marketing festivals', *Journal of Travel and Tourism Marketing*, 28, 644–655.

Gratton, C., Dobson, N., and Shibli, S. (2001), 'The role of major sports events in the economic regeneration of cities: lessons from six World or European championships', in Gratton, C., and Henry, I., eds., *Sport in the City: The Role of Sport in Economic and Social Regeneration*, Routledge, London, pp. 35–45.

Gratton, C., and Henry, I. (2001), 'Sport in the city: where do we go from here?', in Gratton, C., and Henry, I., eds., *Sport in the City: The Role of Sport in Economic and Social Regeneration*, Routledge, London, pp. 309–314.

Gratton, C., Shibili, S., and Coleman, R. (2005), 'Sport and economic regeneration in cities', *Urban Studies*, 42, 985–999.

Gratton, C., and Taylor, P. (2000), *Economics of Sport and Recreation*, Spon, London.

de Grazia, V. (1992), 'Leisure and citizenship: historical perspectives', in *Leisure and New Citizenship*, Actas VIII Congreso ELRA, Bilbao.

Green, M. (2004), 'Changing policy priorities for sport in England: the emergence of elite sport development as a key policy concern', *Leisure Studies*, 23, 365–385.

Green, M., and Oakley, B. (2001), 'Elite sport development systems and playing to win: uniformity and diversity in international approaches', *Leisure Studies*, 20, 247–267.

Griffin, T. (2014), 'The evolving nature of hosting friends and relatives for immigrants', paper presented at Leisure Studies Association Conference, Paisley.

Gripsund, G., Nes, E. B., and Olssen, U. H. (2010), 'Effects of hosting a mega-sport event on country image', *Event Management*, 14, 193–204.

Grunewald, R. de A. (2002), 'Tourism and cultural revival', *Annals of Tourism Research*, 29, 4, 1004–1021.

Hanson, D. (1982), *The Professionalisation of Fun*, Centre for Leisure Studies and Research, University of Salford, Salford.

Harambam, J., Auspers, S., and Hourman, D. (2011), 'Game over? Negotiating modern capitalism in virtual game worlds', *European Journal of Cultural Studies*, 14, 299–319.

Harper, R. (2001), *Social Capital: A Review of the Literature*, Office for National Statistics, London.

Harper, W. J. (1997), 'The future of leisure: making leisure work', *Leisure Studies*, 16, 189–198.

Hayden, L. (2007), 'Tourism and climate change', *Travel and Tourism Analyst*, 1, 1–37.

Hayes, G., and Karamichas, J., eds. (2011), *Olympic Games, Mega-events and Civil Societies: Globalisation, Environment and Resistance*, Palgrave Macmillan, Basingstoke.

Heeley, J. (1986), 'Leisure and moral reform', *Leisure Studies*, 5, 57–67.

Henry, I., and Gratton, C. (2001), 'Sport in the city: research issues', in Gratton, C., and Henry, I., eds., *Sport in the City: The Role of Sport in Economic and Social Regeneration*, Routledge, London, pp. 3–11.

Hesmondhalgh, D. (1998), 'The British dance music industry: a case study of independent cultural production', *British Journal of Sociology*, 49, 234–251.

Hesmondhalgh, D. (2013), *The Cultural Industries*, 3rd edition, Sage, London.

Hesmondhalgh, D., and Baker, S. (2010), *Creative Labour: Media Work in Three Cultural Industries*, Routledge, London.

Hill, J. (2002), *Sport, Leisure and Culture in Twentieth Century Britain*, Palgrave, Basingstoke.

Horne, J. (2007), 'The four "knowns" of sports mega-events', *Leisure Studies*, 26, 81–96.

Horne, J., and Manzenreiter, W., eds. (2006), *Sports Mega-events*, Sociological Review Monograph, Blackwell, Oxford.

Houlihan, B., and White, A. (2002), *The Politics of Sports Development: Development of Sport or Development through Sport?*, Routledge, London.

Howe, J. (2008), *Crowdsourcing: How the Power of the Crowd Is Driving the Future of Business*, Random House, London.

Hughes, G., and Boyle, M. (1992), 'Place boosterism: political contention, leisure and culture in Glasgow', in Sugden, J., and Knox, C., eds., *Leisure in the 1990s*, Leisure Studies Association, Eastbourne.

Hultkrantz, J. (1998), 'Mega-event displacement of visitors: the World Championship in Athletics, Göteborg 1995', *Festival Management and Event Tourism*, 5, 1–8.

Hunter, A. (2014), 'Grassroots football in England: abuse, death threats and withering numbers', *Guardian*, 17 January.

Hutchins, B., and Rowe, D. (2012), *Sport beyond Television: The Internet, Digital Media and the Rise of Networked Media Sport*, Routledge, London.

Ingham, A. G. (1985), 'From public issue to personal trouble: well-being and the fiscal crisis of the state', *Sociology of Sport Journal*, 2, 43–55.

Jago, L., and Dwyer, L. (2006), *Economic Evaluation of Special Events: A Practitioner's Guide*, Common Ground Publishing, Altona, VIC.

Jago, L., Dwyer, L., Lipman, G., van Lill, D., and Vorster, S. (2010), 'Optimising the potential of mega-events: an overview', *International Journal of Event and Festival Management*, 1, 220–237.

Jakobsen, J., Solberg, H. A., Halvorsen, T., and Jakobsen, T. G. (2013), 'Fool's gold: major sports events and foreign direct investment', *International Journal of Sports Policy and Politics*, 5, 353–380.

Kane, Y. I. (2014), *Haunted Empire: Apple after Steve Jobs*, Collins, London.

Kay, T. A. (1987), 'Leisure in the life-styles of unemployed people: a case study in Leicester', PhD thesis, Loughborough University of Technology, Loughborough.

Kennedy, E., and Hills, L. (2009), *Sport, Media and Society*, Berg, Oxford.

Kent, S. I. (2001), *From Pong to Pokemon and Beyond ... The Ultimate History of Video Games. The Story behind the Craze That Touched Our Lives and Changed the World*, Three Rivers Press, New York.

Kim, S. S., Yoon, S., and Kim, Y. (2011), 'Competitive positioning among international convention cities in the East Asia region', *Journal of Convention and Event Tourism*, 12, 86–105.

King, P., Town, S., and Warner, S. (1985), 'Leisure provision and ethnic minorities in Bradford', in Henry, I., ed., *Leisure Policy and Recreation Disadvantage*, Newsletter Supplement, Leisure Studies Association, Bradford.

Kingsbury, A. (1976), 'Animation', in Haworth, J., and Veal, A. J., eds., *Leisure and the Community*, Leisure Studies Association, University of Birmingham.

Kirkpatrick, D. (2011), *The Facebook Effect*, Virgin Books, London.

Kokosalakis, T. (2014), 'Money games', *Sports Management*, Issue 1, 32–34.

Kozak, M., Gokovah, U., and Bahar, O. (2008), 'Estimating the determinants of tourist spending: a comparison of four models', *Tourism Analysis*, 13, 143–155.

Kraut, R., Lundmark, V., Patterson, M., Kiesler, S., Mukopadhyay, T., and Scherlis, W. (1998), 'Internet paradox: a social technology that reduces social involvement and psychological well-being', *American Psychologist*, 53, 1017–1031.

Lancaster, B. (1996), *The Department Store: A Social History*, Leicester University Press, Leicester.

Land, C., and Taylor, S. (2010), 'Surf's up: work, life, balance and brand in a New Age capitalist organization', *Sociology*, 44, 395–413.

Lane, C. M. (2011), *A Company of One: Insecurity, Independence and the New World of White-collar Employment*, Cornell University Press, Ithaca.

Lapavitsas, C. (2011), 'Theorizing financialization', *Work, Employment and Society*, 25, 611–626.

Lapavitsas, C. (2012), *Crisis in the Eurozone*, Verso, London.

Lawrence, L. (2003), '"These are the voyages ...": interaction in real and virtual space environments in leisure', *Leisure Studies*, 22, 301–315.

Lee, A. J. (1976), *The Origins of the Popular Press, 1855–1914*, Croom Helm, London.

Lengkeek, J. (2000), 'Imagination and differences in tourist experience', *World Leisure Journal*, 42, 3, 11–17.

Lenskyj, H. (2008), *Olympic Industry Resistance: Challenging Olympic Power and Propaganda*, State University of New York Press, Albany.

Levermore, R., and Beacon, A., eds. (2009), *Sport and International Development*, Palgrave Macmillan, Basingstoke.

Li, Y., Savage, M., Tampubolon, G., Warde, A., and Tomlinson, M. (2002), 'Dynamics of social capital: trends and turnover in associational membership in England and Wales, 1972–1999', *Sociological Research Online*, 7, 3.

Lowe, G. (2002), 'Teenagers and the mall: findings from a survey of teenagers at Royal Randwick Shopping Centre', paper presented at International Sociological Association Congress, Brisbane.

Lyons, K. D., and Wearing, S., eds. (2007), *Cultural Tourism: Journeys of Discovery in Volunteer Tourism: International Case Study Perspectives*, CABI, Wallingford.

MacCannell, D. (1976), *The Tourist: A New Theory of the Leisure Class*, Macmillan, London.

Maguire, J. S. (2008), *Fit for Consumption: Sociology of the Business of Fitness*, Routledge, London.

Malhado, A. C. M., and Rothfuss, R. (2013), 'Transporting 2014 FIFA World Cup to sustainability: exploring residents' and tourists' attitudes and behaviours', *Journal of Policy Research in Tourism, Leisure and Events*, 5, 252–269.

Manes, S., and Andrews, P. (2013), *Gates: How Microsoft's Mogul Reinvented an Industry and Made Himself the Richest Man in America*, Cadwallader and Stern, Seattle.

Manzenreiter, W., and Horne, J., eds. (2004), *Football Goes East: Business, Culture and the People's Game in China, Japan and South Korea*, Routledge, London.

Markovits, A. S., and Hellerman, S. L. (2001), *Offside: Soccer and American Exceptionalism*, Princeton University Press, Princeton.

Martin, B., and Mason, S. (1988), 'The role of tourism in urban regeneration', *Leisure Studies*, 7, 75–80.

Martin, K. (2010), 'Living pasts: contested tourism authenticities', *Annals of Tourism Research*, 37, 537–554.

Mason, M. (2008), *The Pirate's Dilemma: How Hackers, Punk Capitalists, Graffiti Millionaires and Other Youth Movements Are Remixing Our Culture and Changing Our World*, Penguin, London.

Massey, J. (2005), 'The gentrification of consumption: a view from Manchester', *Sociological Research Online*, 10, 2.

McCrone, D., Morris, A., and Kiely, R. (1995), *Scotland – The Brand: The Making of Scottish Heritage*, Edinburgh University Press, Edinburgh.

McCullagh, C. (2002), *Media Power: A Sociological Introduction*, Palgrave, Basingstoke.

McCulloch, A. (2014), 'Cohort variations in the membership of voluntary associations in Great Britain, 1991–2007', *Sociology*, 48, 167–185.

McGillivray, D., and McPherson, G. (2012), ' "Surfing a wave of change": a critical appraisal of the London 2012 cultural programme', *Journal of Policy Research in Tourism, Leisure and Events*, 4, 123–137.

McGuigan, J. (2004), *Rethinking Cultural Policy*, Open University Press, Maidenhead.

McKinlay, A., and Smith, C., eds. (2009), *Creative Labour: Working in the Creative Industries*, Palgrave Macmillan, Basingstoke.

McNamee, M. J., Sheridan, H., and Buswell, J. (2000), 'Paternalism, professionalism and public sector leisure provisions: the boundaries of a leisure profession', *Leisure Studies*, 19, 199–209.

McNamee, M. J., Sheridan, H., and Buswell, J. (2001), 'The limits of utilitarianism as a professional ethic in public sector leisure policy and provision', *Leisure Studies*, 20, 173–197.

Meller, H. E. (1976), *Leisure and the Changing City, 1870–1914*, Routledge, London.

Merrin, W. (2014), *Media Studies 2.0*, Routledge, London.

Metcalfe, A. (2006), *Leisure and Recreation in a Victorian Mining Community*, Routledge, London.

Miles, S. (2010), *Spaces for Consumption*, Sage, London.

Millward, P. (2011), *The Global Football League: Transnational Networks, Social Movements and Sport in the New Media Age*, Palgrave Macmillan, Basingstoke.

Millward, P. (2013), 'New football directors in the twenty-first century: profit and revenue in the English Premier League's transnational age', *Leisure Studies*, 32, 399–414.

Minten, S. (2010), 'Use them or lose them: a study of the employability of sport graduates through their transition into the sport workplace', *Managing Leisure*, 15, 67–82.

Moller, J., and Tubadji, A. (2008), *The Creative Class, Bohemians and Local Labor Market Performance – A Micro-data Panel Study for Germany 1975–2004*, Working Paper 270, Osteuropa-Institut, Regensburg.

Moorst, H. van. (1982), 'Leisure and social theory', *Leisure Studies*, 1, 157–169.

Morgan, M. (2008), 'What makes a good festival? Understanding the event experience', *Event Management*, 12, 81–93.

Morgan, N., and Pritchard, A. (1998), *Tourism Promotion and Power: Creating Images, Creating Identities*, Wiley, Chichester.

Morgan, N. J., and Pritchard, A. (1999), *Power and Politics at the Seaside*, University of Exeter Press, Exeter.

Morrow, S. (2003), *The People's Game? Football, Finance and Society*, Palgrave Macmillan, Basingstoke.

Moss, S. (2009), *The Entertainment Industry: An Introduction*, CABI, Wallingford.

Mottiar, Z., and Quinn, B. (2003), 'Shaping leisure/tourism places – the role of holiday home owners: a case study of Courtown, Co Wexford, Ireland', *Leisure Studies*, 22, 109–127.

Murphy, P. E. (1985), *Tourism: A Community Approach*, Methuen, New York.

Nasaw, D. (1993), *Going Out: The Rise and Fall of Public Amusements*, Harvard University Press, London.

Nash, R., and Johnstone, S. (2001), 'The case of Euro96: where did the party go?', in Gratton, C., and Henry, I., eds., *Sport in the City: The Role of Sport in Economic and Social Regeneration*, Routledge, London, pp. 109–123.

Nichols, G. (2004), 'The volunteer army', *Recreation*, 63, 24–26.

Nichols, G. (2005), 'Stalwarts in sport', *World Leisure Journal*, 47, 2, 31–37.

Nichols, G. (2012), 'Sports volunteering', *International Journal of Sports Policy*, 4, 155–157.

Ofcom. (2015), *Adults' Media Use and Attitudes Report 2015*, Ofcom, London.

Oxford Economics. (2012), *The Economic Impact of the London 2012 Olympic and Paralympic Games*, Oxford Economics, Oxford.

Palmer/Rae Associates. (2004), *Studies on European Cities and Capitals of Culture 1995–2004*, European Commission, Brussels.

Pangburn, W. M. (1940), 'Play and recreation', *Annals of the American Academy of Political and Social Science*, 212, 121–129.

Parker, G. (2007), 'The negotiation of leisure citizenship: leisure constraints, moral regulation and the mediation of rural place', *Leisure Studies*, 26, 1–22.

Parker, G., and Ravenscroft, N. (1999), 'Benevolence, nationalism and hegemony: fifty years of the National Parks and Access to the Countryside Act 1949', *Leisure Studies*, 18, 297–313.

Paxton, P. (1999), 'Is social capital declining in the United States? A multiple indicator assessment', *American Journal of Sociology*, 105, 88–127.

Pegg, S., and Patterson, I. (2010), 'Rethinking music festivals as a staged event: gaining insights from understanding visitor motivations and the experiences they seek', *Journal of Convention and Event Tourism*, 11, 85–99.

Peterson, R. A. and Kern, R. M. (1996), 'Changing highbrow taste: from snob to omnivore', *American Sociological Review*, 61, 900–907.

Philips, D. (2004), 'Stately pleasure domes – nationhood, monarchy and industry: the celebration exhibition in Britain', *Leisure Studies*, 23, 95–108.

Pine II, B. J., and Gilmore, J. H. (1999), *The Experience Economy: Work Is Theatre and Every Business a Stage*, Harvard Business School Press, Boston.

Putnam, R. D. (1995), 'Bowling alone: America's declining social capital', *Journal of Democracy*, 6, 65–78.

Putnam, R. D. (1996), 'The strange disappearance of civic America', *American Prospect*, 24, 34–48.

Putnam, R. D. (2000), *Bowling Alone: The Collapse and Revival of American Community*, Simon and Schuster, New York.

Quinn, B. (2010), 'Arts festivals, urban tourism and cultural policy', *Journal of Policy Research in Tourism, Leisure and Events*, 2, 264–279.

Quinn, B. (2013), *Key Concepts in Event Management*, Sage, London.

Ralston, R., Downward, P., and Lumsdon, L. (2003), 'The XVII Commonwealth Games – an initial overview of the expectations and experiences of volunteers', in Nichols, G., ed., *Volunteers in Sport*, Leisure Studies Association, Eastbourne, pp. 43–54.

Rapoport, R. (1977), 'Leisure and the urban society', in Smith, M. A., ed., *Leisure and Urban Society*, Leisure Studies Association, Manchester.

Rapuno, D. (2009), 'Working at fun: conceptualizing leisurework', *Current Sociology*, 57, 617–636.

Rath, J. (2007), *Tourism, Ethnic Diversity and the City*, Routledge, London.

Rettberg, J. W. (2008), *Blogging*, Polity, Cambridge.

Richards, G. (2001), *Cultural Attractions and European Tourism*, CABI, Wallingford.

Richards, G., and Palmer, R. (2010), *Eventful Cities: Cultural Management and Urban Revitalisation*, Butterworth-Heinemann, Oxford.

Rinehart, B., and Syndor, S., eds. (2003), *To the Extreme: Alternative Sports Inside and Out*, State University of New York Press, Albany.

Ritzer, G. (1993), *The McDonaldization of Society*, Pine Forge Press, Thousand Oaks.

Ritzer, G. (1998), *The McDonaldization Thesis*, Sage, London.

Ritzer, G. (1999), *Enchanting a Disenchanted World: Revolutionizing the Means of Consumption*, Pine Forge Press, Thousand Oaks.

Ritzer, G. (2001), *Explorations in the Sociology of Consumption: Fast Food, Credit Cards and Casinos*, Sage, London.

Roberts, K. (1999), *Leisure in Contemporary Society*, CABI, Wallingford.

Roberts, K. (2004), *The Leisure Industries*, Palgrave Macmillan, Basingstoke.

Roberts, K. (2012), 'The end of the long baby boomer generation', *Journal of Youth Studies*, 15, 479–497.

Roberts, K. (2013), 'Social class and leisure during recent recessions in Britain', *Leisure Studies*. http://dx.doi.org/10.1080/02614367.2013.855939.

Roberts, K., and Brodie, D. (1992), *Inner-city Sport: Who Plays and What Are the Benefits?*, Giordano Bruno, Culemborg.

Robinson, D. (1996), *From Peepshow to Palace: The Birth of American Film*, Columbia University Press, New York.

Robinson, T. (2006), *Work, Leisure and the Environment: The Vicious Circle of Overwork and Over-consumption*, Edward Elgar, Cheltenham.

Roche, M. (1992), 'Mega-events and micro-modernization: on the sociology of the new urban tourism', *British Journal of Sociology*, 43, 563–600.

Roche, M. (2000), *Mega-events and Modernity: Olympics and Expos in the Growth of Global Culture*, Routledge, London.

Roderick, M. (2006), *The Work of Professional Football: A Labour of Love?*, Routledge, London.

Rogers, T. (2003), *Conferences and Conventions: A Global Industry*, Butterworth-Heinemann, Oxford.

Rojek, C. (1993), 'Disney culture', *Leisure Studies*, 12, 121–135.

Rojek, C. (1997), 'Leisure in the writings of Walter Benjamin', *Leisure Studies*, 16, 155–171.

Rojek, C. (2014), 'Global event management: a critique', *Leisure Studies*, 33, 32–47.

Rowe, N. F. (2009), 'The Active People Survey: a catalyst for transforming evidence-based sport policy in England', *International Journal of Sport Policy*, 1, 89–98.

Rushton, D. (2003), *Volunteers, Helpers and Socialisers: Social Capital and Time Use*, Office for National Statistics, London.

Ryan, C. (2002), 'Tourism and cultural proximity: examples from New Zealand', *Annals of Tourism Research*, 29, 4, 952–971.

Sadd, D. (2014), 'FestIM – the development of a low cost impact evaluation service for cultural events using data from online social networks', paper presented at Leisure Studies Association Conference, Paisley.

Sam, M. (2012), 'Targeted investment in elite sport funding: wiser, more innovative and strategic?', *Managing Leisure*, 17, 207–220.

Sandy, R., Sloane, P. J., and Rosentraub, M. S. (2004), *The Economics of Sport: An International Perspective*, Palgrave Macmillan, Basingstoke.

Sassatelli, R. (1999), 'Fitness gyms and the local organisation of experience', *Sociological Research Online*, 4, 3.

Savage, M., Bagnall, G., and Longhurst, B. (2005), *Globalization and Belonging*, Sage, London.

Savage, M., Devine, F., Cunningham, N., Taylor, M., Li, Y., Hjellbrekke, J., Le Roux, B., Friedman, S., and Miles, A. (2013), 'A new model of social class? Findings from the BBC's Great British Class Survey experiment', *Sociology*, 47, 219–250.

Scheerder, J., Vanreusel, B., Taks, M., and Renson, R. (2002), 'Social sports stratification in Flanders 1969–1999', *International Review for the Sociology of Sport*, 37, 219–245.

Schimpfosal, E. (2014), 'Russia's social upper class: from ostentation to culturedness', *British Journal of Sociology*, 65, 63–81.

Scholz, T., ed. (2012), *Digital Labour: The Internet as Playground and Factory*, Routledge, London.

Schor, J. B. (2004), *Born to Buy*, Scribner, New York.

Schulenkorf, N., and Adair, D. (2014), 'Sport-for-development: the emergence and growth of a new genre', in Schulenkorf, N., and Adair, D., eds., *Global Sport-for-development: Critical Perspectives*, Palgrave Macmillan, Basingstoke, pp. 3–11.

Scott, C. (2014a), 'Legacy evaluation and London, 2012 and the Cultural Olympiad', *Cultural Trends*, 23, 7–17.

Scott, C. (2014b), 'Emerging paradigms: national approaches for measuring cultural value', *Cultural Trends*. http://dx.doi.org/10.1080/09548963.2014.897448.

Seabrook, J. (1988), *The Leisure Society*, Blackwell, Oxford.

Sharp, C., Kendall, L., Bhabra, S., Schagen, I., and Duff, J. (2001), *Playing for Success: An Evaluation of the Second Year*, Research Report 291, Department for Education and Skills, Sheffield.

Sharp, C., Mawson, C., Pocklington, K., Kendall, L., and Morrison, J. (1999), *Playing for Success: An Evaluation of the First Year*, Research Report 167, Department for Education and Employment, Sheffield.

Shaw, P. (1999), *The Arts and Neighbourhood Renewal: A Literature Review to Inform the Work of Policy Action Team 10*, Loughborough University, Loughborough.

Sheller, M., and Urry, J., eds. (2004), *Tourism Mobilities: Places to Play, Places in Play*, Routledge, London.

Siebert, S., and Wilson, F. (2013), 'All work and no pay: consequences of unpaid work in the creative industries', *Work, Employment and Society*, 27, 711–721.

Silk, M. L. (2007), 'Come downtown & play', *Leisure Studies*, 26, 253–277.

Skogen, K., and Wichstrom, L. (1996), 'Delinquency in the wilderness: patterns of outdoor recreation activities and conduct problems in the general adolescent population', *Leisure Studies*, 15, 151–169.

Smart, B., ed. (1999), *Resisting McDonaldization*, Sage, London.

Smith, A. (2010), 'Leveraging benefits from major events: maximising opportunities for peripheral urban areas', *Managing Leisure*, 15, 161–180.

Smith, A. (2012), *Events and Urban Regeneration: The Strategic Use of Events to Revitalise Cities*, Routledge, London.

Smith, A., Haycock, D., and Hulme, N. (2013), 'The Class of London 2012: some sociological reflections on the social backgrounds of Team GB athletes', *Sociological Research Online*, 18, 15.

Smith, R., and Maughan, T. (1997), *Youth Culture and the Making of the Post-Fordist Economy: Dance Music in Contemporary Britain*, Discussion Paper DP97/2, Royal Holloway College, London.

Smith, S. L. J. (1995), *Tourism Analysis: A Handbook*, Longman, Harlow.

Snape, R. (2004), 'The Co-operative Holiday Association and the cultural formation of countryside holiday practice', *Leisure Studies*, 23, 143–158.

Snape, R., and Pussard, H. (2013), 'Theorisations of leisure inter-war Britain', *Leisure Studies*, 32, 1–18.

Somnez, S., Shinew, K., Marchese, L., Veldkamp, C., and Burnet, G. W. (1993), 'Leisure corrupted: an artist's portrait of leisure in a changing society', *Leisure Studies*, 12, 266–276.

Sorkin, A. R. (2009), *Too Big to Fail*, Penguin, London.

South-west Economic Planning Council. (1976), *Economic Survey of the Tourist Industry in the South-west*, HMSO, London.

Sport England. (2013), *Economic Value of Sport in England*, Sport England, London.

Sports Council. (1985), *Olympic Review: Preparing for '88*, Sports Council, London.

Stebbins, R. A. (1992), *Amateurs, Professionals and Serious Leisure*, McGill-Queen's University Press, Montreal.

Stebbins, R. A. (2005), 'Project-based leisure: theoretical neglect of a common use of free time', *Leisure Studies*, 24, 1–11.

Steffen, D. J. (2005), *From Edison to Marconi: The First Thirty Years of Recorded Music*, McFarland, London.

Street, J. (1993), 'Global culture, local politics', *Leisure Studies*, 12, 191–201.

Sugden, J., and Tomlinson, A. (1998), *FIFA and the Contest for World Football*, Polity Press, Cambridge.

Supporters Direct Europe. (2012), *The Heart of the Game*, Supporters Direct Europe, London.

Szymanski, S., and Zimbalist, A. (2005), *National Pastime: How Americans Play Baseball and the Rest of the World Plays Soccer*, Brookings Institution Press, Washington, DC.

Tan Ying and Roberts, K. (1995), 'Sports policy in the People's Republic of China', in Fleming, S., Talbot, M., and Tomlinson, A., eds., *Policy and Politics in Sport, Physical Education and Leisure*, Leisure Studies Association, Brighton.

Taylor, P. D., Panagouleas, T., and Nichols, G. (2012), 'Determinants of sports volunteering and sports volunteer time in England', *International Journal of Sports Policy*, 4, 201–220.

Tett, G. (2009), *Fools' Gold*, Little, Brown, London.

Tomlinson, A. (1979), *Leisure and the Role of Clubs and Voluntary Groups*, Social Science Research Council/Sports Council, London.

Tomlinson, A., ed. (1990), *Consumption, Identity and Style*, Routledge, London.

Town, S. (1983), 'Recreation and the unemployed: experiments in Bradford', *Leisure Studies Association Newsletter*, 4, 5–10.

Travis, A. S. (1979), *The State and Leisure Provision*, Social Science Research Council/Sports Council, London.

Treuren, G. J. M. (2014), 'Enthusiasts, conscripts or instrumentalists? The motivational profiles of event volunteers', *Managing Leisure*, 19, 51–70.

Turner, G., and Tay, J., eds. (2009), *Television Studies after TV: Understanding Television in the Post-broadcast Era*, Routledge, London.

Turner, L., and Ash, J. (1975), *The Golden Hordes*, Constable, London.

Urry, J. (1990), *The Tourist Gaze*, Sage, London.

Veal, A. J. (2011), 'The leisure society I: myths and misconceptions, 1960–1979', *World Leisure Journal*, 53, 206–227.

Veal, A. J. (2012), 'The leisure society II: the era of critique, 1980–2011', *World Leisure Journal*, 54, 99–140.

Veal, A. J., Toohey, K., and Frawley, S. (2012), 'The sport participation legacy of the Sydney 2000 Olympic Games and other international sport events hosted in Australia', *Journal of Policy Research in Tourism, Leisure and Events*, 4, 155–184.

Vogel, H. (2004), *Entertainment Industry Economics*, Cambridge University Press, Cambridge.

Waiton, S. (2012), *Snobs' Law: Criminalising Football Fans in an Age of Intolerance*, Take a Liberty, Dundee.

Walvin, J. (1975), *The People's Game*, Allen Lane, London.

Walvin, J. (1978), *Beside the Seaside*, Allen Lane, London.

Warde, A., and Martens, L. (2000), *Eating Out: Social Differentiation, Consumption and Pleasure*, Cambridge University Press, Cambridge.

Warhurst, C., and Nickson, D. (2007), 'Employee experience of aesthetic labour in retail and hospitality', *Work, Employment and Society*, 21, 103–120.

Wearing, B., and Wearing, S. (1992), 'Identity and the commodification of leisure', *Leisure Studies*, 11, 3–18.

Wheen, F. (1985), *Television: A History*, Century, London.

Whitford, M. (2009), 'A framework for the development of event public policy facilitating regional development', *Tourism Management*, 30, 674–682.

Whitson, D., and Horne, J. (2006), 'Underestimated costs and overestimated benefits? Comparing the outcomes of sports mega-events in Canada and Japan', *Sociological Review*, 54, 73–89.

Wicker, P., Prinz, J., and Weimar, D. (2013), 'Big spenders in a booming sport: consumption capital as a key driver of triathletes' sport-related expenditure', *Managing Leisure*, 18, 286–299.

Williams, K. (2009), *Read All about It: A History of the British Newspaper*, Routledge, London.

Wilson, J. (1988), *Politics and Leisure*, Unwin Hyman, London.

Wilson, W. T. (2013), *Hitting the Sweet Spot: The Growth of the Middle Class in Emerging Markets*, Ernst and Young, London.

Witt, P. A., and Crompton, J. L., eds. (1996), *Recreation Programmes That Work for At-risk Youth*, Venture Publishing, Penn State.

Wollenburg, J., Mowatt, R. A., Ross, C. M., and Renneisen, M. (2013), 'Components of partnership agreements in municipal parks and recreation', *Managing Leisure*, 18, 135–151.

Woods, R., Dobbs, L., Gordon, C., Moore, C., and Simpson, G. (2005), *Report of a Thematic Study Using Transnational Comparisons to Analyse and Identify Cultural Policies and Programmes That Contribute to Preventing and Reducing Poverty and Social Exclusion*, European Commission, Directorate-general for Employment, Social Affairs and Equal Opportunities, Brussels.

Wright, K. (2000), 'Charitable change – creating a new culture of giving for Britain', *LSE Magazine*, 12, 2, 19–21.

Wyman, O. (2012), *State of the UK Leisure Industry: A Driver for Growth*, Business in Sport and Leisure, London.

Yu-Hao Lee and Holin Lin. (2011), '"Gaming is my work": identity work in Internet-hobbyist game workers', *Work, Employment and Society*, 25, 451–467.

Zegre, S. J., Needham, M. D., Kruger, L. E., and Rosenberger, R. S. (2012), 'McDonaldization and commercial leisure outdoor recreation and tourism in Alaska', *Managing Leisure*, 17, 333–348.

Zhuang, J., and Girginov, V. (2012), 'Volunteer selection and social, human and political capital: a case study of the Beijing 2008 Olympic Games', *Managing Leisure*, 17, 239–256.

Zimbalist, A. (2015), *Circus Maximus*, Brookings Institution Press, Washington, DC.

Index